MAN, SCIENCE AND GOD

JOHN MORTON

Man, Science and God

COLLINS

LONDON AND AUCKLAND

1972

William Collins Sons & Co Ltd
London · Glasgow · Sydney · Auckland
Toronto · Johannesburg

First published 1972
© John Morton 1972
ISBN 0 00 215510 9
Set in Baskerville
Made and Printed in Great Britain by
William Collins Sons & Co Ltd Glasgow

Contents

Introduction

FOR three years this book has been struggling to be written, as spare time allowed. In much of its subject matter I am patently not expert. But I hold the unrepentant view that theology is as important to the layman as biology, and ought to be equally accessible.

One of the ideas that runs through these pages is that different aspects of religious truth must be held in tension with each other, and that in our own day such a tension has been allowed to slacken and lose its power. This must happen when men emphasize either the sacred or the secular alone. Present-day theology is almost everywhere preoccupied with an immanent God, and with a Christianity secularly understood. In many places this book will seem largely out of sympathy with the views of colleagues and contemporaries. This is perhaps not an arrogance, but in fact the best justification for writing yet another book on theology and science. A different reason could have been that a writer was able to add more persuasion to an already popular view. Dr Robinson's best-selling books could be said to do this, especially his more reflective *New Reformation?* and *Exploration into God.*

We are often told that the theologian must walk with humility in a world confronted with modern science. We must be careful to know what is meant by this. It is certainly good that Christians should be able to enter into genuine dialogue with other points of view. And after the disastrous attempts of the Church in time past to prejudice the issue in arguments of science, the theologian must be continuingly aware of the limits within which his authority runs.

Yet within its own province, theology is not under the dominion of biology, or of any of the sciences, in the sense that, say, physiology must listen to chemistry. Theology deals with the subject matter of a transcendent world in a way that calls for a wholly non-scientific language. This is not however a new language, since its vocabulary will include the familiar words 'consciousness', 'freedom', 'purpose', 'self', 'I' and 'God'.

It can be useful, up to a point, to insist that science and theology are studying the same world in different ways, and learning different things about it. But it will not be an objection to theology, only a definition of it, to say that its whole content seems vacuous and unnecessary to science. Charles Davis wrote, in *God's Grace in History*,

> Precisely because [God's] causality is total, it does not appear when what is sought is the intelligibility inherent in the universe itself. God is indeed immanent in the universe, but as its transcendent cause not as part of its system.[1]

When we reserve these transcendent things for the special study of theology, this does not mean we are using what C. A. Coulson called the 'God of the Gaps' as a provisional explanation until a better one is put forward. There are many who will assume that, in talking of God at all, we are conjuring some entity to fill gaps. They will hold that I am keeping open illicit refuges for God, if I am not willing to concede that the progress of science, in this century or the next, may come to explain everything about values, purposes and minds in terms of memory, molecules or behaviourist physiology. With the astonishing growth of science in our own day, these sceptics assert that there will soon be no metaphysics left. They can genuinely see no difference in kind, but merely in complexity and the adequacy of our understanding, between statements about a perception and statements about a brain.

The scientist can be forgiven if he feels some concern with all this. He finds science, loaded with acclaim for the modern revolution in thought and technology, now being appealed to on matters never before thought to be within its scope. In an age when men feel increasingly insecure in the vastness of space and time, even clergy are letting go by default the claim that it is not for theology but for astrophysics to lay bare and explain the ultimate nature of the world.

The impact of science is being felt today in attitudes to both history and authority. Technology has given us enormous advances in communication and education. Public enlightenment and social conscience have widened. There is a new depth of humanity perceived, and even sometimes realized, between men and races, for which history affords no parallel. It is difficult not to equate these benefits with the growth of modern science. It is widely accepted that a man of five centuries ago, or even of 1900, without the advantage of a scientific world-view, can be no safe guide for us in ethics or philosophy of life. The same tribute has probably been paid to the contemporary idols of every age. But it is the more compelling today when revolutions in concepts and techniques happen so rapidly, when problems of world population are said to have overturned a whole morality, and when – in certain fields – the sixth-form student can know much more than Darwin, Mendel or Rutherford. At no time has the historical dimension been less regarded, even within the universities.[2]

This must prove a particular handicap in dealing with an historical religion. If we are to allow that God has shown us his nature in some special way in historic time (and this is what Christianity is centrally about) such a revelation must needs be taught and transmitted under some kind of authority. Imposed authority is today widely discredited. Personal and political liberty is part of the native element we live in; it seems, too, to be the necessary condition which allows any creative activity to flourish.

In the outlook science has called into being there is no place for received authority. In the laboratory no questions of tradition or credibility need ever arise. Controlled experiments can be repeated here and now, and the facts laid open to every man's inspection. It is assumed that there can be no other way for knowledge to be acquired, and that if facts are not so verifiable they cease to be knowledge worth having.

For the present distrust of authority the Church herself must take a heavy share of blame. In the past she has widely misused authority and in the face of today's stirring to renewal she too often presents a conservative resistance. Far too often received dogmas have become petrified as if engraved in stone, and alien to living men's hearts and minds. It has been forgotten that 'belief is being' and that the historical revelation must be apprehended afresh, in all its timeless relevance, for each man and generation.

Impatience with authority and the Church is being shown in the new value given to existential Christianity. This is a religion of the spirit, finding cogency above all in the present 'situation' and in the individual's personal insight. One of the themes of this book is that our present awareness of Jesus must be focussed upon and related to an historical revelation, if Christianity is to remain viable or able to be passed on as a coherent body of truth. Our faith has far stronger involvements with history than the modern demythologizers are willing to allow. A due regard for its historic elements will insist not only on the importance of the Scriptures, but on the crucial significance of the Church. It exists as a society among men with a visible and continuing form and order. In a full vista of man's psychic and social biology, it has the place that Teilhard de Chardin finds for it in *The Phenomenon of Man*.

Along with the revolt from history and the Church, the idea of transcendence is being widely rejected. Yvonne Lubbock, in her essay in *The Future of Catholic Christianity*, speaks of the almost exclusive emphasis on immanence throughout the world outside Catholic orthodoxy (whether Roman or Anglican).

> The power of Christian truth, already attenuated, will melt away once it is severed in men's minds from its transcendent source; and it is unrealistic to suppose that this deprivation can lead to anything but the ultimate extinction of the Christian religion however numerous the pseudo-Christian philosophies to which such a dispossession may give rise.[3]

My own theological reading has been palpably English and

Anglican, much of it from a generation unfamiliar to many contemporaries. It cannot moreover be possible that I have digested as they deserved each of the books in my own reading list. But I have been conscious that a student of Christian theology today is still in a great tradition. As Professor Mascall has reminded us,[4] we do not each have to begin all over again: we are part of something greater than ourselves, being the heirs of the Christian ages.

Of a great contemporary man, Bertrand Russell, it was said at his death that he had treated the search for God as a form of self-indulgence from which his intellectual austerity called him back. If it be so with modern men, our plight is sad. We shall be in peril if we pass over God's transcendence even for the loftiest humanism and devotion to fellow man. These, to be sure, are works every Christian will want to bring to fruition. But his first allegiance is more immediate: 'This is the work of God, that ye believe on him whom he has sent.'

Auckland, New Zealand, JOHN MORTON
4 *August* 1970

CHAPTER I

Causes

Laws of nature are not fiats.

Gilbert Ryle[1]

WHEN we speak of the 'causes' of a thing we may be confusing ideas of very different kinds. Ever since Aristotle, philosophy has been using the word in four different ways. If we take, for our object to be explained, a bottle of claret, we can try to see what each of these sorts of cause would entail.

First, the wine could not exist at all without its *material cause*. This is the pre-existence of certain substances: grape juice containing glucose sugar, grape-skins with the purple pigment anthocyanin, and carrying the white 'bloom' of a microscopic plant called a yeast. These can produce nothing until some event initiates chemical reactions between their molecules. This is true whether the molecules be produced by living things – as in yeast or with our own bodies – or are entirely inorganic.

We can recognize, then, with the wine an *efficient cause*, by which glucose molecules are broken into smaller and simpler molecules of alcohol and carbon dioxide. Other factors too contribute, as part of the efficient cause, to the end-product. The skin pigments provide the wine's colour; other substances will affect its taste and bouquet. Control of temperature stops fermentation at the right time. Differences in grapes, sunshine or soil determine whether the wine is to be a St Julien, rather than a Médoc or a Pomerol. Finally there will be the subtle change brought about by years in cask or bottle.

In all this, instead of accounting for my particular bottle of claret, I have been giving a description of the way the laws of nature work. To analyse these 'material' and 'efficient' causes exhaustively, we should have to pursue them from complex biology, through chemistry down in the end to the few starkly general laws of physics. To become more and more general, until ultimately universal in application, is a property of scientific statements. Though they purport to describe claret-making, or the splitting of Amoeba, or the eruption of a volcano, they come in the end to deal with the behaviour of a few sorts of elementary particles, such as protons, neutrons and electrons. Our accounts of phenomena are brought into a form that will obey the same laws anywhere in the universe.

Yet we do not live in a world of elementary particles but one with grapes and yeast and men with brains. Living things have limited and very specific attributes, and conditions on our own planet are rather suited for such phenomena. In the sun, as elsewhere in the universe, elementary particles are held together by atomic bonds. The positively charged protons of the nucleus are balanced by the negative charges of the electrons in orbit round them. There are more than a hundred sorts of atoms, forming 'elements' with distinctive properties; and there is reason to believe that there cannot be many more kinds anywhere in the universe.

With others in the solar system, our planet is made up of materials from the sun. With its lower temperature the separate atoms are slowed down so as to remain bound together in stable molecules. As the earth continued to cool these molecules have joined together by other bonds into elaborate and long-lasting compounds. Even today the earth is far hotter than the outer planets, where all the compounds have become inert and frozen solid. With the free existence that is possible for liquids and gases the earth has become the scene of a lively chemistry, and of a biochemistry too.

The most interesting of the chemical elements, and a peculiarly abundant one on the earth, is carbon. With oxygen, hydrogen and very often nitrogen, it forms the long chain and ring molecules of living matter. The simplest nitrogen compounds of the body, the amino-acids, are built up into complex chains and spirals, forming the special molecules of life known as proteins. One of the properties of living molecules is that they

sustain and reproduce themselves, 'feeding' upon other substances by incorporating them into their own systems. They
may be broken into simpler compounds to be used as building
blocks, or further decomposed to capture their stored energy.
This latter process is 'respiration'. It is what happens when the
yeast splits glucose into alcohol and carbon dioxide.

The fuels respired are moreover being 'burnt' not at the high
temperatures of the laboratory, but at the lower ones of the
living body. The chemical reactions are carried out in small
steps, made possible by the catalysts called 'enzymes' which are
in themselves proteins. There are enzymes not only for respiration, but for the multitude of the reactions of the body's whole
metabolism. These enzymes are produced by living cells from
'information' coded in the special molecules of nucleic acid
(DNA) inherited in the chromosomes. DNA perpetuates itself
throughout life, as the cells – with their nuclei and chromosomes – divide. A whole instruction book for an organism is
handed intact from parent to offspring at reproduction.

Organisms may be not only living, as plants are, but – like
animals – sentient. Life has developed further properties here:
sensitivity to the environment, and the use of contractile tissue,
such as muscles, to move about or do work. Information gained
from the world outside by the senses is coded and stored in the
nervous system (possibly by the second nucleic acid RNA) and
can then be read out and put to use in the animal's future
behaviour. From elementary beginnings, nervous systems have
evolved into computers of complexity quite beyond parallel in
the world.

At what point sensitivity to stimuli becomes consciousness as
we know it, is hard to say. We cannot tell whether sponges or
starfish, or indeed any other animals, are consciously aware of
the world. We can make no more than inference that other
mammals have self-consciousness like our own. But we can
observe that with each new level in complexity – chemical,
living, sentient and mental – matter is organized in more
comprehensive ways. New properties emerge that could never
have been predicted in advance from earlier levels. While

physiology is still in an important sense chemistry, and psychology still physiology, there is a new complexity that was nowhere evident before. Indeed, with life and mind, we reach phenomena that had better be treated by their own rules. We shall have to find out what each shows in itself before deciding that it is 'nothing but' a previous level, with its molecules arranged in new ways.

FINAL CAUSES

We have been making the sort of digression that is very typical of scientists when pressed to explain something. For in accounting for my special bottle of claret, we can expect no help from the laws of science. We are up against not only the complexity of the world, but the particular things in it, and their separate existence. The bottle of claret that I am now decanting exists because somebody made it.

In doing so, he gave effect to a purpose and fulfilled concretely an abstract idea. It is this that has been called in traditional language the *final cause*. And in the idea of the claret, built up and kept alive by skill and tradition, and including the ideal to which all actual clarets aspire, we can find the fourth category of causation which has been called the *formal cause*.

The expression 'final cause' is bound to cause dissent among some scientific readers. Final enough, perhaps, for non-rigorous, everyday description, such causation must be followed back – they will say – into the laws of nature. Presented with the vintner's act of will, they would want to investigate his personal psychological history, right back – if it were possible – to the general laws that must govern physiology and even chemistry and physics.

Not only would such an enquiry be too big for our computers. It would in principle be wildly misconceived. Final causes are not derivable from the laws of nature. This is not to mean that our purposive actions make breaches in those laws. In Gilbert Ryle's words, the laws that physicists 'have found and will find may, in one sense of the metaphorical verb, govern everything that happens, but they do not ordain everything that happens. Indeed they do not ordain anything that happens. Laws of nature are not fiats.'[2]

Professor Ryle deals thoroughly with the problem of the 'will' in *The Concept of Mind* (and it is fair to point out – as we shall later see – that we could not claim his support for the notion of the self and self-knowledge that we are using here). He uses the example of the game of chess (without maintaining that its laws are necessarily like the laws of nature) to show that there is no contradiction in saying that one and the same process, such as the move of a bishop, is in accordance with principles of two completely different types. Neither of them is reducible to the other, although one presupposes the rules, but is not prescribed by them. The player might ask why the bishop always moves on to a square of the same colour. The answer would be given: by the rules. But the answer to why a player at a particular stage moved his bishop here and not there would be, 'to force the opposing Queen to cease to threaten the player's King'.[3]

Words like 'explanation', then, are used at different levels, and it is wrong to answer questions of purpose in terms of mechanism. 'The discoveries of the physical sciences no more rule out life, sentience, purpose or intelligence from presence in the world than do the rules of grammar extrude style or logic from prose.'[4]

When all our talk of 'final' causation has been allowed for, there is still a large class of phenomena, obviously by far the most of what has ever happened in the universe, for which we can find no cause whatever in intelligence or design. The valley of the River Thames has resulted from the varying hardness and shape of the land mass over which so much water has flowed at certain velocities. We would give similar 'explanations' for the eruption of Vesuvius, the rise of sea level after the glaciers or the origin of the moon. These things can hardly be said to be 'caused' in our present sense at all. They have come about by the laws of matter and energy flow, given the existing physical state of the world.

Are the happenings of biology like this? They seem to have this important difference, that they are proportioned to the consequences that are to flow from them. The enzyme in yeast splitting the sugar, or the pigment responding to light energy in the retina of our eye, is clearly of advantage to the organism through extended time. Though they cannot be called purposeful, they are clearly adaptive in a way that the moon or the River Thames are not. The analogy with purpose is so convincing that it is easy to slip into teleology and talk about 'aim' in biology, when we should be content with 'design'. Even the word design has its pitfalls. But we may be sure that with living organisms we have crossed a truly new threshold that separates them from non-living. Molecules are now so organized that they produce results that would be inconceivable from their properties when looked at singly or separately. The whole of inorganic nature follows a downhill path with progressive loss of organization, until – as we can predict – the world grinds to a standstill. 'Entropy', as we may say, increases. Life is not like this: uniquely in the universe it gains in organization, a tiny enclave winding itself up as the rest of the universe is running down.

Whatever sort of design we can detect in organic nature, and in whatever ways we may find it has come about, we can say that without these particular sorts of organization, final causation could never have become operative in the way we can detect it in organisms like ourselves.

LAWS AND FREEDOM

We have claimed that the laws of nature are not fiats but only rules of action. But how strict may they be? And is there anything that can really escape their causal rigour?

At the end of the nineteenth century, the science of physics was thoroughly deterministic. To the laws of mechanics given us by Newton, the Victorians had added the principles of electricity and magnetism. The sway of physical laws was thought to be all-inclusive and complete. Given sufficient information about the disposition of all particles at the first instant of time –

so the confident assertion ran – we could predict in the minutest detail all the course of history, down to tomorrow's weather, the weight of the next ash to fall from my cigarette, or the precise rise in my blood-sugar level as the horn of a passing car startles me.

Such a determinism would not only paralyse our free actions; it would even disable us from rational thought, in so far as this is related to events in the nerve cells of our brains. The 'rules for action' would be a strait-jacket so tight as to leave in the world no freedom of play. We could react to such a pronouncement in two ways. We could discard it, as all sane men do, without waiting upon the leave of physics; because it would make an illusion of what we intuit to be the most essential fact about ourselves.

Or we could validly ask, is physical determinism true? Do the laws of nature really make necessary such an austere view of the world? This is a question that in a later chapter we shall take up again. We shall find that at the level of elementary particles, physics has found a class of events that is 'free', in the sense of unpredictable and random. In a collection of radio-active atoms we have no means of knowing which one will next disintegrate to emit 'gamma particles' (or electrons). But from previous experiments we can know very accurately how many will disintegrate within the next short fraction of a second. In the same way, my life assurance society cannot predict the year of my death, though its actuary can tell it very reliably the number of claims it should prepare to meet within a given year.

An important question that arises is, whether there are situations in which such small indeterminate events can play a part in the lives of organisms. This has been claimed to happen in the mutation of genes, and in the firing of nerve cells initiating specific pieces of behaviour. These activities, in essence, may both spring from chance phenomena at the level of individual particles. But the result as we see it will be very far from chance. An event that offers advantage will be 'selected'. In the one case this will happen by natural selection of mutant individuals that live longer or produce more offspring. In the other, a single indeterminate neuronal event may be availed of by the decision of a conscious mind.

How far this margin of free play operates in nature, and how far it can be converted from the random chance that is 'freedom' in physics, to a useful or rational outcome, is a question to which we can later return.

SCIENCE AND THEOLOGY

Theology deals with the final causes that spring from the actions of ourselves and of God. By his own working method the scientist is right to allow no point at which a 'final' cause resists further enquiry under the laws of nature. He will reply to our talk about final causes with varying degrees of disdain, telling us that we should keep out of his laboratory, or enter a school of metaphysics or a contemplative order. He will remind us that many scientists find no meaning in the theologian's questions at all, and that they may even, in the short run, be better scientists for rejecting them. For while scientific scepticism can be a sour poison to theology, history gives too many examples where theology – growing in the wrong place – has been a strangling weed.

Science is indeed talking not about causes at all, but about relationships. For the 'efficient' causes we have been mentioning are hardly in our present sense 'causes' at all. They are at bottom a description of the way the world is made. Asked to account for the purple colour of grapes, I will describe the molecules of the pigment anthocyanin, showing these to be so arranged that light of a particular wave length falling on them will be unable to pass through but be reflected back. Focussed upon one of the cone cells of the retina, such light will produce a photo-chemical reaction. Its energy will be transduced into small changes of electrical potential that are relayed to the brain along the fibres of the optic nerve. These, 'somehow', 'somewhere', give rise to the sensation of purple that with our private consciousness we perceive.

A similar account could be given of the sweet taste of grape-sugar. The glucose molecules are held to match up with the surface ultrastructure of specific kinds of taste cell. Minute changes of electrical potential again propagate nerve impulses which – channelled to the brain – produce a conscious sensation. Now it is clear that these pieces of sensory physiology, with the mysterious last bit about perception tacked on, are really explaining nothing. They are describing certain relationships without in the least telling us why there should be glucose or anthocyanin, or certain shapes of molecule, or light of specific wave length at all. The whole of science is a language applying adjectives and adverbs to the structures and functions of raw existence.

What we still have to account for is what someone called these 'opaque realities'; and we shall need another language than science to explain them, that is – if they can be explained at all. It is not only raw existence that presents a problem. There is also the existence and nature of particular things, and of those very rare and untypical entities, our conscious selves. For while the statements of science widen out to become more general and ultimately universal, those of theology do just the reverse. They refer to specific and often unique happenings. As Ian Ramsey has claimed in his book *Miracles*, 'there is a non-inferential awareness more concrete than the observable facts that characterize it abstractly and objectively'.[5]

There are obviously natural laws applicable to human behaviour, and at least these go far enough to make psychology and sociology valid sciences. But it is because these disciplines are unaware of consciousness (or rather could be said to know it only extra-murally) that they are unable to render a full account of what we can know about ourselves.

'That man is an inhabitant of two worlds is at once his glory and his anguish, the source of his *grandeur* and his *misère*.'[6] Here – it would seem – is the real encounter of theology and the real gap of understanding with science. Our nature is involved on both sides of this gap. It can be crossed only by a certain encounter of faith, and the bridge must be held up in a constant tension with doubt.

When we talk of phenomena deriving from mind and mentality, it is often questioned whether these are indeed phenomena at all, or simply 'epiphenomena' carried upon the surface of a stream of events whose course we are powerless to influence. My earliest conscious intimation of my 'self' seems to have raised for me this very problem. I was conscious, as it were, of a vast landscape of mystery in which I found myself set off over and against all the rest of things. Though my natural body, with its brain and sense organs, seemed in some sense an object I could observe, and in an undeniable unity with my conscious self, I could never be quite sure of 'where' I was 'in' it.

With the poet's power alone, perhaps, to express this dilemma, Walter de la Mare once asked, in his essay on 'Desert Islands': 'Does not a voice out of "the little nowhere of the mind" astonish every one of us at times with its insistent – "Robin, Robin, Robin Crusoe, poor Robin Crusoe". Where are you? Where have you been?'

In this introduction I have tried to mark out fairly the field in which science must be allowed to operate without the intrusion of purposes or final causes. In the following pages I shall try to explain the cogency of theology today, and its coherence with the findings of a scientific age. We must ask whether it is really true that our notions of purpose, persons and God will one day be taken up into a wider system of natural law. Will we one day have an empiric science of conduct and creativeness? Will the whole world soon become accountable to science as a naturalistic unity? If so, what will its integrated landscape look like? And will there be room in it for our intimations of ourselves, our freedom and of God?

CHAPTER 2

Man's Unity and Freedom

> Men are not machines, not even ghost-ridden machines. They are men.
>
> *Gilbert Ryle*[1]

> A 'Person,' then, is a self-conscious and self-determining system of experience, and human persons are in process of achieving the complete unification of the experience which constitutes them.
>
> *William Temple*[2]

HERE we shall take a rather different view of man from a scientist's, and we shall draw on evidence that would not be used if we were simply giving a behaviouristic description. It has been sometimes doubted whether an individual can have any privileged vantage point upon himself from what could be called an inside view. We will maintain that there are sorts of knowledge we could not get in any other way, and that these are of such surpassing value that we could not carry on any enquiry without them.

We need not then begin by deriving man's nature from its roots among lower forms of life, or – at the outset – consider how far we might treat man as an organism we could stand aside and observe. Nor, when we talk of human purpose and volition and value, will we assume that these are something determinate by the laws of the physical world, and thereby doubtful or illusory.

There are some things we know of ourselves that we encounter at first hand as primary data. First, we are percipient and self-conscious. We do not know how far this may separate us from the lower animals; but we do not have to adopt Descartes's view that these are nothing but insentient mechanisms, or deny even to the lowest animals some of the rich sensory experience (sometimes – no doubt – in modes unknown to us) that we ourselves may enjoy in supreme measure.

Our self-conscious perceiving, like our purposing, our value-judgements and our volitions, are things we know from our introspection of ourselves, rather than from any comparative study of human or animal behaviour. Perhaps – in a primary sense – they are the only things we can 'know' at all. At all events we have here a peculiar and intimate source of knowledge, set off against the whole 'external' world, even those parts of it we call our bodies and brains. We are all, without sophistication, early aware of such knowledge; but to say this does not mean we are attempting to carve out a last refuge for mysticism or metaphysics. Or, if it is indeed metaphysics, then its dividing line from physics runs cleanly through ourselves and the content of our daily experience.

What we know in ourselves we project into others. But it is still a private experience and we cannot know empirically anything about another's perception or consciousness or whether they are similar in kind to ours. That they are so, however, is one of the axioms with which we approach the objective world.

The scientist, too, believes in an objective world, but his different procedures give him wholly different information about man. He could not for example have stumbled upon the fact of consciousness, if he had not 'unofficially' known about it in himself. The neurophysiologist has instruments to study the input of stimuli from the environment, and the output of responses; and he can reconstruct the whole course of circuitry of the nervous system that lies in between. But conscious perception is an added bonus such a system would never have led him to suspect. We could perfectly satisfy the requirements of physiology by substituting a photo-sensitive cell for the eye and a sensitive enough computer for the brain. We regularly do this in effect when we describe the behaviour of lower animals.

With instruments suitable for him to read, a neurophysiologist blind from birth could find out everything that science can know about colour vision. He could measure wave-length differences in what we call the 'visible' part of the electromagnetic spectrum. He could find the minute differences in electrical potential raised by a light stimulus on a cell membrane; and could follow from these the volley of oscillograph 'spikes' recording the passage of an impulse along a nerve.

But in our conscious perception, we are presented with the richness of colour, the sharpness of contour, the subtlety of perspective, and the myriad discrimination of separate points. We see the complexity of a landscape or a microscopic cell structure, or the play of expression in a human face. To the blind man, these belong to a realm that cannot at first hand be known. The gulf between physiology and perception would seem to be of the same order as that between present existence and those things that 'eye has not seen nor ear heard, nor has it entered into the heart of man to conceive'.

Yet here we meet a paradox. We cannot truly believe there is any unbridgeable gap between our minds and bodies. We would distrust the confident division by Descartes – at the beginning of the age of science – of man into these separate entities. Nor, as we shall see, can the Christian accept the Hellenic notion of the soul ('psyche') as a butterfly anxious to take wing from its bodily prison. For we are aware in two ways of the unity of our persons. Our consciousness is bombarded with what the sense organs tell it, and indeed must apparently rely upon their electrochemical activity for obtaining its only information about the world. Small differences in temperature, salts or drugs can bring with them exhilaration, delirium or despair.

But we also believe the mind holds command of much of the body's conscious action; and we are aware of the wide and still mysterious territory we call 'psychosomatics'. So intimately do we realize the unity that is at the heart of ourselves, that we could begin to understand what we mean in theological language in speaking of the 'interpenetration of the organic by the eternal'. Yet this would not be like an intrusion from outside, rather would the mental and the organic be taken together in a seamless whole. It is, indeed, in the mystery of his own nature that the Christian first sees foreshadowed the principle of incarnation that is at the beginning and end of his creed.

What then can the unity of ourselves tell us about the nature of the universe and of man within it? One of the best modern philosophic statements of the traditional Christian view of man has been given by William Temple in his book *Christus Veritas*.[3] It is his argument, sometimes with the use of his own words, that we shall go on to consider here.

Temple held man to be a progressing unity and began by emphasizing the uniqueness of the individual. Every entity, at whatever level, contains something unique at its core, forming its own underived contribution to the sum of things. Negligible with things at the mechanical level, this uniqueness increases with life, and is found at its fullest in human life. The principle is one of growth. With the appearance of higher forms of life, we escape further from external determinants of character and action in the degree to which we acquire rational self-direction. 'The fact that the individual's actions are not generic but his own is the root of man's moral responsibility.'

Our perceptions are so wide over space and time that each mind is potentially a focussing point for all reality. We grow not by isolation but by receiving stimuli from the environment. Though a great man may seem relatively independent of circumstances, this is because he has a deeper and wider dependence. It is in this way that heroes can appear indifferent to temporal calamities. Our capacity to span time gives us an important dimension of unity. The sense data of the present moment do not wholly engross us; we can contemplate and act with reference to unlimited stretches of time. We can be more interested in the future than in the past or even the present. Even in our being conscious of space and time as a limiting frame, there is that which suggests that mind, in its ultimate affinities is not so limited. To act with reference to space and time leads us to set up ideas and purposes, plans and ideals. Here arises our concept of rights and duties. Man thinks of himself in a society of persons and the same qualities that make him supremely individual make him inherently social. 'Personality is the capacity for Fellowship.'[4]

Man is conscious of his freedom and his capacity for original creativity. It is from creativity that – I believe – our individuality is more completely known, than by referring particular actions to our 'volitions'. In *The Concept of Mind* – as we shall later discuss – Professor Gilbert Ryle makes amusing play with the idea of isolated volitions as the mental sources of action. We may learn from him of the care needed in choosing the philosophic language with which to express our human freedom. We must avoid the Cartesian absurdity of a body inhabited and operated by a separate mind, like an automobile with a little invisible horse inside it. Yet the reality of purpose and choice Professor Ryle would be the last to reject. Probably no considerable school of philosophy would rule out our power, within obvious physiological limits, to bring about a desiderated result in the organic order. The neurophysiologist Sir John Eccles expresses the common sense of the matter:

> We believe we have ability to control or modify our actions by the exercise of 'will', and in practical life all sane men assume that they have this ability. By stimulation of the motor cortex [of the brain] it is possible to evoke complex motor acts in a conscious human subject. The subject reports that the experience is quite different from that occurring when he 'willed' a movement. The distinction arises not in the differences between the movements, but in their different antecedents. In the one case there was the experience of having 'willed' an action which was missing in the other.[5]

Consciousness of freedom and creative power is the most obvious psychological fact about us. Our personalities originate that which is new. Even my everyday ideas and purposes would appear to have a uniqueness lacking in other entities. 'When I exercise will,' writes Professor H. H. Farmer, 'I am conscious, as it were, of a shaft opening up in the midst of the order of things presented to me, and something ultimate, which is not presented but is known simply by being it, flowing out creatively into the world through it.'[6]

We generally speak of creativity when man's ideas and designs issue in something that is uniquely novel: a poem, a symphony, a new hypothesis in science. Yet in its most familiar form, human freedom is shown in those actions we call moral. We say a man is 'responsible' for these because, although heredity and environment may have much to do with them, they are his own in the sense that he does them, not because he is physically compelled to, but because he is 'that kind of person'. If an act expresses what he is, he is in fact responsible.

With some actions of this sort, we can speak of freedom only in a limited way. Thus I can over-indulge myself at a party, alienate my friends and get up at noon next day at cross-purposes with myself and those around me. All this I may call 'doing as I please'. And such actions, done in response to our moods or – as we would say – 'because we feel like them' can be the level at which much human behaviour takes place. Far from being fully free they belong with what Temple has likened to St Paul's 'body of death'.[7] Such people have the freedom of Shakespeare's tragic characters to destroy themselves. 'They are free, for the origin of their actions is themselves; they are bound hand and foot, for from themselves there is no flight.'[8]

To some men, the notion of 'freedom' seems to imply the unconstrained following of impulse, to do what they feel like at the moment. In physics and mechanics the essence of what is called freedom is randomness; it disappears by being predictable. Yet a man whose character we can predict and rely upon is not to that extent less free. In this sense, freedom is to be had only by discipline of emotions and the proper channelling of impulses. The educated man, master of a skill, able to stick to a purpose or ride out the mood of the moment, is in a new and important way free. The freedom to run a four-minute mile is one that – like many a freedom – has to be hard-won. The Christian is accustomed to speak in a familiar sense of the 'service that is perfect freedom'.

How can this unity of character and action, the prerequisite of true freedom, come about? For, as Temple observes, man does not commonly behave like one in whom all being finds a focus. 'He commonly behaves as one with strictly local and contemporary interests . . . for whom the animal desires which are limited to the immediate present count for more than the spectacle of all time and all existence.' The attainment of freedom is then an important part of education. Our unity of personality is at first only formal. The problem throughout is 'out of many to become one'. We are born with a host of different instincts, impulses and capacities. We have also a capacity of selective attention; and this ability to fix attention on one object to the temporary neglect of others is what is commonly called the 'will'. To train it is the main business of education, indeed the only business of early education.[9]

As the seat of purpose, the will is not a separate or detachable faculty. It is the co-ordination of the whole psychic nature for action. While everyone is capable of having it, no one has it in perfection. It varies with age and individuals. 'Will is so much of a Personality as is consciously co-ordinated for action.' It can be, though it seldom is, the whole of the conscious personality. The question whether the will is free is – properly speaking – meaningless: it exists only in so far as freedom has become a reality. With St Augustine, if I 'will' to be good, I am good; the two expressions mean the same.[10]

Even with the will deficient we have from the first a real unity and moral responsibility. As Temple observes,[11] there is unity of physical organization, unity in various aspects of psychic life (memory and consciousness of oneness). But the true unity of the person will be achieved 'in the completely organized and harmonized self which it is capable of becoming. Here, as in every true instance of growth, the end contains the explanation of the process and declares its true nature.'

Such a claim for man, placing its emphasis supremely on what he is becoming, has a profound evolutionary significance. For the most important thing to know about ourselves as a species (biologically as well as morally) is that we stand at the present end of a long series in which animals have been gradually emancipated from automatic reactivity to the environment. And if freedom of the will be a psychological reality, man can be emancipated too – in real if limited measure – even from his individual learning history. 'Just because he is self-conscious he is no merely passive plaything of external forces nor of combinations of forces within himself.'[12]

THE EVOLUTION OF BEHAVIOUR

Our description has so far presented man as a finished rational and moral being. We must now look briefly at the history of animal behaviour to find how such an organism came into existence, and how far it may be called complete.

The simplest pieces of behaviour we know in living organisms are perhaps the responses of growing plants, where a stem turns towards the light or a tendril coils round a twig. Or in those protozoan animals like *Paramaecium*, propelled by a covering of microscopic hairs called cilia, the organism may be steered into the shade by the faster 'rowing' of the cilia on the lighted side. These are all direct responses of living protoplasm to stimuli from the environment. But in animals that have acquired a nervous system we find behaviour taking place at sites remote from the stimulation. A simple flatworm will perform various responses: crawling against a water current, or away from a mild electric shock, or towards food. Here a nerve impulse is being generated by cells sensitive to stimuli, in various parts of the body and especially at the early-warning stations of the head. Among these elementary sense organs are even simple eyes. The impulses such cells generate are relayed by attenuated processes called nerve fibres to a 'central nervous system' or brain. Here a diversity of information is integrated, and motor impulses are sent out to a variety of effector organs, muscles, glands or other parts of the body carrying out specific pieces of behaviour.

The most elementary behaviour in ourselves is what is called *reflex*. We blink protectively as a fast object approaches the eye.

The heart quickens, the stomach muscles contract, a gland secretes adrenalin, our muscles make small corrective contractions to prevent our falling over. All this is silent routine behaviour; there would be no advantage, indeed intolerable distraction, if this activity were projected up into our conscious awareness.

Instinctive behaviour differs from reflex in its greater complexity and the time it takes to enact. There is much of it in ourselves, but to understand it best we should turn first to insects, birds and lower vertebrates where it is the predominant mode of behaviour.[13] An instinct is a built-in pattern of behaviour, adapted to a particular set of conditions relevant to the life of the animal. Instincts are innate, that is, they are not learned during the individual's lifetime but inherited from the parents and held in common with the whole species. The behavioural responses of an instinct are the outcome of the structure of a special part of the nervous system. They are produced by the release of a special drive, in the form (as some behaviourists would say) of stored 'action specific energy'. This is triggered by an appropriate sensory stimulus which is called a 'releaser'.

Releasers may be very specific to particular pieces of behaviour. A parent bird will feed nestlings only on sight of their open bright yellow mouths. A male robin is stimulated to fight at certain seasons by his antagonist's red breast. A mere tuft of red feathers on a wire will release fighting, but a perfect robin without the red will not.

Instincts then are stereotyped and not well adaptable to unusual situations. The responses may look foolish and inept if the conditions change. A herring-gull shows a strong territorial attachment to the nest, but if the clutch of eggs be removed it will show no concern about these, even if they are visible a few feet in front of it. Oyster-catchers will respond maximally to large plaster model eggs three times the size of their own. A hen looking for a lost chick reacts to its cheeping call alone. Muffle this sound under a glass bowl and, though the chick's distress is perfectly visible, the mother will not notice it.

Instincts may operate in chain sequences as in the well-studied courtship of the stickleback. Each response by the female provides a releaser for a new initiative by the male. He leads and she follows, as the reaction chain proceeds, through encounter, ritual dancing, showing of the nest, crossing the threshold, spawning and fertilizing the eggs. In many birds chains of instinctive behaviour are drawn-out over a whole season, with migration, courting, nest-building and care of the young.

There are times when the normal release of a particular drive may be thwarted, or when two opposite drives, such as to stand up and fight or to turn and flee, may be in conflict. The outlet of the drive energy may then be switched to an apparently different track, in the phenomenon known as 'displacement behaviour'. Seagulls in the middle of fighting will break off and pull grass. Courtship is interrupted as birds begin to preen intently. Sticklebacks at the threshold of their territory, poised between fight and flight, dig holes in the sand with their noses. Chewing and smoking appear to be human displacements of the eating instinct. When a woman at a time of stress titivates the face or rearranges the hair, this may represent a displacement of the toilet instinct for the care of the coat, widespread in lemurs and monkeys among the lower primates.

In instinctive and reflex behaviour the performer is normally governed by his evolutionary past. But many higher animals are able to make adjustments to their behaviour by drawing upon their own experience. We describe this process as *learning*: or 'adaptive reorganization of behaviour during the lifetime of the individual'. Even with the simple direction-finding behaviour of flatworms, learning is possible. Animals crawling through glass tubes can be trained to avoid a path where a mild electric shock is given. Reflex behaviour can be readily subject to 'conditioning', as with Pavlov's famous experiments with dogs, which 'learned' to salivate and secrete gastric juice when a bell was rung that had previously been coupled with the presentation of food.

Associative learning is illustrated by the well-known experi-

ments with octopuses by Professor J. Z. Young and his colleagues.[14] Crabs were exhibited to an octopus accompanied
by various sign shapes. Those shown with a white circle
were allowed to be eaten; the seizing of others with a white
square was punished by a mild electric shock. Individuals
can be rapidly trained to avoid the punishment situation
altogether.

Somewhat related to conditioning is the sort of learning
known as 'trial and error'. Rewards are now associated not with
external stimuli, but with the performance of particular
sequences of the animal's own behaviour. Thus a blue-tit
associates cream not only with the sight of a bright milk-bottle
top, but with the doing of the specific action of lifting off the top.
Trial and error learning is often the outcome of 'play', which is
an important undirected surplus activity, especially in young
animals, by which the environment and its possibilities can be
explored.

When learning is indelibly acquired very early in life, we may
speak of it as 'imprinting'. Young birds learn at a brief critical
period the characteristics of their companions, and will there-
after follow and associate only with adults of their own species.
This determines too the direction of later sexual attraction. In
the absence of the mother, young geese were imprinted to the
person of the experimenter Konrad Lorenz. Turkey chicks can
even be imprinted to the image of a moving cardboard box, and
with such objects they will – at sexual maturity – attempt to
copulate.

HUMAN BEHAVIOUR

We shall go wildly wrong in our estimate of man if we forget
how much of his behaviour is non-rational. What distinguishes
man from all other primates is his prolonged childhood, and
hence extended learning period. In a rhesus monkey, by
comparison, infant dependency lasts for one year, as against
eight in man. In ourselves sexual maturity is delayed to the
thirteenth or fourteenth year as compared with the fourth in the

monkey. Full social maturity is postponed from the seventh to near the end of the eighteenth year. This gives an apprenticeship period, full of opportunities for training and acquisition of culture; for man brings little of his behaviour into the world in its finished form at birth.

Yet our behaviour patterns are deeply founded in instinctive drives and it would be true to say that reason scarcely shapes them at all. This does not negate the idea of moral action, indeed it applies strongly to man, the ethical animal. Konrad Lorenz in his book *On Aggression* criticizes the famous assumption by the philosopher Kant that the moral impulse, the 'categorical imperative' that enjoins us to behave justly or lovingly, is derived from rational propositions. No man is likely to organize his behaviour systematically on reasoned criteria. Indeed, Lorenz believes that if man were a purely rational being divested of his animal heritage, he would certainly not be an angel but the opposite.

> Always and everywhere it is the unreasoning, emotional appreciation of values that adds a plus or minus sign to the answer of Kant's categorical self-questioning and makes it an imperative or a veto.[15]

By itself reason cannot set up goals for action, but can only devise means to achieve them. The reason cannot give orders, being in itself like a computer into which no relevant information has been fed, or like a wonderful mechanism without a motor to turn its wheels.

The motive power of behaviour, holds Lorenz, stems from much older sources, not able to be rationally self-observed. 'They are the source of love and friendship, of all warmth of feeling, of appreciation of beauty, of the urge to artistic creativeness, of insatiable curiosity striving for scientific enlightenment. These deepest strata of the human personality are, in their dynamics, not essentially different from the instincts of animals.'[16]

What is different, and peculiar to man, is the great structure of special norms and rights built on these bases and the rational and intelligent control they come under in their highest manifestations. There are both the complicated rules and inhibitions that society imposes, and – bravest of all and probably unique to man – the individual behaviour and creative initiative of the non-conformer.

We are not then to despise our behaviour, or hold it in some sense 'sub-human', because its mainsprings are instinctive. For as well as our instincts, much also of what we learn during our intelligent life-span is afterwards reduced to conditioned habit. This does not mean that freedom and moral responsibility disappear. Conditioning or habit-forming can be an economy by which behaviour learned or voluntarily initiated may with repeated use become more automatic. By analogy a plane may fly with an automatic pilot without reducing the human pilot's ability to resume control. Conditioning frequently reinforces moral behaviour: there are things 'a nice person doesn't do'.

Behaviour may then be subject to rational control, although its patterns have not sprung from rationality. Upon any behaviour taking place in the conscious sphere, we can apply the sanctions of choice and will. This extends even in a limited way and for a short time to such reflexes as breathing and blinking. In some areas of behaviour the inhibition of deep emotional drives may be harder than in others, especially for some individuals. Voluntary restraint may disappear under the influence of alcohol or drugs, or even with high levels of external stimulus.

The sex instinct is a good example of behaviour with an innate background. It may proceed to its fulfilment entirely as a piece of inherited behaviour. There will be first what is called 'appetitive behaviour', the searching and exploring of the environment for the key stimuli. This narrows progressively towards its goal, and is followed by the more stereotyped 'fixed action pattern' that leads the behaviour to its completions, drawing off, as we say, the accumulated energy of the drive. Successive parts of this inherited behaviour may of course be embroidered with learned associations, particularly as new and individual sorts of releasers are built into it. The novelty of the human situation is that so much of this can be brought under voluntary restraint.

Instinctive behaviour can be led to conform with other considerations, enjoining prudence or altruism; it can be brought under the social and moral patterns in which our lives are set. The difficulty of this achievement will vary with temperament, with heredity and especially with the conditioning involved by a particular time and place. We can enter upon situations where we have put rational restraint entirely beyond our powers.

It is helpful, indeed necessary, to know the instinctive and emotional basis of our own behaviour, and to allow for it in our fellows, in forming moral judgements or even realistic laws. But it would be wrong to believe that a thing is inevitable or morally justified just because it is 'instinctive' or a 'part of our old nature'. For man is the last of a line of animals that has been emancipated from automatic reactivity. Such a release must have been gained first from the external environment, later from his own instinctive organization, and even personal psychological history.

Even the earliest animals, as we have already seen, 'regulate' their internal chemical and physical state against the outside world. For example, they control the water and salt content and the temperature of the body. Higher animals develop more and more complex control systems, operating both by nerves and hormones, which we describe by the cybernetic term 'feed-back'. With an increasingly complex nervous system, whole patterns of the built-in behaviour called instinctive could become adapted to the generalized requirements of the whole species. At a higher level still – by his personal learning – the individual has been able to achieve some flexibility against his inherited set of instincts. We are, in Temple's phrase already cited, the first creature that is not the plaything of external or internal forces.[17] For in the reality of plans and purposes, with the power of deliberation and decision, the human animal may from minute to minute assert his autonomy over the conditioned pattern presented by our personal past. We can be emancipated not only from the history of the race, but even from our own.

LANGUAGE

In this novel situation of human behaviour, language has a key importance. Sir Karl Popper in his book *Conjectures and Refutations* could distinguish four levels in the 'language' by which animals communicate with each other. First, and at an early stage in animal evolution, information is already conveyed by symptoms and expressions. At a second level, these are refined into special signals or 'releasers' that we find becoming ritualized in instinctive behaviour. The distinctively human levels of language are the third, descriptive, and the fourth, argumentative. This last and highest function of language involves the development of critical and rational attitudes. Popper has put forward a theory of human rationality that he calls 'freedom with plastic control'. This is a process of trial and error elimination. Its main regulative idea is the distinction of truth from falsehood. The higher functions exert over the lower ones a control with feedbacks, and arguments are the means of control. Language has become refined under the need for better control. We have learned how to 'abstract', to take out from various modes of expressing a theory its invariable content or meaning; and we do the same with aims, proposals and ideas for action.

All organisms, maintains Sir Karl Popper, are engaged in problem-solving day and night: so are evolutionary lines. New reactions, new forms, new organs, new modes of behaviour are tentatively put forward and controlled by error-elimination. A single organism telescopes into its body all the controls developed by previous generations and is in itself a sort of spearhead of progress – 'a tentative solution probing into a new evolutionary niche'. The individual itself, and its behaviour, may both be looked upon as trials that can be rejected by error-elimination. Human rationality makes it possible to eliminate errors without killing the organism: happy are we in having attained to a level where our hypotheses are able to die in our stead!

When an Amoeba solves its problems it is not rational. Einstein is. And this consciously critical attitude to our own ideas is – in Popper's view – the only really important difference between the method of Amoeba and the method of Einstein. It makes it possible for Einstein to eliminate a hundred hypotheses as inadequate before examining another.

The use of language is a very large part of our lives; and it is clear that our 'argumentative' language is uniquely human. In his book *Syntactic Structures*, which has strongly influenced linguistic thought during the past decade, Professor Noam Chomsky, of the Massachusetts Institute of Technology, has moved sharply away from the behaviourist view of language. The learning of language is more than a matter of acquiring verbal behaviour from the environment, as might be likened to mastery of the internal combustion engine by watching the dials on a switchboard.

It is evident according to Chomsky that children learn language (sometimes against enormous handicaps) through a very complex inborn capacity. The study of language, it is claimed, may form for us a 'mirror of consciousness', opening the way to the operating principles of the mind. When children are learning, they are observed to follow certain rules, but they are not copying adult grammar. They appear to be expressing a universal grammar not yet transformed into the appropriate structure of the surface language. Though it proposes a finite set of rules, grammar will characteristically allow an infinite variety of sentences. We can use language creatively where a computer can deal only with clichés.

The language that can be taught to computers is very limited. Even with laborious pauses and emphasis, groups of sounds can hardly be identified as words, let alone groups of words as sentences. Though millions of dollars have been spent on developing computers that can translate from one language to another, we are told that little or no progress has been made. If the real nature of the problem had been understood, it may be that the money would never have been spent.

The processes by which the human mind achieved its great complexity of language organization are still a mystery. Chomsky and his school would doubt whether Darwinian natural selection, or any of the neurophysiological concepts we now know can account for them. We may need to develop principles entirely new.

CHAPTER 3

The Bogey of Determinism

THE idea that a man's conduct is determinate can arise from two levels. First there is the philosophical argument, stemming from an incomplete understanding of physics, and even today this has died hard. Second, there is the behavioural determinism taught by the followers of Freud, that would in practice bring us into a position almost as rigid as physical determinism.

We may begin briefly with the first. Lord Russell, in his *Autobiography*, speaks of the dilemma commonplace at some time to most men: 'At the age of fifteen, I became convinced that the motions of matter, whether living or dead, proceeded entirely in accordance with the laws of dynamics, and therefore the will can have no influence upon the body.'[1] In our own century, both physicists and biologists have addressed themselves with some anxiety to the question of human freedom and responsibility. For the physical sciences were too often assumed by the lay public to be on the way to a millennium where everything, including the phenomena of life, would be explained on their terms. Gilbert Ryle observes, 'people still tend to treat laws of Mechanics not merely as the ideal type of scientific laws, but as, in some sense, the ultimate laws of Nature. They tend to hope or fear that biological, psychological and sociological laws will one day be "reduced" to mechanical laws – though it is left unclear what sort of a transaction this "reduction" would be.'[2]

On practical grounds, no sane man runs his life as if determinism were true. Dr Johnson's pragmatic good sense: 'Sir, we intuit our freedom, and there's an end on't', outweighs many a sophisticated critique of human responsibility.

The determinist view of the mind as an 'epiphenomenon' overlaid upon the body, conscious of the body's causal sequence, yet powerless to influence it, is of course easiest of philosophical claims to reduce to absurdity. In Karl Popper's words:

Pure physical determinism would completely destroy the idea of creativity and morality. History, it has been claimed, would be reduced to a tale of campaigns fought by mindless robots. A deaf musician, it has been likewise said, could write all the symphonies of Beethoven and Mozart simply by studying their precise physiological state and predicting where they would put their black marks on paper. He could even write the different scores they would have written had they eaten lamb instead of chicken. In this way, in short, conscious mind would be no longer a conative faculty, but a powerless voyeur gazing at the whole stream of so-called moral and creative aspiration.[3]

Not only is determinism incredible to common sense. Not only would it be pragmatically the worst of hypotheses – if taken seriously – in negating moral or creative achievement. Its fatal objection is that it is logically impossible to propound. If the behaviour of the nerve cells of my conscious brain is somehow determined by the previous history of the universe, not only do my physical actions, even if I appear to will them, cease to be my own. So do my thoughts and rational processes. My claim to draw valid conclusions is spurious if these are the effect of any 'cause' beyond my freedom to process the data and apply the tests of rationality. It has sometimes been argued that a determinate mind could still be in register with the world outside, and able to compute a valid picture of it, by logical or other rules. Consciousness, even though its content would be determinate, might then be one of the necessary links in a causal sequence. But computers can regularly achieve as much as 'consciousness' of this sort, and do it more efficiently. And the obvious fact that minds can make mistakes or come to different conclusions from the same data would seem to invalidate them as determinate registers of truth.

If determinism were true we could never validly affirm it. The mental events leading to such a statement would depend not on the cogency of the evidence, but on the past history of the world. Yet many people are strangely troubled by the determinist claim today. A friend (and in sad truth he was a clergyman) recently argued with me: 'You assure me I am not determinate, but you say this as a biologist, and moreover one with a known theistic bias. Suppose that a psychologist told me that my belief in freedom was illusory, should I go on clinging to it just for fear of the consequences of losing it?' To which the only reply can be: 'Sir, I am not asking you to accept my scientific authority nor to discount it by my theological prejudice: only to inspect my logic. Denial of your freedom is the one proposition no man – be he psychologist or other – can ever validly put to you.'

MODERN PHYSICS AND DETERMINISM

Few physicists today would claim that the course of all nature is fixed beyond all uncertainty. The behaviour of the smallest particles is individually unpredictable, and the regularity of nature is seen as a statistical regularity applying to particles in large aggregates. The new outlook of physics in this century has come from the growth of quantum mechanics, dealing with the behaviour of the smallest particles such as the electrons or protons of the atom, or the units in which light travels, called photons.

The best known ⌐f the quantum laws to the ordinary man is the Principle of Un ertainty, enunciated by Werner Heisenberg in 1927, which tells us that the position and velocity of a particle such as an electron cannot be precisely determined. It is important to understand that this need not be due to the crudity of our instruments or even to any present lack of knowledge. Uncertainty seems to be a property at the real heart of nature.

We can make this clearer by an actual experiment as suggested in the accompanying picture. If a beam of electrons is passed through a narrow slit it will impinge on a wider area of a screen at the other side. We cannot predict where any individual electron will fall and the width of the diffraction pattern on the screen is a measure of this uncertainty. If we try to make the uncertainty of position smaller by narrowing the slit, the diffraction pattern will widen as we have increased the un-

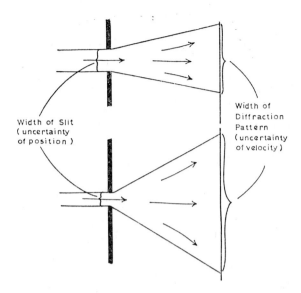

FIGURE I. (*above*) A beam of electrons passed through a narrow slit to form a diffraction pattern on a scintillation screen. The two diagrams show how by narrowing the width of the slit (reducing the uncertainty of position), the width of the diffraction pattern (and the uncertainty of velocity) is increased. (*below*) A diagram to represent a photon as a 'probability wave packet'. The intensity of shading at a given spot represents the probability of finding the photon in that location. (After Rothman.)

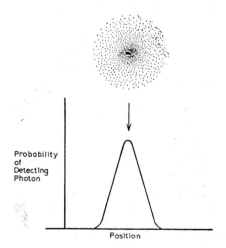

certainty of velocity. The more precisely we try to locate the electron's position, the less we can know of its velocity. There is no way we can determine both at any instant.

With a single photon of light passing through a slit, we can likewise make no exact prediction of its behaviour, though we can calculate the probability that it will impinge on one spot of a photographic plate rather than another. A photon could be said indeed to be represented by a 'probability wave packet'. Where the shading is darkest, there is the greatest probability of locating it. But its real uncertainty of location, like that of the electron, must represent a fundamental property of nature.

Such uncertainty applies in principle to all single bodies. But the uncertainty of velocity greatly decreases as the mass increases. Protons with a mass 1,800 times greater than an electron have a diffraction beam 1,800 times narrower. Uncertainty may operate even on a very gross scale of particles. Milton Rothman, in his very readable introduction to *The Laws of Physics*,[4] takes the example of a vacuum chamber free of vibration containing two spheres the size of a baseball. One is glued to the floor, the other is dropped upon it. Classical physics would predict that if the two spheres are perfectly elastic, the dropped ball will bounce up and down indefinitely. But from the uncertainty principle there is a probability that this ball will land slightly off centre each time it falls. Each bounce will magnify this tendency and after ten or twelve bounces there is a large probability that it will land far enough out to hit the floor rather than the fixed sphere. The ball behaves as if by chance, and we cannot precisely predict its direction at any bounce. Rothman writes:

> Scientists and philosophers of the 'deterministic' school (to which the late Albert Einstein belonged) would say this is nonsense: if we knew all the variables involved, we could tell exactly which way the ball would bounce. But most physicists working in the field of quantum theory believe it is really impossible to predict exactly where a particle will go, and the best we can do is to predict probabilities.[5]

The laws of science begin to operate then with a probability approaching certainty only when we come to deal with large aggregates of particles, such as the molecules in a jar of gas or with any of the familiar situations of physics and chemistry in the life-sized world. For our predictions about these we are using the mathematics of probability.

What relevance – if any – can the random behaviour of small particles have for human freedom or any living process? It has been suggested that gene mutations may be caused by the random impact of particles from cosmic or X-irradiation. It is possible too that in the nervous system certain inherently unpredictable events, originating in 'noise' at the level of very small particles, could be amplified to initiate behaviour at a large-scale level. To this speculation we shall have to return in the following chapter.

But even if the uncertainty principle were established for human brain cells, we should not like to think of our behaviour as having randomness or 'freedom' in the quantum sense. People displaying this sort of freedom are usually put under psychiatric care! The uncertainty principle would solve nothing for human freedom in itself. It will simply allow that, if there are purposive events in the world that originate with our own minds, the laws of nature are not such as to confine these in a determinate strait-jacket set up thousands of millennia before we existed.

Biologists have sometimes sought for physical models of human behaviour that would allow the choice implicit in our freedom by invoking the margin of uncertainty offered by quantum physics.

The philosophers are apt to be scornful of such attempts in advance. Professor Ryle objects that 'the modern interpretation of natural laws as statements not of necessities but of very, very long odds is sometimes acclaimed as providing a desiderated element of non-rigorousness in Nature. Now at last, it is sometimes felt, we can be scientific while reserving just a very few occasions in which appraisal-concepts can be properly applied. This silly view assumes that an action could not merit favourable or unfavourable criticism, unless it were an exception to scientific generalisations.'[6]

With great respect, what appears to be silly is Professor Ryle's missing of the point. No suspension or exception to natural laws is being sought for human behaviour; merely the demonstration that the laws of nature can still operate in situations where human action enjoys a real freedom of choice.

But some impatience is justified when the validity of our freedom is held to depend upon the Heisenberg principle. We are of all men most miserable if we can be philosophically shaken by the day-to-day fluctuations of quantum theory. Jonathan Swift's Laputans, with their obsessional anxiety over the state of the sun's health, would seem by comparison rational and strong-minded.

The antinomy of freedom and the laws of nature would draw us to some strange conclusions if we let it. The physicist Erwin Schrödinger, in his book *What Is Life?*, involved himself at the end in an odd form of pantheism. Maintaining that his body functioned as pure mechanism, yet allowing that his introspective consciousness of free-will was valid, he was forced to the 'only possible inference . . . that I – I in the widest sense of the word, that is to say every conscious mind that has ever said or felt "I" – am the person, if any, who controls the "motions of the atoms" according to the Laws of Nature'.[7]

FREUD AND HUMAN BEHAVIOUR

Even if we no longer believe in a physical determinism of behaviour, it is popularly believed that the findings of Sigmund Freud and his followers about motivation and conduct force us into the same sort of strait-jacket. Our thoughts and actions – we are taught – are strictly governed by causes very different from those we imagine. True, such causality may not be mathematically rigid; the Freudian would not predict trivial actions inside certain limits of precision. But causal laws are firmly held to apply to the drives of human behaviour and to the broad patterns of conduct in which they issue.

Behaviour originates – in the Freudian view – not in our rational motives nor in our intelligent reaction to stimuli. Its sources are deep-seated. Every mental fact – thought, idea or overt action – is controlled by factors that are either congenital (hereditary) or historic (resulting from the influence of environment). Every experience leaves lasting traces, and though sited deep in the unconscious it is never forgotten. Nothing that happens to the mind is lost or ceases to exert its influence. The foundations of our behaviour lie then in the personal issues of our past emotional life. They may be uncovered by analysis, or they can be revealed – most significantly – when the intellect is least in control, as in dreams, under drugs or alcohol, or by unintentional slips of the tongue.

The causal continuity of personality brings us to the role of the unconscious mind. We have found already, as with conditioned learning, that the subject responds to a contemporary stimulus not directly, but in a context of past mental history. Conditioned reflexes, the Freudians hold, replace the sort of discriminatory behaviour usually postulated for our higher mental functions.

As it is put by J. A. C. Brown, in his useful volume *Freud and the Post-Freudians*,[8] the unconscious mind is a dynamic force playing a predominant part in mental life, rather than a wastepaper basket of trivial memories that have fallen below the threshold of consciousness because they were unimportant.

On the contrary, ideas may be kept out of consciousness because they are so significant to the ego that they are repressed. And in disguised form these memories of unpleasant things we shrink from recalling may issue in devious ways as neuroses or various sorts of phobia. A conflict thus arises between primitive drives seeking an outlet and learned behaviour patterns that must inhibit these as unrealistic. The concept of 'drive' can be compared with the 'homoeostasis' or maintenance of the physiological state of the body, as with the level of our blood sugar, or salt and water content. There is a similar constancy of psychic equilibrium: what is inhibited in one way will break out in another to an exact and compensating degree. The ego can learn a 'detour behaviour' that may inhibit the direct or immediate satisfaction of drives in the interests of the individual's more general well-being as a social organism. Or the more unviable attempts at drive-gratification may appear as the neurotic symptoms of various disorders.

Behaviour is thus motivated and goal-directed. Its symptoms are to be explained in the context of psychic determinism; and we should be able to detect their specific goal. Freud not only looked for general laws describing the occurrence of symptoms. In a way no one had done before, he looked for their *aim*. He claimed that the individual showed two vital and overriding drives, towards self-preservation and towards procreation. It is around the latter – most often blocked from expression – that Freudian psychology is centred. The drive energy of procreation, called 'libido' or sexual energy, can in the broadest sense be equated with pleasurable sensation arising from any of the bodily functions. By the detour paths of sublimation it is associated too with tenderness, altruism, pleasure in work and friendship.

According to Freud, three orifices of the body are involved in the satisfaction of the libido, and interest centres in these in definite sequence from birth upwards. To the new-born, the mouth is the primary organ of pleasure and the first desire is to suck the breast. Substitute satisfactions come from sucking the thumb or other objects, and the phase of oral interest continues through life by pleasure in eating, smoking and kissing. The mouth is soon supplanted as a centre of interest by the anus. In this phase the aim is at first to expel the faeces aggressively, but later (as the anal sphincter begins to work effectively towards the end of the first year) to retain them. About the end of the third year, pregenital sexuality is succeeded by early genital or phallic interest, centred on the penis or its female homologue. Unlike previous drives, the phallic one requires an external object for its satisfaction. The latent period of sexuality continues to the tenth year, until the glandular changes begin that lead to sexual maturity.

Adult sexuality may continue to embody pregenital along

with genital drives, and if these become primary – in the adult – we speak of perversion. The pattern of adult sexuality can be much determined by early parental attitudes, as for example to bowel-training and masturbation, and prohibitions in early life generally. The Freudians would see the development of adult character in terms of pregenital drives that have changed their object and disguised their mode of expression under social pressures. The 'anal character' may show forth in such traits as stubbornness, independence and possessiveness. The value attached to possessions, especially the accumulation of money, equates with the faeces-retention pleasure of the child, modified in its expression. Faeces are represented by possessions, especially money: so it is significant that we speak of 'filthy lucre' or 'throwing money down the drain' or of 'rolling in it'.

Not all of the teachings of Freud would be generally accepted by analytical psychologists today. Nor should we think of Freudianism as a body of theory obtained by the methods of science, or open throughout to experimental verification. It is a system largely of intuitive hypothesis that has been found successful in analysis. Some of its arguments can be shown to be circular, relying for proof upon facts deducible only from the arguments themselves. And if Freudian theory purports to show that psychology is wholly determinate, it will be as vulnerable as any postulate of physical determinism, for it would invalidate rational thinking. It has been amusingly maintained by one of the critics, Dr Rudolf Allers, that Freudianism is just the system that, on Freud's own principles, a man with Freud's background might be expected to develop.[9]

But none of these criticisms need remove the pragmatic value Freudianism may have in the treatment of patients, even if – like other systems of ministration by the physician or priest – it can be said to have developed a mythology of its own.

Few theologians will want to deny that our behaviour contains far more irrationality than we have traditionally cared to believe. For the picture we have just presented, of our lives lived by our subconscious, and of our minds in bondage to past history, stands strangely at odds with our earlier vision of man

as a self-organizing system, increasing in freedom and rationality. It is disturbing to recall H. G. Wells's assurance that the
God-like intellect of man is no better designed for discerning
ultimate truth than a pig's snout.

Is this true? And is the gulf in outlook between Christians and
deterministic psychologists really too wide to bridge? The
Christian teaching about freedom and responsibility must be
looked at – I believe – as the dynamic expression of what
Freudianism is viewing statically. Christianity adds a forward
dimension to our view of man. We are to expect to find freedom
and rationality in a continuing process of growth. This is what
the Christian looks forward to, with what must seem – to
outsiders – an ever-unrealistic hope. There is to be progress in
both the short and long run. The Christian's ultimate hope of
the world may have the long reach of Teilhard's vision of point
Omega where our whole species is to be redeemed and unified.[10]
There is hope in our individual lives too. For we are part of a
progressing order we believe is already inaugurated for us. In
our present condition, looked at statically, we can hardly be
called free. Indeed Freudian determinism has given us yet
another picture of what is a familiar human dilemma. Knowing
the good, we choose the ill. Ovid has written: '*Video meliora
proboque, deteriora sequor.*'[11] St Paul has pictured for us in the
Epistle to the Romans the same plight: 'The good that I would
I do not: but the evil which I would not, that I do. . . . O
wretched man that I am! who shall deliver me from the body of
this death?'[12]

A darkly realistic view of man's plight is, then, no special
attribute of St Paul or St Augustine, or of a medieval Church
obsessed with original sin. Indeed where Christianity and
Freudianism draw closest together is in rejecting the shallow
humanistic optimism about the state of man. But the disability
that the analyst sees clinically from outside, the sinning man has
the grief of knowing from within. What another might call in us
'*privatio*' – deprivation of enlightenment or understanding – we
know in ourselves to be moral guilt or '*pravatio*' for which we
carry responsibility.

This is the guilt that both Christianity and analytical psychology offer, with their diverse means of therapy, to cast out. Both recognize that human freedom is a difficult and exceptional attainment. It can only be slowly and partially reached in a lifetime. There can be no disharmony with Christian teaching if the analyst tries to show how much of our present behaviour is in bondage to the unconscious, and what a massive obstacle this presents to moral and rational progress. Freudian determinism can disable human freedom no more than the 'fault and corruption' Christianity finds in the nature of every man.

It would be foolish to claim that Christians and psychologists always see these things as one; but even more wrong to tie all the analytical school (some of them Christians) to the personal attitudes of Freud. He himself would have claimed to be an atheist, and one of his objectives was a protest against all religion. The search for moral values was, with Freud, centred in the nature of the individual organism itself. Such an outlook would be considered by most psychologists and sociologists today an over-private one, with excessive emphasis on nineteenth-century individualism. They would look rather for a system of personal relationships spelled out with reference to man's duties and obligations to his fellows. Far more than Freud would have allowed, the basis of morality is social.

CHAPTER 4

Mind and Nature

The brain secretes the mind as the liver secretes the bile.[1]

I cannot admit that the connection of soul and body is really
either intelligible or explicable.

F. H. Bradley[2]

THE human brain is the most intricate structure, living or
inanimate, ever realized. Sir Charles Sherrington spoke of it as
'the great ravelled knot' by which we feel, see, hear, think and
decide. Obviously it is in anatomical terms the master tissue of
the body. Its complexity is hard even to imagine. If we think of
the expanse of grey cells of the folded cerebral cortex as a
computer system where information is processed and stored and
recalled, there are three million sensory nerve cells relaying on
to it. These have long trunks or axones along which nerve
impulses are propagated. Though they travel fast, at a hundred
metres per second in a mammalian axone, they show
nothing like electronic speed, being merely handed on step by
step, by self-propagated depolarization of the axone membrane.
If the sensory neurones were linked up two by two in every
possible way, the number of combinations would be $2^{2,783,000}$, a
number that would take a larger book than this simply to write
out. It would be vastly greater than Eddington's 10^{79} for the
particles in the universe. In fact the smaller number of 10^{10}
interconnecting cells of which the cortex is built up would
appear to be ample to integrate the greatest conceivable range
of cross-patterns.

The cortical neurones themselves are short cells without
axones but linked into systems by branching twigs or dendrites.
The body of each cell receives from others perhaps hundreds of
fine processes, swollen at the tips into tiny knobs (*boutons*

terminaux). These do not quite touch the membrane of the adjacent cell, being separated by minute gaps of no more than $\frac{1}{30,000}$ of a millimetre across. Across these gaps impulses are passed from cell to cell, by the liberation of short-lasting traces of chemical transmitter substances. Such transmission sites or gates between cells are called synapses.[3]

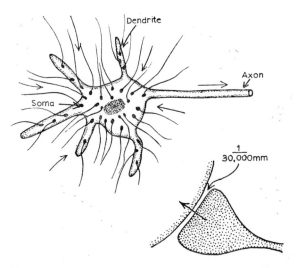

FIGURE 2. The cell-body of a neurone, with the numerous synaptic knobs reaching it from other neurones. The thick outward trunk is the beginning of the long axone. The inset sketch shows the synaptic knob even more magnified with the narrow width of the synaptic cleft.

Conscious thought comes into play only when the cerebral cortex is active. But both here and in other parts of the brain, a high complexity of information can be stored. We no longer reckon in terms of special areas of the brain with specific information written in. By removing large tracts of the cerebral cortex of rats, Lashley showed that the learned behaviour of rats in mazes was left unimpaired. We are taught today to think of units of experience leading to the production of appropriate 'memory molecules' of protein, specified by brain-cell RNA.

Rather than spatially localized, these are widely dispersed in the cortex, and able to be 'recognized' and experience re-called on repetition of the stimulus that produced them.

The interconnections between neurones, as illustrated in the sketch overleaf, are sufficient in number and variety to give the complexity needed for the highest activities of the brain. Using information theory we could suggest that it is the brain's function to set up a reduced copy or a working model of reality, preserving or abstracting all the essential features of the original. An interesting discussion on the brain as an engineering problem is to be found in R. L. Gregory's chapter in Thorpe and Zangwill's *Current Problems in Animal Behaviour*.[4]

Even our creative imagination can be physiologically pictured. Sir John Eccles has suggested[5] that the subconscious working of the brain could involve intense and unimaginably complex interplay of the separate 'engrams' or written-in ideas. What we call imaginative insight would happen when a new combination produces an emergent pattern transcending any existing one. Images of beauty and subtlety, verbal, musical or pictorial, can be evoked by association with other experiences. Such associations could happen even under hallucinogenic drugs such as mescaline.

From what we know of artificial computers there is in principle no difficulty in conceiving the brain as storing and recalling information in this way, or in making comparisons between neurones and computer units. An electronic engineer, Dean E. Wooldridge tells us:

> The neuron possesses not only some of the characteristics of an on/off switch, but also other properties . . . The body of the neuron, in electronic terms, is like a summing amplifier that adds the effects of a number of inputs and compares the sum with a threshold value to determine whether the axone is to fire, and, if so, what is to be the frequency of its output pulse train.[6]

We can readily enough grasp that a central nervous system

and a computer could achieve the same results, from a similar kind of processing; and it matters little that the functional units are different, the one electrochemical (and incidentally working at rather slow speed), the other electronic with impulses flashing at the speed of light.

The real mysteries that the nervous system confronts us with are at a different level. They concern the involvement of the brain in our consciousness and volition. We cannot yet formulate even suitable questions to compare our subjective experience with the lucid demonstrations of physiology. The brain-mind problem is dwelt upon by Sir Charles Sherrington, the father of neurophysiology, in his Gifford Lectures, published in 1940 as *Man on his Nature*. The final conclusion has about it a deep note of resignation:

> Where the brain correlates with mind, no microscopical, no physical, no chemical means detect any radical difference between it and other nerve which does not correlate with mind. . . . To correlate with that physiological entity [of the brain, we find] a suite of mental experience, a complex of thought, feeling, conation, an activity no doubt, but with what if any relation to electrical potential, heat and chemistry? For myself, what little I know of the how of the one does not, speaking personally, even begin to help me toward the how of the other. The two for all I can do remain refractorily apart. They seem to me disparate; not mutually convertible; untranslatable the one into the other.[7]

We are tempted too to involve philosophy with brain physiology when the perennial problems of volition and the freedom of will are raised. We have already mentioned the randomness of events allowed to us by the Heisenberg uncertainty principle under the laws of quantum physics. If such randomness could operate in the nervous system, it could be the basis of inherently unpredictable events, originating at the level of minute particles and enormously amplified by the nervous system.

In their large work on the invertebrate nervous system, Bullock and Horridge write:

> Some encouragement for such speculations has been found in the occurrence of apparently random events at the level of subthreshold junction potentials in certain nerve-muscle endings, miniature end plate potentials arising spontaneously with the frequency character of noise. But the reality of 'indeterminate' events at the level of the organism has been questioned. .... It is a consequence of our knowledge of the code used by neurons that a source of randomness is available without appeal to molecular events, in any case where several active neurons converge on one. Even if the frequencies of the individual cells are not random . . . a modest number of independent cells will together make up an input experimentally indistinguishable from true noise. But while there is no difficulty making models which would provide randomness, how and where it is actually done is quite unknown. [8]

We must be quite clear what we are entitled to ask of the brain in the name of human volition. We are clearly not seeking indeterminism as an explanation of purposiveness. Sheer randomness would be the last thing we are seeking in behaviour; penny-tossing choice would be a worse basis for rationality than determinism, for freedom and responsibility stop when chance begins.

We are simply seeking a system with a sufficient degree of freedom to allow an event to happen without the necessity that it should be inevitably *this*, and not anything else, by virtue of the antecedent physical state of the brain and the world. No natural law need be broken. In theological language, freedom presupposes nature, not violating it but perfecting it.

Sir John Eccles has given prolonged thought to the physiological situation where human 'volition' is involved in an act of free choice. [9] A Nobel laureate widely acclaimed for his discoveries about the mode of transmission of impulses between cells, he also holds a philosophic conviction of the reality of human freedom. A journey to the frontier of volition and neurone would seem – on the face of it – the most promising such a scientist could attempt.

We can begin by asking: is there any unique sort of activity by which the brain enters into liaison with the mind? Our 'volitions' impinge upon the world by the contraction of certain muscles that operate our limbs, our vocal chords or other organs of overt action. Muscle contractions are initiated in particular neurones of the cerebral cortex, linking with the outgoing cells that we call motor-neurons. Special areas of the brain are evidently organized by the interconnections of their cells to activate special bits of behaviour.

The passage of impulses from cell to cell is regulated by the synapses. These are gates that can be momentarily opened and shut, as controlled by minute changes in electrical potential across the cell membrane of the knobs. Whatever we are calling the 'will' could operate by opening particular gates. If at these points indeterminate events were available at molecular level or as noise, one of these – at the selection of the will – might initiate a firing pattern through a whole circuit of neurones. We must remember first the high speed of propagation of impulses between cells (pedestrian though it be as compared with electronic events). If each neuron had three inward and three outward gates, the number that could be activated within a fiftieth of a second is of the order of 10,000. With five gates in and five out, the number would rise to 800,000. The actual number of synaptic contacts of one cell with others is found to be more like a hundred, of which we could assume four or five were in operation. This assumes participation by only one cell, where in fact whole fields of neurones may be co-operating to initiate a complex pattern in space and time.

The real question is not whether such a model is adequate for the job, but whether such questions are the right ones for biologists to ask. Eccles has himself – I believe – managed to avoid the Cartesian trap of positioning a gap between the brain and the mind. From his close approach to the frontier he has – in his latest writings – drawn back, sensing that the journey, however exhilarating, was part of an unreal situation. Unreal not because the brain and mind lie irreconcilably asunder, but because they are aspects of a unity that is indivisible. In his 1964 broadcast lectures, 'The Unity of Conscious Perception', he recognizes the primacy of our intuitions about ourselves and our freedom. He concluded:

> The prime reality of my experiencing cannot with propriety be *identified* with some aspects of its experience and imaginings such as brain and neurons and nerve impulses . . . I believe there is a fundamental mystery in my existence transcending any biological account of the development of my body (including my brain) with its genetic inheritance and evolutionary origin . . . I woke up in life as it were to find myself existing as an embodied self with this body and brain – so I cannot believe that this wonderful divine gift of a conscious existence has no further future, no possibility of another existence under some other unimaginable conditions.[10]

MIND EMERGENT?

Not all biologists have been deterred by the difficulties that Sherrington and Eccles confess. 'Explanations' of mind are regularly attempted, which are simply descriptions of its assumed past history. Accustomed to the spacious time-scale of evolution and to the development of the simple out of the complex, we have the mind accounted for by its 'emergence' from the material body. When physical units such as molecules are arranged in new ways – so the argument runs – new structures with new properties may arise, living from non-living, sentient from merely alive, mental from sentient. Mind is the physiological behaviour of an advanced nervous system: like other functions such as temperature regulation, or control of blood sugar level, it is achieved by the evolution of appropriate structures. Mentality is simply the highest way we know in which life manifests itself and could be explained like everything else living, from biochemistry. 'When behaviour reaches a certain level of complexity it will begin to have a conscious or mental aspect.'

If this last *non-sequitur* be thought too much, the Victorian biologists were more euphoric still. Diagrams were drawn, showing the neuron as 'the organ of the mind', like Descartes's allocation of the seat of the soul to the pineal body. To T. H. Huxley, 'the thoughts to which I am now giving utterance and your thoughts regarding them, are the expression of molecular changes in that matter of life which is the source of our other vital phenomena'. It was at the British Association meeting in Belfast in 1874 that Professor Tyndall affirmed that as the bile is the secretion of the liver, so is the mind the secretion of the brain.

In our own day, Sir Solly Zuckerman has argued the same thing with more sophistication. To him mind is a convenient cloak for processes that can be scientifically observed, on the analogy of artificial brains responding to patterns recognized out of past experience. 'The difference between real and artificial brains is, however, ceasing to be absolute, since machine brains have been made which, even if only in a rudimentary way, are also dynamically responsible for the establishment and working of their own controls.'

There is much popular misunderstanding about human and artificial brains, and even of the potential superiority of the latter. An artificial brain might in principle reproduce efficiently everything that a physiologist could observe empirically about a man. But apart from the different construction and enormous bulk of a computer, its 'intellectual superiority' lies simply in the speed with which calculations can be handled, when translated into its binary or other notation. Electronic pulses flash with the speed of light as compared with the pedestrian rate of nerve impulses. Calculations can be done in a few seconds that would take the brain many months. Logic becomes a matter of automatism.

Yet since all the manipulations of the computer are automatic, anything like genuine invention or creativity is beyond it: 'the problems, the purposes and the scale of values which a machine involves are merely those of its manufacturer.'[11]

Whatever the value of artificial brains as physiological analogues, they touch none of the problems raised by our concept of the mind. For the mind cannot, with a proper use of language, be called the 'function' of any organ system at all. Functions, as we know them in physiology, including the performance of work, the generating of nerve impulses or the secreting of hormones, are straightforward physical activities. They can be expressed in terms of energy and can be predictably modified by doing things to the physical system.

It is true, but aside from the point, that the events of the mind are in close register with what happens to the body. We can evoke specific sensations by electrical stimuli or drugs. We can procure the movement of a limb by applying an electrode to an appropriate nerve. But there is a world of difference between the sensation then experienced and the awareness of having 'willed' the action to happen.

The 'function' of any brain cell can be verified by experiment: it is to generate a wave of depolarization passing in precisely measurable quantities along a nerve axon. We could do the same experiment equally well in ourselves, in a jellyfish, or in a decapitated blow-fly. Consciousness has no part in the sequence.

Professor Otto Lowenstein has concluded his short but illuminating book, *The Senses*, with a philosophic discussion of perception. He affirms:

Redness is a private experience. Though it may be triggered off by the arrival of nerve impulses in a highly specific part of the brain, there does not seem to be a physical connection between it and the nerve impulse. I mean a connection of the kind we find in cause and effect relationships, say between the heating of a block of ice and its melting into a corresponding volume of water . . . We have so far no reason to suppose that conscious experience is a form of energy and we cannot say in fact that nerve impulses are converted into experience in the same way as heat is converted into motion in a steam engine.

The process seems to be irreversible and outside what we could call the laws of thermodynamics.[12]

The 'emergent' view of the mind confuses two orders of things fundamentally unlike. It is not merely that they cannot be equated point by point, as with the disparate terms 'yellow' and 'hot'. For these can be properties of a common reference object, such as flame; they can be measured in degrees centigrade or millimicrons of wave length, and amount of yellow can be re-expressed as amount of heat. Mind and consciousness are not entities we can do this with; and we could not imagine a scientific equation where they could be substituted for any term in a way that would be meaningful.

It is true also that only with an advanced nervous system can the mind hold any relation with the organic world; and this seems to be the only modality under which we can ourselves discover it. Lower animals probably have earlier levels of mentality, though this can never be directly known. But to use an emergent theory of mind as its *explanation* is really to side-step the problem by giving a lesson in brain anatomy or the evolution of behaviour instead. We can build a plausible enough theory of mind unfolding if we assume it is already there in early orders of life. The pantheist indeed looks for its rudiments even in plants, rocks and molecules. Possibly this helps us towards a unified view of nature; or perhaps – as a colleague suggests – it is like finding Amoeba has spectacles (though only very elementary ones).

IS THERE A BODY–MIND PROBLEM?

And if there is, could it be cleared up if only our neuro-physiologists worked harder, or learned to ask better questions? In a symposium of talks arranged by the BBC,[13] we find even scientists still conjecturing about the stages in a process where the 'liaison' between mind and body is assumed to take place. Lord Adrian, author of the distinguished Waynflete Lectures on brain and perception,[14] conceded that at the present time physical mechanism cannot explain all that happens in the brain. We should have to decide when and where the mind intervenes, at what stage in its passage through the office the file is brought out of the sorting machines and submitted to the director for his personal scrutiny and decision. He concludes that 'before the trouble comes to a head it will have been solved by some enlargement of the boundaries of natural science, by the progress of psychology, for instance. In fact, psychology can scarcely get along without coming to terms with the relation of body and mind.'[15]

Sir Russell (later Lord) Brain holds out the same hope that physiology working with psychology will throw a real light on the relation between brain and mind, 'but you must not expect me to give you a clear idea of how that will happen. . . . My guess is that in the nervous system we are looking at the threads while with the mind we perceive the patterns, and that one day we shall discover how the patterns are made out of the threads.'[16]

To such hopes of the scientists Professor A. J. Ayer gives chill discouragement. The problem, if it is a problem at all, is a philosophical one. Further information about the brain will not solve it; if a river is unbridgeable it will not help if we raise one of its banks. The mind is not the sort of thing that can have a 'place' in the brain, or any locus in space at all. It thus makes little sense to talk of signals 'reaching it', mental processes being interleaved with disturbances of nerve cells, or 'messengers travelling through the brain, reaching a mysterious entity called the mind, receiving orders from it, then moving on'. In Ayer's conclusion 'the two stories will not mix'.[17]

THE STATUS OF MIND

One way to break the deadlock would be to remove one of the stories altogether. Gilbert Ryle has attempted this in *The Concept of Mind*. He has elsewhere told us that the umbrella terms 'mind' and 'matter' are words of the hustings and 'prejudice the solutions of all problems posed in terms of them'.[18] We have so far been freely using these concepts in our own enquiry; and we must now see what is the worst that can be brought against us by the radical critique of Professor Ryle.

First, as we have done, he would disallow Descartes's dichotomy of mind and body, or the 'ghost in the machine' concept of two independent substances. As two untaught peasants might look at a steam engine and conclude 'of course there is a little horse inside it', so we have been apt to imagine we lead two separate existences, with a ghost horse called Mind inside us.

Mental processes are not the same as physical processes. They are merely, contends Professor Ryle, what we infer from witnessing the sorts of things men do. 'Overt intelligent performances are not clues to the workings of mind: they *are* those workings.' Description of them in mental terms may be a convenient shorthand; but it is in the last resort simply a description of certain forms of bodily behaviour. In principle, I could draw up a language without loss of sense where I could cease to talk of mind and put the description in terms of behaviour instead. By watching a man play chess, I could study his behaviour and predict his motivation as readily as if I were myself the chess-player.

It may well be that some forms of behaviour allow us to infer motivation more readily than others: for example, where a man is playing a game with a rigorous set of rules. It could be easier too to predict the course of behaviour of a man acting egotistically, or with calculation for a selfish end. For it is a characteristic of ill-doing that its pretensions can often be so foreseen: the enactor seems to be under a determinism from which creativity, altruism and self-surrender are altogether free.

The 'myth of volitions' comes under attack in *The Concept of Mind* as one of the curiosities of philosophical history. First, it is said, no one describes his own conduct in such terms. By what sort of predicates, it is asked, can volitions be described? Can they be strong or weak, difficult or easy? Can they be accelerated? Can we take lessons in volition? Can I do two, or seven, at once? Can I forget how to do them? Second, no one ever witnesses the volitions of another. Third, the connection between volition and action is a complete mystery. Fourth, there is the question, if it be volition which makes action meritorious or the reverse, is volition itself voluntary or involuntary, meritorious or not?[19]

Professor Ryle would allow us no privileged access to ourselves on account of self-knowledge. But he claims that this is made up for by what we can observe of other people, and can be brought to parity with knowledge about ourselves. 'I learn that a certain pupil of mine is lazy, ambitious and witty by following his work, noticing his excuses, listening to his conversation and comparing his performances with those of others. Nor does it make any important difference if I happen myself to be that pupil.'[20]

Professor Ryle's thesis would seem to leave important parts of our awareness simply unacknowledged. Dr Mascall observes that part of the difficulty is the high level of clarity he will insist upon for anything he would regard as knowledge worth having and goes on to chide him: 'However vigorously he may have repudiated the Cartesian doctrine of the ghost in the machine, he has accepted wholeheartedly the Cartesian doctrine of clear and distinct ideas. What is not known with the immediacy of sensation or the transparency of logical implication "isn't knowledge".'[21]

Like an earlier sceptic, David Hume, Professor Ryle writes in a captivating way. If we compare his style with that of the physiologist-philosopher Sherrington in *Man on his Nature* we find the latter sensitive and individual, breaking at times into a poetic flash. Yet it is Sherrington, the 'amateur' among these problems, who brings with him a patience open to every nuance and subtlety that the problem, a real one, possesses. His insight rather than Ryle's may be the one we need when we are looking not into the hard brightness of science or logic, but into the half-lights of a non-rational kind of truth.

Can we know more about ourselves than Ryle will allow? I believe we have kinds of self-knowledge the neglect of which in his book is so surprising that we inevitably find ourselves asking 'Is this all?' at the end of this dismissal of introspection. The author does not in fact validate an exclusively behaviourist view of man. He is simply relying without acknowledgement on a rich background of subjective knowledge, without which he could infer nothing about his pupil's temperament, motivation or purposes, or about his own. Self-awareness must remain our primary datum about the world. It comes from 'this side' of the world of sensible phenomena. It is in its immediacy different in kind and unreplaceable by any knowledge I can get from outside.

If I am in myself a self-determining and self-unifying system of experience, I cannot then be *simply* an integration of such outside information as my sense organs can gather together. Professor Ryle heads part of a chapter 'The Systematic Elusiveness of "I" ',[22] which is a property he seems to find remarkable. Would it not be more extraordinary if some part of 'I' were not elusive; even in the sense that God is elusive to the natural order which is organic to him or results from his transcendent direction? As Ryle very fairly reminds us, even Hume – after he had sketched out all the items of his experience and found nothing to correspond to 'I' – still suspected that something important remained, without which his sketch failed to satisfy his experience.[23]

Professor Ryle would, then, drastically restrict our sources of useful knowledge. When the questions are about our own being and ultimate nature, or about God, he would oblige us to let go of important kinds of knowledge altogether. Yet it is here that answers that were models of intellectual clarity would be bound to seem facile and insufficient. Twentieth-century man, by every impulse from his scientific training, would want to have the answers plain; but the profound mystery of fundamental things is still very expectably part of the philosophic world he has to deal with. For too long, in the past, the religious man feared to admit the cold light of science with its bogey of determinate mechanism. It could be that a commoner disability today is the opposite shrinking from the mystical or transcendent.

The entities of 'mind', 'volition' and 'freedom' are qualities of the transcendent world that we partly live in. However necessary this statement may seem to us, we would still be loath to build upon them an ultimate dualism of the world. We are reluctant to set them definitively in inverted commas, just as it is anathema to the scientist to talk about entelechies or '*élan vital*' or disembodied spirit. Christian teaching has never affirmed the necessity of these dualities. Professor Mascall has fairly pointed out that Ryle has been led into his sceptical position by 'a failure to realize that there can be any doctrine of the soul as a real entity other than that of Descartes'.[24] In his short and readable book *Nature and God*,[25] the biologist L. C. Birch likewise devotes much space to a refutation of the Cartesian view of the world. He appears to believe at the end that he has shaken radically some tenet of traditional Christianity, which he declares to be irreconcilable with modern science.

Christians apprehend well enough that we are 'not machines, not even ghost-ridden machines. [We] are men'.[26] In most of us the philosophical craving for unity is very strong. Though Sherrington has suggested[27] that the idea that our being should consist of *two* fundamental elements offers no greater inherent improbability than that it should consist of one, few scientists or theologians can believe that this is in fact so. I find I am in a real sense a unity, and this knowledge is a prime part of all my apprehensions. It is such awareness, together with misconceptions about what Christianity really teaches concerning the body and soul, that has led to the widespread disdain for theology as 'supernaturalistic dualism', in some way part of the Cartesian package.

Yet transcendent reality, being truth about God and ourselves, will never (if it exists) be objectively perceived. If man be in some sense an inhabitant of two worlds, he cannot have access to one by using the criteria of the other. We are in fact constantly concerned with knowledge of two quite different sorts. We have potentially two ways of viewing not only the objects of physics or of metaphysics, but the undivided whole of reality. It is as if not aspects or parts but the total of being could be apprehended from either aspect, convex or concave. The normal territory of physical science, and this must include the bodies of other organisms, and men and their brains, we approach from outside, *convexly*. This, it would seem, must be the whole method of physical science. But being a person myself enables me to have a view of personality *concavely* or from within. Though I can think about myself objectively or convexly, as I can think about God through the science of theology, I believe I can understand personality only – as it were – immediately and concavely. Such a vantage point I cannot myself assume towards the physical world; but this realization of personality may be the sort of apprehension (partial and imperfect) that the believer has of God.

We have often assumed that life is an anomalous and altogether exceptional property within the cosmos; and that mind and consciousness form an anomaly even rarer in the midst of the living. Teilhard de Chardin, in *Man's Place in Nature*, makes a protest against so hesitant a view. He takes an analogy from the discovery of radium by the Curies, when it was thought a puzzling anomaly in the physico-chemical world, one more rarity for the curious to add to their collections. Today we know that the phenomena of radio-activity are in the profoundest sense explanatory of the atom and all its properties. But a similar hesitance, says Teilhard, still persists in assimilating the more important phenomenon of life.

If we try to 'psycho-analyse' modern science, we are forced to this conclusion: that life, in spite of the extraordinary properties that make it unique in our experience, and in fact *because* it is so infrequent in appearance and on so small a scale (so ridiculously localized, for no more than a moment of time, on a fragment of a star), is still in practice looked upon and treated by physicists – as radium was initially – as an exception to or an irregular departure from the great natural laws: an interesting irregularity, no doubt, on the terrestrial scale, but with no real importance for a full understanding of the basic structure of the universe. That life is an epiphenomenon of matter – just as thought is an epiphenomenon of life – is still too often, what too many people, implicitly at least, hold to be true.

It seems to me essential then to protest without delay against this depreciatory attitude, by emphasizing that (again, as with radium) there is another solution to the dilemma . . .; that life is not a peculiar anomaly, sporadically flowering on matter – but an exaggeration, through specially favourable circumstances, of a universal cosmic property – that life is not an epiphenomenon, but the very essence of phenomenon.[28]

The two kinds of knowledge, involving our approach to the physical order and to personality, bring us in the end to something like the distinction made by Sir Arthur Eddington when he spoke of 'symbolic' knowledge and 'intimate' knowledge.[29] Our more usual processes of everyday reason are developed to handle symbolic knowledge. This is observational: it deals with the world outside and is susceptible of logical analysis. Intimate knowledge can however be neither codified nor analysed; or when this is done it is turned into symbolic knowledge. Theology is in this sense symbolic knowledge, whereas experience of God is intimate knowledge.

As 'intimate' knowledge Eddington cites not only our mystical feeling for nature and God, but even – at a homely level – our enjoyment of humour. The scientific explanation of the structure of a joke cannot compel laughter. In the same way a philosophical discussion of God's attributes is likely to miss the intimate response of the spirit in which the religious experience really consists.

If I were to try to put into words the essential truth revealed in the mystical experience, it would be that our minds are not apart from the world; and the feelings that we have of gladness and melancholy and our yet deeper feelings are not of ourselves alone, but are glimpses of a reality transcending the narrow limits of our particular consciousness – that the harmony and beauty of the face of Nature is at root one with the gladness that transfigures the face of man.[30]

Of the physical world we build our ultimate pictures in terms of the atoms and their elementary particles. These would tend to show us that our picture of a familiar object with its properties of hardness and solidity must be an illusion. To provide its 'reality' as we perceive it, our sense organs, writes Eddington, have to weave images about it. So, to man, the first way to the revelation of the wider world must be to awaken image-building in connection with the higher faculties of our nature. These are then no longer blind alleys, but open out into a spiritual world,

> a world partly of illusion no doubt, but in which [we] live no less than in the world, also of illusion, revealed by the senses.[31]

For those who would discount the insights and preoccupations of the mystic, leaving him to his harmless spiritual playground while the practical man goes on with the 'real' business of making the 'real' world go round, Eddington warns that 'mysticism may be fought as error or believed as inspired, but it is no matter for easy tolerance'. In the busy involvement of human achievement and aspiration, it is the mystics that give creative impetus to the world.

> We are the music-makers
>   And we are the dreamers of dreams
> Wandering by lone sea-breakers
>   And sitting by desolate streams;
> World-losers and world-forsakers,
>   On whom the pale moon gleams:
> Yet we are the movers and shakers
>   Of the world for ever, it seems.[32]

CHAPTER 5

Psychosomatics: A Short Digression

THE liaison of the mind with the body we commonly associate with conscious action, as of the voluntary muscles for movement and speech. There are however other interactions we would think of as involuntary; the symptoms of our emotional state such as blushing or increased rate of heart beat are for example produced when the hormone adrenalin is secreted under stress. All of our organs are strongly under the influence of our emotions, especially perhaps the skin, which may sweat, dry up, suffuse with blood, or develop distressing allergic reactions. There is an enlarging territory too where the unconscious mind is registered upon the body in the conditions we call psychosomatic. Today we can have no doubt that the unconscious mind is an informational system with a wide effect upon bodily functions and structures.

A large range of illnesses are today regarded as psychosomatic. They may present us with two sorts of pathologies, medical and psychiatric, with cause-and-effect relations still impossible to untangle. Dr Clark-Kennedy in his Pelican volume *Human Disease* speaks of the complex causative cycle with the itching of the skin.

Thus the mind becomes sensitized to the skin and the skin to the mind, and the vicious circle piles up until areas of eczema are produced. Accurate diagnosis is always difficult. Every case depends in part on the constitutional sensitiveness of the skin, in part on peripheral stimulation, in part on physical health, and in part on the emotional reactions of the patient. Indeed, exact analysis of the causative facts may be quite impossible. But to cure eczema the vicious cycle must be broken somewhere.[1]

Large philosophical questions, as well as medical ones, are raised as Dr Clark-Kennedy goes on to ask:

> Can a state of mind start rheumatoid arthritis, or initiate the vaso-constriction ... that ultimately leads to heart failure? Can the mind get a carcinoma going in the body? Can the fear of a disease initiate that disease? Can emotion, disappointment, worry actually lead to cardiac infarction? Can a man really die of a broken heart? Could the news of Napoleon's victory at Austerlitz, as the history books say, have killed Pitt?[2]

Dr Stephen Black has recently written a challenging book *Mind and Body* that I shall mention in some detail in this section.[3] A physician conducting research into the method of hypnotherapy, he puts forward a theory of the unconscious mind that gives a new realization of its influence over the body.

Our psychosomatic ills include those commonly called allergies, such as asthma and hay-fever and the skin reactions of urticaria. These are the 'immediate type hypersensitivity' (ITH), while among the 'delayed type' (DTH) are eczema, psoriasis, contact dermatitis and tuberculosis. All these are of known pathology and psychopathology. Others where only the psychopathology is known include the aches and pains of 'neurosis', hypertension, tachycardia, and run as far as slipped disc, peptic ulcer and sexual malfunctions.[4]

Psychosomatic illnesses have been dramatically relieved by hypnotherapy among the rather small part of the population – some five per cent – that is susceptible to deep trance hypnosis. Hypnosis may be defined as a state of decreased or altered consciousness, found not only in man but most animals, and produced by constrictive or rhythmic stimuli imparted by another individual. With the increased suggestibility the hypnotic state allows, contact can be made with the unconscious mind.

This level of the mind is held by Dr Black to be an informational system derived from early primeval mechanisms. It lacks the means of verbalizing experience possessed by the conscious mind, but whatever the nature of the divide between them, access can only be gained through the senses, whether through psycho-analysis or hypnosis.

It is now known that the unconscious mind, as stimulated by direct suggestion under hypnosis, can act upon the skin to inhibit the ITH reactions of allergies. With hay-fever and asthma, not only are the skin reactions abolished, but this can be done in a controlled experiment by progressive suggestion, limb by limb.

The Mantoux reaction of tuberculosis was also found by Black to be susceptible to hypnotic suggestion.[5] Patients who have had in childhood a harmless bout of tuberculosis can become allergic to the Koch bacillus. This is why, before antibiotics, a second infection was often fatal. Allergy normally appears as a skin redness and swelling after injecting attenuated bacillus under the skin. Hypnotic treatment can change a Mantoux positive to a Mantoux negative subject. One can even see histological changes in the skin cells under the microscope.

In 1952 a remarkable account appeared in the *British Medical Journal*[6] of a cure by hypnotherapy of the fish-skin disease or ichthyosis in a fifteen-year-old boy. This is a congenital malfunctioning of the skin glands, and the skin is greenish grey and scaly, often with an offensive smell. Previously thought incurable, this condition was cleared up in controlled treatments, first in one arm, then the other, then each leg and finally on the body. In a few weeks the scales were replaced by normal skin, and the relief over the five years since was permanent. A reviewer wrote that this single case alone would call for a revision of the current concepts of the relation between mind and body.[7]

Therapy such as this does not appear possible through conscious channels. Allergic reactions are evidently to be manipulated only through the unconscious mind; we cannot simply tell an asthmatic to get better.

The structural basis of allergic reactions is ultimately molecular. A foreign substance to which the body reacts by an immune response is known as an antigen (or in this special case an allergen). When these enter the body, their complex molecular forms carry a high 'information' content that has not been lost – as in food molecules – by being broken down and digested. Antigens are taken up by the white cells or phagocytes and the substances called antibodies are produced from special clones of cells originating in the thymus gland and other centres. These recognize and immobilize the specific antigen molecule by having an exact fit with its molecular surface. There is an almost infinite variety of antibodies possible, to fit any new-coming antigen. The antibodies are based upon the structure of the protein molecule of gammaglobulin. The molecular chain can be complexly folded, with new secondary and tertiary and quaternary structures, so that its possibilities of molecular form are virtually inexhaustible. The determinant of the antibody is a limited chemical configuration on the surface of an antigen molecule. As early as the 1920s Landsteiner, by attaching small molecular groups to proteins, made entirely synthetic antigens that had never occurred before. All these evoked antibody formation.

Beyond their value in therapy, the results of deep hypnosis could be vastly important in our theoretical understanding of the relation of mind and body. As Arthur Koestler wrote, they could make the world look different not only for the scientist but for the philosopher and theologian too. If we look at the brain and the nervous system as the physical representation of life and mind, both can be characterized in terms of information. Life, says Dr Black, is 'a quality of matter that arises from the informational content inherent in the improbability of form'.[8] The universe is filled with matter of which every particle holds a standing potential of information. Life feeds on this informa-tion flux, and the greatest quantity of information (which is to say, the highest improbability or the most complex organiza-tion) is incorporated in the nervous system.

Information can shape the cells and tissues of all living things. It is no longer true, says Dr Black, that 'sticks and stones may break my bones but words will never hurt me'.[9] For a verbal command can change the reactivity and form of tissues at cell or molecular level. The informational content of the environment can be vital to physical health. This access between mind and pathology is as mysterious – no more or no less – as the transaction between neurone and volition. The mind would seem to be supremely sovereign over what happens in the body; and this appears both in our voluntary action and in the pervading role of the subconscious.

Our moral life must be involved in these conclusions too. The exploitation of man by man, deeply resented by the subconscious mind, with the greed and violence of today's world, could be responsible for our high incidence of mental illness. Our callousness or exploitation of others can cause lasting trauma for them and for ourselves too. This may be why the soundest therapy the Christian knows was accompanied – and can still be – by the assurance 'your sins are forgiven you'.

For in the conclusion of his whole book, Dr Black comes close to accord with the picture we have already drawn of man as a free and moral being:

Vice may be our inheritance in the somatic mind of the unconscious – but so is the inspirational quality of the artist. And virtue is **acquired** both consciously and unconsciously – so that what counts in the end is what we build into the body through the cybernetics of experience. In this, as Christian doctrine makes so clear, we undoubtedly have freedom of will.[10]

CHAPTER 6

The Status of Nature

Mind no longer appears as an accidental intruder into the realm of matter; we are beginning to suspect that we ought rather to hail it as the creator and governor of the realm of matter – not of course our individual minds, but the mind in which the atoms out of which our individual minds have grown exist as thoughts.

Sir James Jeans[1]

WE have found it unsatisfying to think of mind as simply a latter-day emanation from the rearrangement of material molecules; and it is now time to consider the increasingly abstract pictures scientists are drawing of matter itself, and the particles of which it is composed.

The philosophic discussion of 'mind' and 'matter' may begin for us with the seventeenth-century English empiricists. To John Locke the real world was simply like the model our senses give. The 'ideas' the mind forms of the world have attributes actually like the qualities in real things. Of these qualities, some, such as shape, size, number, motion and solidity, are 'primary' and truly inherent in the things themselves. The 'secondary' qualities, such as colour, sound, odour, even if they are not in the real thing as the mind receives them, nevertheless can be said to 'represent' the qualities of reality.

Early in the following century the Irish philosopher, Bishop Berkeley, held that this separation of primary and secondary qualities was fundamentally unsound. The 'ideas' of the mind, he believed, were all we had to reckon with: nothing except an idea could fittingly correspond to, or represent, an idea. An idea cannot exist without a mind, and the essence of a thing lies solely in its being perceived by a mind, man's or that of a Supreme Being. In a magnificent and often quoted passage:

All the choir of heaven and furniture of the earth, in a word all those bodies which compose the mighty frame of the world, have not any subsistence without a mind . . . so long as they are not actually perceived by me, or do not exist in my mind or that of any other created spirit, they must either have no existence at all, or else subsist in the mind of some eternal spirit.[2]

Berkeleyan idealism could be a comfortable view of the world for theism, or for any school that takes the status of mind seriously. It could not be challenged effectively from the side of empiric 'common sense', as Dr Johnson tried to do, by kicking a large stone and claiming: 'I refute it thus.' Nor would it have been different even if the stone had taken him by surprise and fallen upon his head. But it was open to the sceptic David Hume to apply the same criticism to mind as had been levelled at the material order. If we have no evidence of things behind our perceptions, neither can we have any certainty of the existence of our minds. All we can know is a flux of ideas, sensations and mental images. In this stream of experience no separable 'self' can be recognized as engaged in the experiencing.

Some varieties of this radical scepticism (or 'phenomenalism') are current today, just as many men of a 'scientific' cast of mind lean to some form of realism or empiricism. But with the coming of relativity and quantum mechanics, a number of physicists (and these – of all scientists – are the people most concerned with problems of existence and reality) were to move far from scepticism or materialism. As someone has said, they began to talk of God in a manner their Victorian grandfathers would have found very shocking.

A generation ago, the mathematician and astronomer, Sir James Jeans, in his popular classic, *The Mysterious Universe*, came close to an idealist view of a world created out of pure thought.

Of the universe revealed to us by the theory of relativity, Jeans develops for us the classic picture of a soap bubble with a wrinkled surface.[3] This is a continuum of four-dimensional space-time, and across it run broad bands made up of countless small threads which are the world lines of its atoms, occupying their distinctive positions with respect to time and space. As we move in one direction – timewards – along the tapestry, its threads shift about and change their positions with relation to each other. In doing so, they obey the set of harmonies that are the laws of nature.

The world lines representing our bodies have the special property of conveying information through our senses to our minds. They alone have the power to affect our consciousness directly; and we can most simply interpret consciousness as something lying entirely outside the picture and making contact with it only along the world lines of our bodies.

The effect of this contact we feel as the passage of time: we appear to be dragged along our world line to experience different points on it as different states at successive moments of time. Though time may be spread before us from beginning to eternity, we seem to make contact with it at only one instant, as a wheel with one point on a road. Alternatively we could be likened to a fly caught in a dusting mop and dragged across the surface of the picture; events are not happening, we merely come across them. Or if the feeling of influencing parts of the picture is more than mere illusion, consciousness might be better likened to the feeling in the finger of the painter as he guides the brush over the unfinished work.

This space-time model of the world can serve only as a statement of the large-scale phenomena of nature. Not only are we to think of consciousness going on outside it. Even such a simple event as the meeting of two electrons requires not four but seven dimensions to depict it, three each for space and one for time. For three electrons we need ten, and so on, the time dimension serving as a mortar that binds together systems that would otherwise exist in separate and non-communicable three-dimensional spaces. The nearest approach to actuality may be to think of the electrons as objects of thought and time as the process of thinking.[4]

The spaces required for these pictures of wave mechanics can

be said to 'exist' only so far as they give an adequate mathematical representation of what happens. For the wave motion
of a single electron, even though its configuration corresponds
with ordinary space, should not be taken too literally to exist. It
could be likened to the waves of probability that a single
diffracted electron will hit a sensitive plate at a particular spot.
More drastically, it may be that the ultimate phenomena of
nature do not admit of representation on a space-time framework at all. Just as the shadows on a wall project three dimensions into two, so the phenomena of space-time may be
projections of realities that occupy more than four dimensions
and of which the real explanation is to be located outside our
familiar continuum.

As Jeans many times stressed, nature – in revealing her
ultimate secrets – has shown herself modelled on the principles
of pure mathematics. These concepts had already been worked
out by abstract thought, being arrived at with virtually no
contribution from the observational world. Such are, for
example, the laws of probability, the manipulation of imaginary
numbers such as square roots of negative quantities, and multi-
dimensional geometry.

Nature's ultimate laws, then, do not correspond to those
suggested by our whims or our passions, or by our muscles and
joints, but by our *minds*.[5] This statement does not, of course,
refer to the empirical observations of *applied* mathematics,
which are the familiar large-scale mechanics worked out to
describe what had first been seen in nature.

Jeans has set out the concepts fundamental to our understanding of nature:[6] a space that is finite, and that is empty so
that one point differs from another solely in the proportion of
the space itself; a space that expands; four- – or more – dimensional spaces; and a sequence of events that follows the laws of
probability instead of the laws of causation, or – alternatively –
that can only be fully described by going outside space-time.

All these seem to be constructions of pure thought, incapable
of being realized in any properly material way. If the universe is
a universe of thought, its creation, concluded Jeans, must have

been an act of thought. Such a creator, infinite mathematician, would then be at work outside the time and space which are part of his creation, as the painter works outside his canvas or the sculptor outside the clay to which his creativity is giving shape.

From the world presented to us by relativity and quantum mechanics, scientists have had to re-draw the pictures of matter that Victorian mechanists would have held alone to be real. True, those models of nature that we endow with substance and solidity can still be used for everyday, normal-scale purposes. But if we are looking at the very large or very small, we find that a working model may not be a help but a hindrance to our understanding. Professor E. L. Mascall amusingly comments on the insufficiency of mechanistic thought:

Gyroscopes and indiarubber and wax and beer-froth were made of matter, and matter was made of ether. But when we enquired what ether was made of, it turned out to be gyroscopes, indiarubber, wax and beer-froth on an ultra-microscopic scale, or at any rate something with properties very like theirs. [7]

The fact that our pictures of the real world will no longer be mechanistic ones should give new liberty both to the scientist and the theologian. To recognize that the physical world is an abstraction generated from consciousness, does not mean we must abandon belief in the 'reality' of the natural order. Yet it may confirm our picture of a universe in which mind has a commanding status, and its intimations may be heard with respect for what they may tell us of the nature of that world. The spiritual domain we construct from them will be as valid and as immediate as the physical world constructed from sensory data, however more complex and elusive we may find it.

If the validity of nature does not then rest solely in the mind perceiving it, what in the last resort *are* real things? And what are the properties we may know them by?

Obviously, many of the sub-microscopic objects of chemistry and biology can be very well visualized by working models. Thus the molecular lattice of a salt crystal, the alpha-helix of a protein molecule, the double strand of DNA, have unarguably a structure that is responsible for their observable functions. If we could see them with the microscope as today we can see muscles of mitochondria, they would undoubtedly look much as we depict them in our diagrams. Where most of us would think of pictorial solidity disappearing is at the level of atomic structure. Here we have the empty space of a miniature solar system puzzlingly substituted for what we had thought of as a solid particle. Are neutrons or protons or electrons real, and if so in what sense? Lord Rutherford once affirmed that electrons were as real as that dessert-plate (but this was said to be in an after-dinner speech).

On scientific theories as descriptions of the real world, Professor Mascall has given a lucid discussion in his *Christian Theology and Natural Science*.[8] The real world, he argues, is intelligible and as such can be known by our minds. It has therefore a structure that is a proper object of study for mathematical physics. The mistake the post-Newtonian physicists made was in supposing the real world must be like the world we *sense* 'with the so-called secondary qualities left out and a few mysterious non-sensible qualities, such as mass and electric charge, brought in'. Such a real world was held to be essentially 'sensible' (that is, apprehensible by sense data), however hard it was in fact to sense. However, we now know that atoms, though apparently solid, are in reality full of empty space. Thus the world we sense is not the real world, though somehow we sense it.

To Locke and the empiricists, the world of perception was only a refined version of the world of sensation. But if perception is really sensation and all theories must at the last be reduced to sensible shapes, then all that is perceived must be sensible. In fact, however, the objects of the real world – electrons and other particles – appear not to be the ones we sense.

With relativity and quantum theory, the idea of the sensible world as something with a reality in itself is doomed. If reality and sensibility are the same, reality goes if sensibility is lost. And if we cannot explain the world any longer in terms of sensibility all we have left – concludes Professor Mascall – would be to discuss the language-habits of physicists. Thus reality must be wider than sensibility. For the world does not lose its reality by being no longer imaginable in time and three-dimensional Euclidean geometry; and to get it back we do not have to bestir ourselves to make a picture of a four-dimensional balloon covered with wrinkles. 'The paradigm of a real world is not its sensible imaginability but its intelligent apprehensibility.'[9] This sort of intelligibility is what the formulae of quantum physics express.

To the question, are electrons real?, the answer may be that they are real patterns of events in the physical world but that the things we have discovered about them are different from those that are familiar in the man-sized world. We need only worry about whether they are 'real' if we continue to think of reality in terms of hard sensible particles.

PROCESS AND ORGANISM

In his well-known account of the universe, Alfred North Whitehead has conceived the whole of reality to be an organism.[10] At a single instant of time, which is not a primary entity but an abstraction, we are unable to perceive the full reality of matter at all. For not only mind and life but also matter are inherently and essentially activity. The qualities of matter do not depend upon some static aspect such as the atomic weight of an element, but upon activity in extended time, as for example the pattern of electrons revolving in an orderly way about the atomic nucleus. 'Process, activity and change are the matter of fact. At an instant there is nothing.'

To Whitehead, the cosmic process is not merely rhythmical. It has direction and drive, and in an evolving world its characteristic is not only extensiveness but *aim*. Nature is permeated by the drive to the creation of 'wholes', or larger, more comprehensively integrated systems. This was the theme of Jan Smuts's well-known work *Holism and Evolution*. Each successive stage is distinguished by the emergence of a new and more comprehensive type of individuality. Each new stage transcends the earlier stages as the whole does its parts. Though we can give a mechanistic description of a new stage in terms of a lower stage, we can never satisfactorily account for its novelty in such a way.

In his Gifford Lectures,[11] the philosopher Samuel Alexander took a wide-ranging view of this process of ascent through complexity. 'At each change of quality, the complexity as it were gathers itself together and is expressed in a new simplicity. The emergent quality is the summing together into a new totality of the component materials.' As life has arisen from matter, so mind – according to Alexander – has arisen from living organisms, using life as its substratum. Mind is presently engaged in evolving out of itself something as different from itself as mind is from life. This next order of complexity is deity, and God is the being to whose emergence the whole process of cosmic evolution is directed. Far from God being creator of the world, then, the world itself could be called God in an anticipatory, as yet unrealized, form. The world is moving towards God.

Alexander's thesis cannot reveal *why* there should be such a leaning or predisposition of the cosmic process, why life should emerge from matter or mind from life or God from mind. Like any system based from within the natural order, it is an empirical one with no apparent logical necessity. R. G. Collingwood has criticized this concept of God as being in fact a constructive atheism.[12] It would make God hardly as yet a creature, much less a creator. He would be nothing but a picture, however supremely worth drawing. Being what Alexander calls a 'qualified infinite' he cannot exist and it would seem intrinsically that he never will exist. For all the nobility with which such a construct of God is expressed, it comes in the end to a denial of his transcendent quality as author of the system and of whatever values the system may disclose and portend.

Whitehead's conclusions about God drew much closer to the traditional statements of Christian theology. In a climate of thought when many theologians themselves are ceasing to resist a naturalistic view of the world, we are apt to find scientists taking a dependent view of nature. The world that science is interested in forms only one aspect of being, and that aspect is a secondary one derived from something prior to itself. To Whitehead, the properties and values we see being realized in the natural process are not solely immanent in it. If nature be indeed finite, certainly in space and probably in time, then the activity that science identifies with matter cannot be a self-created or ultimately self-dependent activity.

The properties we find expressed in the natural world transcend it, being the properties of an eternal world beyond the process. Such a world is the reality necessary for the explanation of the cosmic process and its apparent aim. God becomes, in Collingwood's phrase, 'the infinite lure to which all process directs itself'. 'He is the lure for feeling, the eternal urge of desire. His particular relevance to each creative act, as it arises from its own conditioned standpoint in the world, constitutes him as the initial object of desire, establishing the initial phase of each subjective aim.'

Such a view of the cosmos, with its properties of direction, drive and creative advance, could bring us close to the Christian's traditional conception of God as creator, 'initiating and directing the entire cosmic process through its love of him'. We are indeed nearing the point where the nature and attributes of such a God must be further investigated. But first in the chapter to follow, we shall have to look more closely at the evolutionary process itself. In the closing words of his *Origin of Species* Charles Darwin spoke of this 'most exalted object which we are capable of conceiving, namely the production of the higher animals'. 'There is grandeur in this view of life, with its several powers, having been originally breathed by the Creator into a few forms or into one; and that, whilst this planet has gone cycling on according to the fixed law of gravity, from so simple a beginning endless forms most beautiful and most wonderful have been, and are being evolved.'[13]

We must now ask what may be the significance of this process from the standpoint of man and his origin.

CHAPTER 7

Life Evolving

L'Homme . . . seul, dans l'univers, n'est pas fini.
Villiers de l'Isle-Adam

IF we can think of mind as in some sense holding the sovereign status in the real world, the most important chapter in cosmic history must have been its involvement with biological forms in the natural order. In such a way the universe has become conscious of itself.

The plain man naturally thinks of his own species as the spear-point and culmination of evolution. We ought not simply to dismiss this viewpoint as anthropocentric. In our human condition it could hardly be other. If this gives an astigmatism to our cosmic outlook, we are entitled to ask, where are the philosophic ants, or technological tapeworms that could help us to a corrected world-view?

Still, to the man of science with his long vista of evolution and cosmogony, the notion of a creator's special concern with this one species is hard to accept. Even if he be a religious man, it strains belief – in a universe expanding through space and time – that a unique significance should attach to this speck of a planet or this species so newly arrived. Whether or not life is unique on this planet (both scientists and theologians can leave this an open question), the claim that man is centrally important has about it what G. K. Chesterton called a star-defying audacity.

Yet how rational in themselves are our bogeys of astronomic time and space? Size is relative to the bigness of ourselves; and we are about midway in mass between a planet and a molecule: a good size to cope with the hazards of the physical laws, big enough not to blow away, or stick down by surface tension, small enough not to need all our energy for refuelling our body mass, or to crumble our limbs beneath us when we stand.

In a creative economy we need not measure wastage of materials with human frugality. A cod produces fifteen million eggs, only a dozen or so destined to reach adulthood. For each egg thousands of spermatozoa are expended for every one that fertilizes. A system so wasteful of gametes could be equally prodigal of galaxies. There are several orders of size between them, but at our distance the Milky Way looks similar enough to cod-sperm! The outstanding difference is indeed that each microscopic sperm cell has a far more intricate organization than the whole mass of a barren star.

The profusion of species of animals and plants has also made man sceptical about his own special significance. What can be the value of all these side-ventures of evolution – sponges, flatworms, starfishes and spiders – if the production of man has been a central theme? At a conservative estimate there are between two and three million species of animals living today. Few have any common name at all, being known only to the expert who studies them. Many are microscopic, living in unlighted depths, in the ground or hidden in the bodies of others. The total might be multiplied a hundredfold to take in former species now extinct.

Without being a biologist one can scarcely comprehend the stupendous diversity of life. In the tropics this is especially lavish. In the Solomon Islands, for example, I recently studied more than two hundred species of crabs. They differed in size, shape and colour, in body design and camouflage and in habits and food-catching. They lived on coral, in algae, in sand and mud, inside the shells of clams, amidst the tentacles of anemones and in the rectum of sea cucumbers. Each was a new and ingenious expression of the original crab idea.

In the rain forests of the same islands there is unimaginable prodigality of plants. Beneath the hundred-foot tree canopy, the vegetation is arranged pavilion upon pavilion: with vines, lianas, perching lilies, mosses, strangling plants, ferns, epiphytes, intricately structured orchids and the outrageous form and colour of the fungi. Below visible size are the microscopic moulds, algae and yeasts. And in all this many-tiered world, hardly a fragment exists that is not living or the product of life. Between plants and animals there are adaptations for intimate co-operation, as for securing pollination, or for dispersal by seeds, or fleshy and luscious fruits. Each floral design is a detailed lure matched to the habits of an insect or bird. Of a hundred or so species of figs, each kind is penetrated by its own species of minute wasp, subtly adapted to crawl into the fleshy pseudo-fruit and fertilize the invisible flowers within.

Those who are naturalists or gardeners can best attain a glimpse of the delight a creative God might have in the whole organic order, undiminished, surely, by any special concern he might have for one of its species. The panorama of life provokes in us an awe that is needed for our fullest understanding of the world. Yet an unchecked wonder in creation may still be inimical to a scientist's working temper. Let theologians beware of too readily acclaiming the evolutionary process as a guide to God's nature. To some, evolution has offered the appeal of a creator leading forward his cosmic process stage by stage rather than in a few precipitate days of creation. Evolution is thus given a moral content that is highly dubious; and it is time to correct our perspective by examining the process of natural selection in the way a biologist must see it.[1]

THE SUBSTRATE OF LIFE

Life is not only scarce in the universe, but of startling novelty. The inorganic world – including, it may even be, the whole extra-terrestrial universe – discloses no apparent adaptation or internal design. Its behaviour could be predicted from our knowledge of the laws of physics and chemistry.

One of the fundamental principles often brought into discussions about life and organisms is that of the Second Law of Thermodynamics. This speaks of entropy increasing, the universe 'running down hill' towards a state of greater randomness or loss of order. On a grand scale this can be illustrated by the sun shining and emitting heat. In its strict terms, the law proclaims that heat will not of itself pass from one body to a hotter body. If I hold a spoon in a flame, it becomes at first hot at one end while remaining cool at the other. But the end I am holding will soon also become hot as the state of improbability lessens and heat becomes uniformly distributed throughout the spoon. In the operation of any machine – whether engine or refrigerator – energy flows from a hot place to a cold place and we may say the amount of organization in the universe is reduced. As an unvarying principle of nature, Milton Rothman puts it in this way:

> In a closed system, there is a tendency for organization to change into disorganization, or for the amount of information available about the system to become smaller as time goes on.[2]

It is to this rule, operating so far as we know throughout the universe, that the living world has appeared to offer a tiny local exception. It is often said that where the total tendency of all matter (organic things included with the rest) is to run down or increase in entropy, living organisms form a small enclave that for a time resists this general rule. They gain in complexity, producing organized and non-random structures that have a high capacity for ordered activity. Energy is stored by the molecule ATP after breaking down fuel substances. The system is wound up by the use of energy in the patterned synthesis of biological molecules and complex tissues. The living organism could be compared to a pump that raises water above ground level to store it as potential energy, reversing the tendency of water to lose this energy by running groundwards to the lowest level.

We should be clear how much we are saying here. We do not mean that life breaks the Second Law about entropy increasing. Where order is acquired and energy stored, a precisely equivalent amount is lost to the world outside; entropy thereby increases to the extent of its apparent decrease in the organism. We can in fact usefully talk of entropy only in relation to the whole system, where its amount always increases. Like book-keeping, the transactions must always balance. When a living organism adds to the amount of order in its own part of the system, energy is gained by a transaction with the environment. In Schrödinger's words, 'Life feeds on negative entropy'.

Molecules from both the living and non-living world are incorporated into the organism, in the chemical reactions known as metabolism. The compounds of living matter are proteins, nucleic acids, carbohydrates and fats. These are built into self-maintaining systems we call cells. A property of an organism is not only to maintain its state, but to extend itself. It increases its bulk and space occupied at the expense of its surroundings. Plants can synthesize compounds such as sugar from molecules of the inorganic world. Animals must feed on other living matter, dismantling the chemical compounds and building them into substances of their own. The reverse aspect of metabolism is the breaking down process called 'respiration', equivalent to burning fuel. Energy-rich molecules such as fats and carbohydrates yield this energy for the organism's own requirements.

By their synthesis of new materials, living organisms grow, divide and reproduce. They maintain their 'steady state' against the environment and its whole tendency to disrupt them. This is achieved by self-regulating systems, both biochemical and physiological. Such controls include, for example, 'thermostats' and feed-back devices to stabilize salt and water content, or organs of equilibrium to counteract the tendency to fall over. Living things, especially animals, act too upon their environment by manipulating parts of it, or moving about in it by effector organs such as muscles.

A 'steady state' is also maintained from generation to generation. New individuals are produced like the parents. This is ensured by information carried in the genes of the chromosomes. The instructions known as the genetic code are spelled out by combinations of four substances called nucleotide bases (adenine, thymine, guanine and cytosine) contained in the nucleic acid DNA. The DNA code not only replicates itself exactly at every cell division, but throughout life provides the information for building the organism's distinctive proteins. Some of these proteins are the biological catalysts called 'enzymes'. It is by these that the chemical reactions of metabolism are carried out in many small steps, like the operations of a factory production line. Importantly, these enzymic reactions take place at body heat instead of the high temperatures that would be required without their living catalysts.

To perform all these functions, organisms have a unique complexity. Their components, from enzyme molecules up through cells and organs to whole behaviour patterns are quite manifestly *adapted* to their role. It is in studying this design for function that biology differs from physics and chemistry and could be likened to engineering or architecture. But we must remember that the designs of man involve a cognitive purpose; in biology, if we are to be allowed the word 'design' at all, we can speak of no conscious purpose, indeed no purpose discernible within the system itself at all.

Many observers, with the sense of mystery that is an impediment to science, have talked of a special life force, or vital principle. It is natural to feel wonder at the perfection with which an organism develops through egg and embryo, or an amputated newt's leg is regenerated from an unorganized bud of tissue. But the scientist's task is to analyse such systems in terms of orderly mechanism and causative laws. This is why, within the working territory of science, the old arguments over vitalism against mechanism are profitless – and finished. Biochemistry may be a very unexpected, or unpredictable sort of chemistry, but it is still chemistry. To the student who uses '*élan vital*', or entelechies as explanatory terms, we must give the same low mark as to the theological examinee who ascribes the authorship of the Epistle to the Hebrews to the Holy Spirit.

THE MEANS OF PROGRESS

Offspring are never entirely like their parents, nor like each other. In any population, as Darwin was the first to stress, individuals vary, for each characteristic, over a wider or narrower range. Some of this variation, as for example in human height, will be contributed by the environment in which the organism has grown up. Far more – and the important part for evolution – is hereditary. It arises from small differences in the genetic instructions handed on to the individual from its parents. Brother and sister may well be unlike because their germ cells will, in the shuffling of the chromosomes, have received certain different genes.

Evolution is based simply upon the occurrence of variation and competition between variant individuals. A gene transmitted to an offspring will form part of the total pool we call the individual's 'genotype'. It may be 'recessive' in making no present contribution to the organism's discernible structure or function. But if it is actively expressed, it becomes also a part of the 'phenotype'; and it is not until this happens that natural selection can act upon it.

All organisms, even potentially elephants and men, reproduce in far greater numbers than living space exists for. There is thus a struggle for survival in which each individual is in competition with his fellows. Certain individuals will have characters in various ways advantageous to them in the struggle. Those that are enabled to get more food, escape enemies and live longest can be said to be successful, and they will transmit their genes to the greatest number of offspring. If, for example, insects are sprayed with DDT or bacteria are treated with an antibiotic, there is likely to be in each population a tiny proportion – it may be less than one per cent – with genes conferring resistance to the toxic substance. These individuals and their progeny will have such an advantage that they will rapidly increase to form the entire population. By the death of those with less advantageous genes, they will have been 'naturally selected'.

A British moth, *Biston betularia*, has normally a grey and white speckled appearance, giving it camouflage against lichens and the bark of trees. In the industrial North and Midlands, where the trees are darkened with soot, a dark melanic mutant form became prominent by the end of last century, and by its superior ability displaced the grey and white over large areas.

Competition is sometimes strong between brothers of the same species. There may be a contest for food or space, or in fleetness of foot that will leave the slower individual as food for some predator. Young marsupials such as kangaroos spend several weeks after emerging from the birth opening attached fast to a nipple in the mother's pouch. With wombats six young are born at one time. Blind and prematurely entered into the world, these must contend with each other in crawling along the mother's belly to the pouch. The two slowest are always eliminated, for the provision of nipples is not six but only four.

The novelties in the genes that provide the raw material for natural selection are known as 'mutations'. These represent small alterations in the order of the DNA code-words in the chromosomes, and they arise constantly and spontaneously in every organism. In a number of animals, including man, where the frequency of mutations has been calculated, a mutation for a given gene is found to occur approximately once in every 100,000 cell divisions. There are about 10,000 human genes, so that for every 10 germ cells (egg or sperm) formed, one can be predicted to contain a mutation for some one gene.

The geneticist H. J. Muller found in 1927 that the rate of mutation could be greatly accelerated by dosage of fruit-flies with X-rays. Other types of radiation (gamma rays, neutrons, ultra-violet light) also induce mutations, as do the chemical mutagens such as mustard gas. Artificial induction of mutations always looks dismal in the result. As with natural mutations, the vast majority of artificial mutations are not only disadvantageous but even lethal, and they produce a host of errors and malformations. And even natural mutations are changes that appear randomly without respect to their usefulness to the individual.

The production of new mutations and the rate of evolution are naturally faster in organisms like fruit-flies that reproduce weekly, or in bacteria that divide every twenty minutes, than in men or elephants where reproduction is a rare event in a long life.

Evolutionary novelty does not appear by mutation alone. Every act of sexual reproduction gives an opportunity for the reshuffling of the genes. Chromosomes are rearranged by 'crossing over' of genes from one to another. The interchange of sex cells between parents provides new combinations out of the large gene pool every individual possesses. Each species has a great store of variation, much of it lying unexpressed in the 'phenotype'. It has been calculated by Sir Ronald Fisher that such stored-up variation could be enough to provide as much evolutionary change in the future as we have seen in the past, even if new mutations were wholly to cease.

Not only are most mutations deleterious, and eliminated by natural selection. Even the results of natural selection can be harmful to efficiency. The gorgeous tail of the peacock, or the cumbersome antler spread of stags are an absurd encumbrance to the wild animal. But since females give preference in choice of mates to the finest adorned males, these genes for over-ornamentation will be favoured by selection, at least until the decline of a whole species through inefficiency. Natural selection may sometimes be as unreliable in securing the long-term welfare of the species as *laisser faire* individualism in promoting the health of the economic system.

Competition within a species undoubtedly improves efficiency. Sometimes it can lead to exquisite refinement of detail. The familiar orange and black monarch butterfly is distasteful to birds, which reject and avoid it. The viceroy butterfly is nonnoxious, but deceives birds by mimicking the monarch pattern. A rather rough general resemblance might have been sufficient; but in a competitive situation, where one individual goes beyond what is 'good enough', the contest is heightened. Mimicry – like all adaptive design – is sharpened towards virtual perfection.

Evolution by natural selection is directed then to the advantage of the individual in the particular time and circumstances. It is not at once easy to see how this *laisser faire* principle, the apotheosis of selfish opportunism, can lead to long-term improvements, such as the conquest of the land by early vertebrates, or the beginnings of social organization in primates.

With a successful pattern of adaptation, an organism becomes progressively more confined to a single track. Plasticity is reduced. Straight-line progress of this sort may give the appearance of 'orthogenesis' or 'directed evolution' that teleologists have frequently believed in. But some linear evolution may be retrogressive. Parasites lose complexity and become degenerate. The large dinosaurs developed huge baroque excrescences of armour and ornament. Natural selection will ultimately operate to eliminate the inefficient, but if the animal be large and powerful, or competitors few enough, extinction may be long delayed.

There are also lines of advance that lead to higher levels of efficiency. Certain characters already possessed may offer advantages in entirely novel directions, and it is these that are sometimes referred to as 'pre-adaptations': a particular organization may be pregnant with new possibilities. Thus the vertebrates probably discovered the land habitat only fortuitously, pushing into it almost reluctantly as eels come on to moist ground from intolerably stagnant water. Primitive fishes had already acquired a lung for nostril breathing of atmospheric air while still living in oxygen-poor swamps. From the fleshy fin of the lung-fish the five-toed limb became splayed out, with which our ancestors crawled laboriously over swampy ground, seeking not the land but new pools as the old ones dried up.

In our own order of mammals, the primates, it was from the tree-climbing life that the lemur-like ancestors acquired the versatile clinging and grasping hand. With this came a highly developed tactile sense, a regression of the snout and the sense of smell, and efficient stereoscopic and colour vision. Our small-bodied, large-brained forbears were thus adapted for tool-bearing and the accurate manipulating of objects picked up by the hand.

THE INEVITABILITY OF PROGRESS?

Can we detect anything in the evolutionary process that will of itself lead to progress? Given the nature of living matter, could we for example have expected sensitivity to the environment, or the complex brain? Is there even a forward thrust that makes man inevitable?

These are natural questions to be asked. For most of us - even scientists – are reluctant to believe that the emergence of our own species was fortuitous; or that if variation and selection had at times gone a little differently, man might as easily not have happened.

None the less questions about the 'inevitability' of man are wrongly based. It is true that with hindsight, each step in the origin of man may seem explicable from natural selection; just as there is nothing in the writing of this book that could not be explained – when it is finished – under the laws of physiology. But – as we have already stressed – specific instances are not the sort of things for which natural laws are to be held responsible. If it be postulated that there exists a creator who had a design for man, there is nothing in this a scientist need be concerned to deny. But we can be sure that no trace of such purpose will appear from the study of the natural order in itself.

There are two notions about evolution that we shall have to avoid. First, there is the naive teleology of a God with itching fingers, intervening to give mutation and recombination a creative push this way or that. Second, we cannot as scientists look within the process for any self-determined outcome that 'had to be'. Eloquent of design as the world may be, there can be no trace of plan inherent in evolution itself. If I am asked what the study of evolution can of itself tell me about God, the answer – if I am to be honest – must be bleakly 'Nothing'. God, it has been observed, is not a scientific word, even a high-grade one. We shall never find any empirical relevance for God by working the word into a scientific sentence. Whether or not mankind-grown-up must be 'able to get along without him', the man in the laboratory must surely do so. Charles Davis has well written, 'Precisely because his [God's] causality is total, it does not appear when what is sought is the intelligibility inherent in the universe itself. God is indeed immanent in the universe, but as the transcendent cause not as part of its system.'[3]

Is progress, then, in itself fortuitous? Are not only its direction and end-point but even its occurrence at all unpredictable from the natural system? We meet with this question at two stages: first, with the tendency of living things, once launched in their course, to increase in complexity; second (though prior in time), the origin of the living itself from the non-living.

Within the natural order with its overall tendency to increase in entropy, we have shown that life occupies an exceptional position. It alone shows an exception to the cosmic tendency to run down, to lose energy from the system – or, as we say – to decrease in organization.

The idea of increasing *fitness* has generally been linked with increasing complexity. And though the 'fit' are merely by definition those forms that do in fact survive, it is an observable fact that survival and improved organization go together. The geneticist, Sir Ronald Fisher, argued that a 'law of increasing fitness' could be shown to operate in all living things: 'The rate of increase in fitness of a population at any time is equal to its genetic variance in fitness at that time.' Regularity of progress – through the means of variation and natural selection – is 'guaranteed by the same circumstances that make the particles in a gas bubble obey the laws of gases without appreciable deviation'. While the second law of thermodynamics (that entropy always increases) holds the supreme position among the laws of nature, Fisher has observed of his own theorem: 'It is not a little instructive to find that so similar a law should hold the supreme position among the biological sciences.'[4]

For both laws, in describing the behaviour of populations, hold true irrespective of what units compose them. Species numerous in individuals, with a wide range of mutants and ample store of variation, must evolve and adapt and increase in fitness faster than rare species. Abundant species thus increase in relative abundance. Rare species become rarer.

THE BEGINNINGS OF LIFE

Can the theory of evolution by natural selection explain how living systems first arose? Did the key substances of bio-chemistry, the nucleic acids and proteins, appear fortuitously? Or could there have been a selection, even from the first, that favoured the generation of 'living' molecules from simpler organic substances, or the organic itself from the inorganic? It was these questions that the biologists A. I. Oparin in Russia and J. B. S. Haldane in England began to ask over 40 years ago. The recent book *The Origin of Life* by Professor J. D. Bernal gives a highly readable account of their conclusions as they have lasted to the present day.[5]

The earliest atmosphere of our planet must have consisted of a mixture of gases, hydrogen, ammonia, methane and water vapour. In a classical experiment, an American chemist, Stanley Miller, has combined a mixture of these gases by a spark discharge in a flask. Small yields of amino-acids were obtained. It is feasible that the earliest steps in organic synthesis could have come about in this way. The primordial energy sources before the dawn of life could have been the electrical discharges of storms or the ultra-violet solar radiation that is now mostly blanketed from the earth by the ozone layer in our modern atmosphere.

It is a property of amino-acids to link up in chains to build polypeptide sequences and ultimately proteins. The simple nitrogenous bases (purines and pyrimidines) of the nucleic acids can also be produced by non-living reactions. With phosphate and the sugar ribose, these could have been assembled to form molecules of DNA and RNA, and also the energy-carrying compound ATP.

The next step in biogenesis would have been to bring the key molecules together. These could have built up complexes upon materials with high surface energy, such as particles of clay; or they could have been concentrated in tiny pools of water. The nucleic acids might then have served as templates, as they do today, for building proteins out of amino-acids. As a next advance these chemical aggregates – at a stage we must call 'pre-cellular' – would have begun to draw upon outside molecules – inorganic or, presently, other organic – as building materials. 'Life' may be said to have come into being when the complex molecules thus began to feed and to replicate their own kind of structure.

Some sorts of molecule, either by peculiarities of their chemical structure or by the special efficiency of their reactions, would have had a special ability to take up outside molecules. Hence they could monopolize these supplies by excluding other molecules from access to them. A 'competition for substrate', or for molecular food and fuel, would thus have arisen. This contest would selectively favour the multiplication of the more successful systems. For the first time in the planet's history we can now properly use the terms 'efficient' and 'adaptive', and natural selection has begun to operate at the earliest level we can call biological.

The first living things were probably 'chemotrophs' feeding upon non-living chemical substances. Then would have followed forms that fed and grew at the expense of other living matter, being thus called 'heterotrophs'. We may take it that these respired anaerobically, without oxygen, just as yeast cells do today. A new atmosphere now began to develop, still lacking oxygen, but rich in the carbon dioxide produced by anaerobic respirors. This in turn served as the substrate for photo-synthesis. Green plants began to appear with pigments that could capture radiant energy, and the simplest of the carbo-hydrates, glucose-type sugars, could now be produced from carbon dioxide and water.

The other end-product of photosynthesis is oxygen. For the first time since the earliest history of the planet (when metals and other heavy elements took up the oxygen to form ores in the rock crust) free oxygen was now restored to the atmosphere.

This was a revolution with momentous consequence both for chemistry and biology. It was first brought about and has been sustained ever since by living green plants. First, the presence of oxygen allowed the progressive development of an ozone layer 70 miles up, cutting off from the earth's surface all but a minute amount of ultra-violet solar radiation. We have now lost for ever access to the energy that we took to be so important in the first stages of biogenesis. Second, with an oxygen atmosphere, aerobic respiration is now possible for the majority of plants and animals. Fuel compounds can be broken down to yield far more energy than is obtained by anaerobic respiration, and a greater percentage yield from the fuel than in any combustion machine yet devised.

'THE UNIQUENESS OF MAN'

Human evolution fully justifies such a claim. Under Fisher's law, progress is the reward of the abundant and fast-reproducing; but man is in large areas of his life protected from the operation of natural selection. Yet his ecological dominance is immense, unquestioned and unprecedented; and there is every ground to believe that his is the line from which alone further progress can come. Sir Julian Huxley wrote:

> One of the concomitants of organic progress has been the progressive cutting down of the possible modes of further progress, until now, after a thousand or fifteen hundred million years of evolution, progress hangs on but a single thread. That thread is the human germ-plasm. As Villiers de l'Isle-Adam wrote in *L'Eve Future*, 'L'Homme . . . seul, dans l'univers, n'est-pas fini'.[6]

The human species has two characteristics: the achievement of a nervous system of unparalleled complexity and the initiation of what has been called 'exosomatic evolution'.

A comprehensive view of human biology must take account of new structures not developed by organic adaptation but fashioned from the materials of the outside world. These include new sense organs (cameras, amplifiers, oscilloscopes, electron microscopes) and new effector organs (cars, knives and forks, jet planes and cyclotrons). They can even be called hereditary, in a valid biological sense if not in the genetic mode. For human culture and technology are transmitted not by genes in chromosomes, but by schools and libraries, patent offices and museums. Our books are our exosomatic chromosomes.[7]

Side by side with his exosomatic achievement, man has remained – the brain apart – a surprisingly conservative mammal. His line is highly advanced only in cerebral development and in the key senses of vision and touch. Even the human hand, with its high behavioural plasticity and refinement of nervous connections, is structurally almost as primitive as in the five-fingered amphibians that first colonized the land.

Whatever the future vistas of our social and mental evolution, human bodily structure is unlikely to change greatly. There are some modest changes a captious critic could ask for: improvement in the weight-carrying pelvic and lumbar region, better drainage of such cul-de-sacs as the nasal sinuses, complete elimination of the often troublesome third molar tooth. But even these changes are less likely in that our species has tended to reduce the impact of natural selection.

It would be clearly wrong to say selection has entirely disappeared. It is true that many genotypes may survive today that would have previously been eliminated (for diabetes, Addison's disease, poor antibody formation). But natural selection still comes to bear in many characters, affecting the vigour or viability of the individual. Good examples are shown by the immuno-proteins of the blood serum, the different ratios for the gene for 'sickle cell' haemoglobin in regions with and without malaria, and the elimination of deleterious genes as for haemophilia. Natural selection may often operate by pre-natal mortality; and there is in most human communities today a selection arising from unequal reproduction among different intelligence and social groups.

But selection pressures change, and are relaxed by welfare

programmes and medical advance. With today's population expansion almost unrestrained, the harsh Malthusian checks of famine and epidemic could begin to operate again, under conditions of poor nutrition, over-crowding and break-down of relief services.

It will not be without precedent if our species continues physically unchanged for millions of years ahead. The New Zealand tuatara, the coelacanth and many other 'living fossils' have done exactly this, though always as relict types in relative decline, never as ecological dominants such as man.

Human evolution illustrates two important biological principles. First, man has kept to a minimum his investment in specialized adaptations. Continued plasticity is needed to keep open further options. Long-term progress has been denied, for example, to anteaters with attenuate snout and tongue, and eyes and teeth reduced; or to the dolphin, which – despite its renowned intelligence and acuity – has lost much of its manipulatory range by sacrificing the hand and foot.

Second, man exemplifies again the saying that 'every characteristic is both inherited and acquired'. We inherit an active and questing intelligence. A large part of our cultural attributes we re-learn in each generation, especially during the beneficially prolonged childhood that distinguishes man from other mammals. Behaviourally, we bring little into this world; from the time of birth we rely supremely on conditioning, training and intellectual exploration.

THE POTENTIAL OF MAN

[In the gospel of Christianity we find] the only biological outcome proper to or conceivable for the phenomenon of man.[8]

Teilhard de Chardin has given us in his writings, and in particular *The Phenomenon of Man*, a far-ranging vision of human evolution. In a true sense this is a work of prophecy with a theme nothing less than man's future in relation to the whole cosmic process. Catholic priest and palaeontologist, Teilhard was in his own right a scientist of distinction. But though he opens with a plea that his book be read simply as a scientific treatise, this it is manifestly not. A work of fine intellectual and spiritual discernment, it is an apocalyptic construction placed upon the whole of evolution, through primal stuff to life, consciousness and man. Its language may be found heady and exhilarating, used not to describe but to open and explore new and raw concepts. This has, only naturally, opened it to critical onslaught by those who cannot share its preconceptions, most of all in the sustained cruelty of Sir Peter Medawar's famous review of 1961, in the periodical *Mind*.[9]

On the other hand, many humanists have warmed to Teilhard's glow. Outstandingly among scientists, Sir Julian Huxley, from his eminence as an evolutionist, has interpreted, and largely identified himself with, Teilhard's message. If Huxley's introduction to the English translation be tackled first, the argument will come home far more succinctly to the ordinary reader.

Man's significance lies not in his origin or present attainments but in his direction and promise. The appearance of life imposed an additional layer, the 'biosphere', upon the inorganic 'lithosphere' of our planet. With the arrival of man, a 'thinking layer' has appeared, involving conscious rationality, inventiveness and union between souls. This new reality, the 'noosphere', is constituted by thought and purpose revealed under biological forms.

The Phenomenon of Man refers many times to a unique property of human evolution that Huxley was the first to stress. Man is the only dominant biological type that has remained as a single species, or potentially interbreeding group. All other dominant forms have rapidly sub-divided into separate lines: the birds with 8,500 species or the insects with almost a million, fill the different available niches by adaptive radiation. With man, freer migration and intermarriage has prevented the break-up from going further than races. A convergent or centripetal tendency replaces the general tendency to diverge and differentiate.

Human psychosocial evolution has indeed produced different and discordant cultures. But these are still 'interthinking groups'. They have never become established as separate species. With improving communications, an intensified cultural convergence is leading the human species into a single framework that Teilhard calls the 'noosystem'. Theories of innate racial superiority have no scientific basis known to the evolutionist. Racial or national separatism pulls against strong natural tides. The United Nations Declaration on Human Rights makes as good sense to the biologist as to the Christian or the humanist.

A pivot of Teilhard de Chardin's argument is what he calls 'complexification', the building up of increasingly elaborate organic systems. Beginning with subatomic units, organization proceeds by way of atoms, molecules, complex carbon compounds, cells and multicellular animals, to man and civilized societies. Biology flows into sociology. The whole world stuff is engaged in an '*enroulement organique sur lui-même*'. It is the same tendency that Huxley has called 'self-integration', leading to a greater intensification of mental activity, to more conscious and integrated mind, and to more pervasive and effective purpose.

Human personality is the culmination of two major evolutionary movements, towards more perfect individuality, and towards more extensive interrelation and co-operation. The ultimate convergence and integration is towards the point Omega, at which Teilhard sees the universe intensely unified with a hyper-personal organization.

The postulate Omega is not merely a remote goal extrapolated into the far future. It is, on the contrary, 'already in existence and operative at the very core of the thinking mass'. It would thus seem inevitable that some trace of its presence should appear. 'Either the whole construction of the world presented here is vain ideology or, somewhere around us, in one form or another, some excess of personal, extra-human energy should be perceptible to us if we look carefully, and should reveal to us the great Presence.'

Teilhard finds the Christian phenomenon deeply significant

for man's biological destiny. It brings us the 'crucial confirmation' we need, the perspective of a universe dominated by energies of a personal nature. We find this in the substance of the Christian creed, in its 'existence value' and in its extraordinary power of growth.

> In the centre, so glaring as to be disconcerting, is the uncompromising affirmation of a personal God: God as providence, directing the universe with loving, watchful care; and God the revealer, communicating himself to man on the level of and through the ways of intelligence.[10]

With prophetic sweep, Teilhard sees the biological achievement of man move upwards towards the new level where God will fulfil and purify the world by uniting it organically with himself. By partly immersing himself in it, by becoming element, God will then from this vantage point in the heart of matter assume the control and leadership of what we now call evolution. Then, as St Paul has foreseen for us, 'God shall be all in all'.

In a moving passage upon Christian love, Teilhard places this value at the very heart of cosmogenesis.

> Christian love is incomprehensible to those who have not experienced it. That the infinite and the intangible can be lovable, or that the human heart can beat with genuine charity for a fellow-being . . . But whether it be founded on an illusion or not, how can we doubt that such a sentiment exists, and even in great intensity? We have only to note crudely the results it produces unceasingly all round us.[11]

Just as we have held the mind to be no latter-day emergence from biological mechanism, so Christ in the world can be no alien intruder at a receding point in history. He is the continuing and enlarging revelation of the cosmic plan. It is profoundly confirmatory of such a plan that a zone of thought has already appeared in which a genuine universal love has not only been conceived and preached, but has been found psychologically and existentially possible.[12]

'The Christian fact stands before us. It has its place among the other realities of the world.'[13] Here we find the very cross-check needed with the world process, 'the reflection onto what is ascending of that which is already on high . . . The palpable influence on our world of *an other* and supreme Someone.'[14]

CHAPTER 8

The Existence of God

The sole object of genuine worship is a
transcendent God.

H. D. Lewis[1]

A God comprehended is no God.

Tersteegen

THE secularist objections to the traditional idea of God are
scarcely surprising: they are statements of the very properties
we should expect a transcendent God to have. For we cannot
exclude God from nature, as the working method of science
must require, and at the same time expect him to be 'non-
supernaturalistic'. We must not deplore the survival in the
twentieth century of a 'God out there' while still holding possible a God whose existence could be explanatory of the world.

If we are searching for ultimate explanation – and if we
believe that the search is one worth making – we shall assuredly
find mystery before we reach the end. The natural system is still
patently incomplete. Whatever it fully portends is evidently as
yet unrealized. It could be pointing towards a level more unified
and comprehensive than the physical or biological one, just as
life presents us with an integration beyond the terms of the
physical order.

We can expect, however, that study of the natural order itself
will be sterile of final explanations. For a creator God will be
logically transcendent to his whole creation, at least if he be the
sort of God that retains any philosophical usefulness. Being the
cause of the whole system, he is not therefore to be thought of as
one of its ingredients or observable properties. He cannot even
be the unattained goal towards which the system is transforming
itself. Current theological writers seem no longer happy with

the term 'supernatural'. In much of its contemporary use, it has overtones of anti-scientific mysticism that have taken away most of its value as a useful theological word. Many writers have tried alternatively to get along with the concepts of the 'sacred' and 'secular', which Charles Davis has defined in terms of their kind of intelligibility to man.[2] 'The secular is the domain open to human investigation . . . where the enquirer can expect the insight that . . . penetrates its intrinsic truth.' The sacred is in principle hidden before man's scrutiny. Nevertheless he is aware of its presence as 'of a darkness he knows to be light but cannot see, of an intelligibility too bright for his gaze, of a transcendence that evokes his adoration'.[3]

If we can understand this distinction, which is elementary to theology, much of the modern controversy, for example Julian Huxley's spirited passages in *Religion without Revelation*, comes to look naively off the point:

> The god hypothesis is no longer of any pragmatic value for the interpretation or comprehension of nature, and indeed often stands in the way of better and truer interpretation. Operationally, God is beginning to resemble not a ruler, but the last fading smile of a cosmic Cheshire cat . . .
>
> It will soon be as impossible for an intelligent, educated man or woman to believe in a god as it is now to believe that the earth is flat, that flies can be spontaneously generated . . . or that death is always due to witchcraft.[4]

Yet Dr J. A. T. Robinson quotes this passage with some sympathy in his book *Honest to God*,[5] in claiming that a 'psychological – if not a logical' blow has been delivered by science to the idea of a 'God out there'. If he were right, this might, of course, be not an invalidation of God but an impediment to man's understanding of the world and himself. It could be a reflection, too, upon the clarity and cogency of our theologians; for I believe that Dr Robinson's own argument about God has brought him into a logical morass.

Anxious to avoid 'a super-world of divine objects', Dr

Robinson turns to Paul Tillich, to commend his reinterpretation of 'transcendence', which defines it in such a way as to 'preserve its reality while detaching it from the projection of supra-naturalism'.[6] 'Within itself, the finite world points beyond itself. In other words, it is self-transcendent.'[7]

God is frequently spoken of by Dr Robinson as the Un-conditional in the Conditioned, evidently in the sense that we shall find certain values, such as love, wholly compelling of our assent, and in this sense transcendent over every other. For to what 'beyond itself' could the finite world point? To an order of existence not finite? Or even to something 'out there'? What are we to understand by the Unconditional existing in and under the Conditioned, if not a principle emergent from the natural order and even contingent upon it? Has not God, or the Unconditional, become simply a metaphor for the values realized in and by the universe, or foreshadowed perhaps in the ultimate aim of the cosmic process?

Though Dr Robinson is at pains to avoid the reproach of 'secularism' or 'naturalism' (in the same way few modern writers would in so many words own to 'pantheism'), he would appear to be deriving not merely our own apprehensions of God, but God himself from 'our own' ultimate depths. He is even prepared to call ultimate reality 'deeply personal', but by this he evidently means simply that certain types of personal relationship among ourselves have for him supreme value. This is not very different from maintaining that 'Love is God', though Dr Robinson disclaims this. The truth seems to be that for such a God, fashioned out of *our* ultimate depths and *our* existence, he has been prepared to forget the role of God as creator and sustainer of the world. What – if we may ask a Robinson-type question – would the God he envisages have been doing at the middle of the Jurassic age?

Dr Robinson has of course not a philosophical but a pastoral concern. He has been bravely seeking to reconstruct a basis of belief credible to scientifically oriented man in an age that is widely sceptical or indifferent to religion. Such a belief, he maintains, can arise from existential sources and be, in effect, self-demonstrating and atheist-proof. 'One cannot argue whether ultimate reality *exists*. One can only ask what ultimate reality is like . . .'[8]

David Jenkins has commented somewhat brusquely on this passage.[9] 'You can only ask whether pretentious phrases like "ultimate reality" are wanted at all and . . . whether there is any case for bringing the word "God" within smelling distance of the argument.' Dr Robinson's God posited in the depths of our ultimate concern, or in what we think important without reservation, is in short no more atheist-proof than any other. Ultimate reality no more refers to some self-evident reality than does the name 'God', or the 'Perfect Being' of the old ontological proof of God (see below, p. 111).

Jenkins continues: 'One can refuse or be unable to believe in God and one can refuse or be unable to believe that "ultimate reality" has the character asserted . . . Further, *if* ultimate reality does have the character asserted of "it", then it looks very much as if it remains true that there exists a personal God who is other than and more than the stuff and phenomena of our life, however true it must be that he is to be encountered only in and through this stuff.'

For God is eminently subject to doubt. Even if I do not doubt him, I observe that many men, with better intellects and philosophical training than mine, do. No species of rational demonstration can impose belief in God on the resistant mind. If we are to allow the sceptic or the positivist his choice of ground, the contest is already lost. To them, the idea of God is vacuous because of the very property we would expect God to show, his inability to be substituted meaningfully for any term in a scientific description.

The alternative to God is one that many of our contemporaries prefer: that the world is not explicable at all. Whatever internal coherence science may find in the natural order, man is ultimately alone in a meaningless world. This is a position from which none of the resources of intellectual philosophy will by themselves avail to rescue us.

It is true that it cannot be a conclusive objection to theistic belief that some men have none; though if they had seriously sought it and lacked it still, this might raise another problem about the justice of the world. But any explanation of the world's existence will not be a mere description of the way things function and have evolved. It will be a statement about the metaphysical and the transnatural. Etienne Gilson in his lectures *God and Philosophy*[10] considers various answers to the question of God. The best, he concludes, is the one that grasps the deepest implications of the problem, and bows freely 'to the metaphysical necessity of its only solution'. As to him who would reject it: 'Let him have at least the satisfaction of turning down the only pertinent solution to a true problem: not the supreme carpenter of Paley, or the supreme watchmaker of Voltaire, but the infinite act of self-existence, by whom all the rest is, and as compared with whom all the rest is as though it were not.'[11]

Of the traditional properties of God, we shall have little difficulty today in accepting his oneness. The earliest Hebrews, with the primary religious impulses common to most races, had not yet come to look for a unity in ultimate explanation and authority. Only at a maturer stage was the Lord our God recognized as one Lord, so that – wherever men might travel – Yahweh, to the exclusion of every local deity, remained one and supreme.

To the Hellenic world, with the crowded hierarchy of Mount Olympus, the multiplicity of deities remained a permanent obstacle to religious profundity. As in secular Rome, the gods were finally displaced to the gallery of mythology, and the educated minority had grown no mature belief to take their place. But with the religious genius that showed the Jews as a chosen people, as with the dawn of Hellenic philosophy, we find the recognition of one God being related to the philosophical problem of existence. The first enigma is, why anything is at all. The mainstream of Christian philosophy was to follow not Plato, but Aristotle 'christianized' by Aquinas to produce the great Thomist tradition of Catholic thought. Here too Existence is the first problem handled; and it is in Existence rather than in Creativity that I believe we can find our first intimations of God today.

THE 'PHILOSOPHICAL PROOFS'

Whatever the ultimate source of our beliefs, we can put them under the scrutiny of philosophy to see whether they are in harmony with the sort of world that on other grounds would appear possible or reasonable. This is the value for us of the traditional 'proofs' of God's existence. The Catholic Church, while never doubting that God's prime revelation was given in his own self-showing, would employ the system erected by St Thomas Aquinas to show the rationality, and indeed the philosophical necessity, of belief in him.

The reformed churches have generally been more austere in their hopes of philosophy. Their emphasis has been upon the revelation to the believing mind, or on the power or 'kerygma' of the preaching of the gospel. To many of the reformers, man's nature was so vitiated by its sinning, that it had no possibility of recognizing God through any power of its own. The sternest representative of such a tradition in our own day was Karl Barth. To him, man's response is as much a miracle as God's revelation itself. God's impact on the world is solely vertical and one-way. Man can have no insight upon him through history, or the processes of nature, or even his own nature.

The oldest of the 'proofs' is the ontological one. It was first maintained by the English St Anselm (Archbishop of Canterbury, 1093-1109), but was rejected by St Thomas Aquinas (1225-74). Its reasoning seems – to modern minds – to involve a certain sleight-of-hand, though in fact Dr Robinson's finding of God in ultimate reality is a resuscitation of this 'proof'. The existence of a perfect being is argued from the idea of such a being that our minds can conceive. One of the attributes of perfection is existence. If such a being does not exist, it is not perfect, for it would be possible to imagine another being superior to it, namely one that does exist.

According to this argument, what can be thought of thereby has existence. Descartes was later to take a similar view in affirming values to exist because we can powerfully conceive them. Since we can form an idea of perfection, the only adequate cause for such an idea must be perfection itself. Kant's critique of the ontological argument was that bare existence is not a real predicate, and that when you say of a thing that 'it is' you have added nothing more to its attributes.

Of St Thomas's five 'proofs' of God's existence, no fewer than four centre round the cosmological argument. This would posit the existence of a first cause that would explain all other existences but is in itself neither needful nor capable of proof. For though we may explain all things by their causes, an endless regress of causes is impossible. Something must be reached that moves other things without being moved. Similar arguments are those of an ultimate source of all necessity, and a completely perfect source of all the various and relative perfections in the world.

From these arguments, we could envisage a first being whose existence is not – like every other existence – contingent, but is necessary. The title 'He Who Is' is then the most appropriate to God, because it signifies 'to be' and the word being, as a noun, denotes some substance. Gilson writes:

> [In the natural order] we first conceive certain beings, then we define their essences, and last we affirm their existences by means of a judgment. But the metaphysical order of reality is just the reverse. . . . what first comes into it is a certain act of existing which, because it is *this* particular act of existing, circumscribes at once a certain essence and causes a certain substance to come into being. . . . 'to be' is the very act whereby an essence is.[12]

Plato spoke not, like the Jews, of 'Him Who Is', but of 'That Which Is'. But to Hellenic philosophy, as to Jewish, the ultimate explanation lay not in those elements that are always being generated and are therefore 'contingent' but in something that, because it has no generation, truly exists. Not only for the deepest layer of reality, but as the supreme attribute of divinity, the best that can be said is 'He exists'.

Christian philosophy does not begin then with the God of Descartes with his primary function to create and preserve the world, still less with the deist's withdrawn caretaker God that has set the world going by undeviating laws. These Gilson likes to call merely the 'by-products of the philosophical decomposition of the Christian God'.

> The essence of the true Christian God is not to create but to be. 'He who is' can also create, if he chooses; but he does not exist because he creates, nay, not even himself; he can create because he supremely is.[13]

The cosmological proof too has been criticized by Kant, who austerely maintained that all we can know is phenomena. We must not carry such modes of thinking as cause and effect beyond sense data to the supersensible; and we cannot argue from finite apprehensions to the infinite. The modern positivists of our own day would hold that there is no legitimate knowledge beyond what is empirical, and that questions incapable of answer in such terms are not meaningful.

It has also been argued that the cosmological proof would establish not a deity but only an all-inclusive system. It would bring us to a form of pantheistic naturalism, the absolute reality being the whole, of which particular experiences are a part. But pantheism is not fundamentally explanatory at all. It gives us no inkling of why the total system, or any part of it, is. It can shed no light on the existence of values. It points to a closed and static system in which everything that is, is settled and final. If we are to hold – as with 'emergent' or 'evolutionary' explanations – that the supreme existence is 'immanent' or comprehended within the system, this is in fact to offer no light upon it at all.

If the cosmological proof can bring us no further than an all-inclusive system, and if we are to continue seeking for explanation at all, we may turn next to St Thomas's fifth or teleological proof. In its various forms, this proof is the demonstration of God and his nature from the purpose disclosed in the existence and design of the world.

Inanimate and non-conscious things disclose ends not explicable from themselves. From such designs we are led to the arguments for a designer that undoubtedly appeal to a plain man's commonsense view of the world. These will not necessarily be anthropocentric, or human-oriented. But among the attributes of 'Him Who Is' (if he is to satisfy our full intimations of him) must be something not less than the purposiveness we can in a limited degree identify in ourselves.

One of the mysteries left in a scientifically explained world (though a mystery so familiar that we have learned to live with it daily) is that of personality with its criteria of consciousness, judgement, purpose and value. Not only is this the most direct and compelling datum we can have about anything. It also resists involvement with science, and leaves the findings of science intact and unimpugned.

The teleological theme, with its argument based on purpose, is a leading strand in William Temple's great works, *Christus Veritas* and *Nature, Man and God*. For another masterly treatment of the argument from design I am indebted to Dr W. R. Matthews' classic *The Purpose of God*.

If we are to ask for an explanation of the universe at all, we are bound to formulate it (so runs the argument) in terms of purpose or will. Indeed the two imply each other. When we find as the cause of some phenomenon, that an intelligent will chose to bring it about, we raise no further question. When we find a will, we have reached an ultimate term, the end of the causal regress. 'The only explanation of the Universe', writes William Temple, 'that would really explain it, in the sense of providing to the question why it exists an answer that raises no further question, would be the demonstration that it is the creation of a Will which in the creative act seeks an intelligible good.' This – it is acknowledged – is theism, and if it is untenable, the universe remains ultimately inexplicable. 'Merely to show how it fits together as a rational system does not fully explain it, for we are left still asking – Why does it exist at all?'[14]

Persuasive as we might find its reliance upon purpose, the teleological argument – considered as a formal 'proof' of God – has also been much criticized. The first objection must come from Hume, and it is that the design of the universe need not of necessity imply a mind at all. Given infinite time, it would have been conceivably possible for the chaos of an utterly disordered universe so to arrange itself as to constitute the intricate order under which we live. Dr Matthews' answer to this is that we should need to be sure the number of particles in the universe was finite, not infinite; and to fix a definite term for the number of particles in the universe is to destroy the state of disorder postulated by the objection.[15]

More serious still is the philosophic objection to postulating purpose at all in the governance of the universe. Purpose is said to be a psychological construct appropriate to man which we can have no warrant for placing in the cosmic seat of control. The ideas of cause and effect, however indispensable they may be as vehicles of human thought, are not to be extended beyond the immediately sensible world of phenomena.

How disabling need this objection be? First, we should be clear that, despite the anxieties of the scientists, the theist is not – by the teleological argument – putting any purpose *into* the natural order at all. Whether he is a believer in God or not, the scientist will insist that nature must be a coherent system, explicable throughout by observation and experiment. The scientist is reluctant to concede any boundary to this territory over the whole field of human knowledge, not always because teleological arguments are disapproved of in principle, but lest they may *de facto* discourage the scientist from fully exploring his own ground. Nevertheless, explanations involving purpose – whether our purpose or God's – leave the whole possible realm of natural laws intact. If it still seems necessary – after our inspection of the world and our introspection of ourselves – to postulate purpose in the design and regularity of the world, this might be not because man has put the concept into nature, but because, in the eternal foundation of nature, he has found purpose already there.

To take issue with teleology is really to enquire whether the categories of human thinking are eternally valid. The theist is taking the option of believing that, on the whole, we err least in ascribing to the highest level of being something *not less* than the sublimest, most creative and most heroic capacities that we can detect in minds like our own.

The alternative the physicist Sir Mark Oliphant has confidently predicted, that the explanation of the universe is to come not from metaphysics or philosophy, but from astronomers and astrophysicists, we can venture to rule out. Explanations from scientists are not really final explanations at all, unless – like the conjectures of Eddington or Eccles – they come from thoughtful men standing aside from their own discipline to use the insights of theology.

There is a further objection to the teleological argument, considered as an invincible 'proof'. As Hume expressed this, the cause ought to be proportioned to the effect, and any effect that can be cognizable to us is not infinite. What right have we from finite causes to attribute infinity to a divine being? Nothing we can infer from phenomena can ever be equal to demonstrating a God one, perfect and unique. As Kant teaches us, no bare experience can ever be adequate to an idea. It is alleged, moreover, that the design of the world does not reveal a perfect or loving God at all. And this is an objection more powerful because it is not formal or theoretic but starkly empiric. In a memorable passage, provocative with what W. R. Matthews truly calls Hume's 'adorable style', it is suggested that this world may in fact be a poor example of world-making.

This world for aught [a man] knows is very faulty compared with a superior standard, and it was only the first rude essay of some infant deity who afterwards abandoned it, ashamed of his lame performance; it is the work of some dependent inferior deity and is the object of derision to his superiors; it is the production of old age and dotage in some superannuated deity, and ever since his death has run on at adventures from the first impulse and active force which it received from him.[16]

The argument for the 'dysteleology' of the world can be put into a form we must presently take more seriously than Hume's. It is that the evil and suffering so evident in the world suggest that the Creator is no loving God, or that if God be loving, then he is severely limited in his powers.

Still the weight of the argument from design may with a judicious mind be very great. Many a non-Christian has had to appeal to it as an ultimate argument in the way the Christian would not do. To Albert Einstein it appeared to offer firm evidence for a God in the austere sense a mathematical scientist could accept: one who 'reveals himself in the orderly array of what exists, not a God who concerns himself with the fates and actions of human beings'.

In our search for God the teleological argument will bring us, then, to a deity at once just, aloof and invariable. Spinoza (1632–77), held by Bertrand Russell,[17] and not by him alone, to be the noblest and most lovable of the philosophers, finds in God the only possible substance of existence, in whose being all individual souls and separate objects are but partial aspects. Spinoza's view of the world is purely pantheistic. The strict logical necessity of God's undeviating purpose rules out both free-will and chance. Everything that happens is part of God's inscrutable nature and purpose. Even the evil that appears to us as sin, is not evil at all when seen by God as part of the eternal and timeless whole. Our minds are capable of forming an adequate idea of God's nature, and can even deduce a system of ethics, with axioms, theorems and Euclidean proofs. But our knowledge of the divine will is apt to be distorted by passions. Among these are hate and strife – and love, too, at least the limited love that arises from the individual's desire to persevere in his own partial being. The mind's highest good is the knowledge of God, and the mind's highest virtue is to know God. Love towards God must occupy the highest place in the mind. But he who loves God cannot wish that God should love him in return. A man who loves God *cannot* want God to love him, for that would be to desire that God should be less than God.

CHAPTER 9

Towards Knowledge of God

Man's property is to surpass himself.
Pascal

THE philosophic arguments do not in themselves lead to anything like the Christian's God. However philosophically useful God may be as ultimate existence and as creator and mover of the world, we shall have to pursue him further in an area where rational means are not alone sufficient. We may at the outset accept Isaacs' definition of religion in *The Survival of God in the Scientific Age*: 'any type of belief, experience, or observance which affects human behaviour and depends on the concept of a supernatural agency.'[1]

In man the universe becomes conscious of itself; so that the mind is potentially a focus of all existence. It is our singular quality as an animal that we are widely interested in the outside world. Other living things are self-centred by first definition; and while the lower animals continually respond to the environment they do so to maintain themselves as individuals. As their sensory range increases, higher animals can discriminate more of their world; but they still take notice of only that small fragment that is relevant to their lives and releases appropriate instinctive behaviour.

The mammals – and to some degree the birds too – explore more widely. Mammals indulge in the important activity of 'play' by which the environment could be said to be 'enjoyed'. Trial-and-error learning or environmental conditioning becomes possible as the young animal becomes familiar and adept with its living and inanimate world. Play is then a surplus of activity beyond the immediate needs of survival. Professor W. H. Thorpe (in *Learning and Instinct in Animals*) has stressed this growing mastery of the environment as the essential first step 'not only for play but for all those activities which transcend mere maintenance and which underlie the mental and spiritual development of man'. Though originating in play, this new comprehension of the world 'may, for all we know, offer vistas of advance in the millennia to come, compared to which our present understanding will seem puny and infantile in the extreme'.[2]

The same self-overflow is then a quality of our cerebral evolution. The brain cortex – as we have seen – has a complexity utterly without parallel. Sir John Eccles, in an article we have already noticed (p. 54), has shown how the interplay of neurone activity in the cortex gives a basis for the recall and re-experiencing of mental images. One group of patterns evokes another, and so on with an ever-enriching spread. 'When these images are of beauty and subtlety, blending in harmony and expressed in some language – verbal, musical or pictorial – to call up transcendent images in others, we have artistic creation of a simple, lyrical kind.'[3]

At such times, as revealed by the waves recorded by the electroencephalograph, there is increasing withdrawal from the mind's ordinary activities. There may be a deeper sort of image formation, as well, which can include the profoundest of human activities, 'creative imagination'. This must arise from the mind's subconscious operation, involving the intense and unimaginably complex interplay of stored images or 'engrams'. With their repeated activation, we may experience as in a flash the sudden illumination of a new hypothesis in science, or a wholly novel organizing of ideas. While a hypothesis might thus owe little of its origin to the rational process, it will of course be submitted afterwards to experimental and rational critiques.

A complex brain will not inevitably construct an imaginative world. There is in fact a poor correlation between brain size and intelligence; and a chimpanzee with a neurone population 80 per cent of our own appears to have little or no creative imagination.

With ourselves, the imaginative life is no exceptional or

occasional surplus. It is found to be the activity supremely worth pursuing. At its highest we will give it a priority over physical comfort, and even over the preservation of life itself. For man has become pre-eminently an evaluating animal. He has a highly developed symbolic language. This allows ideas to be detached from their concrete reference, in the timeless process of abstraction. We customarily think of the 'traditional values' as the Platonic beauty, truth and goodness. But however they are to be classed, their property seems to be to exist – as it were – entirely outside our own ego-centres. They make their claim on us without regard to time or circumstances, or to our personal needs and wishes. They suggest that the Self is capable of ultimate satisfaction only as it is left outside the field of its own attention.

AN EVALUATING ANIMAL

Moral judgements are not intellectual, nor is goodness to be proportioned to intelligence. The moral impulses by which values are invoked seem to spring from deep sources. Our moral behaviour is built on an ancient inheritance; and we have already remarked on Lorenz's conviction that a purely rational being divested of his animal heritage would not be an angel but the opposite. Though man can bring up his actions for rational appraisal, we are not to think of him as having dismantled his old psychic nature, but rather to have built upon it.

Love or moral goodness, among the values, has a foremost and unique claim upon us. It would everywhere seem to compel the assent of free men acting with the best part of their nature. There is an important question here, that we could have asked when we discussed the freedom of man in Chapter 2: Why cannot a man, as a 'self-determining system of experience', be in this sense a free creature, and yet will to act evilly?

The answer can come only from an empiric experience of man. The Apostle, in bidding the Galatians who were called to be free men not to turn their freedom into licence, declares: 'If you are guided by the Spirit you will not fulfil the desires of your lower nature. That nature sets its desires against the Spirit, while the Spirit fights against it.'[4]

The things that belong to the lower nature: idolatry, contention, quarrels, envy, anger, self-seeking, jealousy, orgies and intemperate indulgence, are empirically found *not* to satisfy the fully free nature. They are by all experience *not* the things in which a man can rejoice at having expressed his whole nature. The fruits of the Spirit, in which the whole personality will take delight, are – we find – 'love, joy, peace, patience, kindness, goodness, fidelity, gentleness, and self-control'.[5]

The compelling force of these qualities tells us, in itself, a good deal about the world. In a sermon on 'The Universality of Christ' William Temple spoke of the supremacy of the value of love. Of truth, he observed that we can always desire this, just as we can always desire beauty. But it can in addition be said of truth that we can always be actively promoting it, as we cannot always be promoting beauty. Even so, we may still not always be able to attain the truth we seek.

But love is to be ranked higher still. 'There is no conceivable situation in which it is not possible to show absolute perfection of love. I do not think there is any other quality of which that can be said . . . love is one of the things, possibly the only thing, that can never be excluded by circumstance.'[6]

By its self-vindicating quality, by the authenticity with which it speaks to us, and by being uncontingent on any expediency, moral goodness must be an important part of the world's ultimate constitution. It is not really able to be rationalized or intellectually explained, as for example Kant attempted to do with his demonstration of morality as the categorical imperative. Nor – as I believe – can we satisfactorily account for it as something generated by man's primeval fears and psychic needs. It is true that love, like the other values, abundantly satisfies such needs, and opens for us a way beyond ignorance, insecurity and loneliness. But our profound personal need of these values is not to be put up as a critique of their ultimate reality.

St Paul, writing to the Christians at Corinth, has left us his undying words about love. Not all the gifts of heaven are for all men, but he will now show them the best way of all, that all men can know.

There is nothing love cannot face; there is no limit to its faith, its hope, and its endurance. Love will never come to an end. Are there prophets? their work will be over . . . . Is there knowledge? it will vanish away; for our knowledge and our prophecy alike are partial, and the partial vanishes when wholeness comes . . . . In a word, there are three things that last for ever: faith, hope, and love; but the greatest of them all is love.[7]

In the upward sweep of evolution, Teilhard de Chardin (see Chapter 7) finds in the phenomenon of love – towards God and towards fellow men – a specifically new state of consciousness emerging. To him, this is in a deep sense confirmatory of the world's real character:

Christian love is incomprehensible to those who have not experienced it. That the infinite and the intangible can be lovable, or that the human heart can beat with genuine charity for a fellow-being, seems impossible to many people I know – in fact almost monstrous. But whether it be founded on an illusion or not, how can we doubt that such a sentiment exists, and even in great intensity? We have only to note crudely the results it produces unceasingly all round us. Is it not a positive fact that thousands of mystics, for twenty centuries, have drawn from its flame a passionate fervour that outstrips by far in brightness and purity the urge and devotion of any human love? is it not also a fact that, having once experienced it, further thousands of men and women are daily renouncing every other ambition and every other joy save that of abandoning themselves to it and labouring within it more and more completely.[8]

FROM VALUE TO PERSONALITY

The Old Man in the Sky is only a mythological symbol for
the Infinite Mind behind the scenes.

John Wren-Lewis

Am I a God at hand, saith the Lord, and not a God afar off?
Jeremiah 23:23

Just as we have done here, the secular theologians would find
their nearest-to-hand evidence for God's existence to arise from
the relationship of love as practised among men. Dr Robinson
has written that 'to believe in God as love means to believe that
in pure personal relationship we encounter, not merely what
ought to be, but what is, the deepest, veriest truth about the
structure of reality'.[9] What Dr Robinson finds harder than
accepting this, is to take the next step to the existence of a
'supreme Person, a self-existent subject of infinite goodness and
power, who enters into a relationship with us comparable with
that of one human personality with another . . . the creator and
most sufficient explanation of the world as we know it'. To him
these are the characteristics of 'theism', with the inference that
he rejects them. We must now ask whether anything more
remains in Dr Robinson's concept of God, than the idea of the
mythical personification of the vital energy of human life, of
personal values such as love, beauty and justice.[10]

When we claim to locate the 'deepest, veriest truth' about
the world in the ground of *our* being, we are surely displaying anthropocentricity to a degree that would have shaken
Archbishop Ussher and the old-time special creationists off their
feet. Since Sir Charles Lyell's famous *Principles of Geology*,
published in 1830, we have come to realize that the world's
time-scale does not run from a mere 4004 B.C., the creation date
allowed by the Archbishop, but something like 10,000,000,000
years. But the earliest humanoids appeared at the most one
million years ago. Without more than the 'ground of being'

which theologians are willing to posit about God, it is hard to see why our own late and palpably imperfect development should have anything to disclose about the ultimate quality of the world. Cosmologically, the 'vital energy of human life' dismally fails to satisfy our philosophic need.

But the idea of God as transcendent personality comes under attack today because of what are called the psychological barriers to belief in it. We can at the outset assume that by a 'personal' God, no one imagines today a deity invested with human shape, attributes and apparel. Clearly the refutation of anthropomorphism – if any adult Christian was indeed ever worried by it – has no bearing on the question of God's personality. Whatever our difficulties of believing in this, they can have nothing to do with the fact that we no longer think in terms of a 'three-decker universe' or that radio-astronomy has flushed God from his location in astrospace.

Objection is taken also to God's personality as implying 'a being beside others and as such a *part* of the *whole* of reality, having a definite space and endless time, being in short a being and not being itself'. Such a conception is of course, like the knockabout references to spacemen, Father Christmas and rich aunts from Australia, a travesty and a Robinson-strawman. As a fair statement of the other side's position, it ranks almost with Bishop Wilberforce's question whether T. H. Huxley claimed descent from a monkey on his grandfather's or on his grandmother's side.

If there really be anyone who holds the image of God to be a part of the whole of reality, this has never been the teaching of traditional Christian theology. St Thomas Aquinas specifically called God 'being itself' without feeling compelled to abandon the concept of him as transcendent. We have already found Etienne Gilson, as a contemporary Thomist, regarding God as the infinite act of self-existence 'by whom all the rest is'. Creation thus implies not more being (*plus entis*) but more beings (*plura entia*).[11]

Even while we have that separateness from him and dependence on him that must belong to creature as against creator, this transcendence of God has never been allowed to obscure his indwelling. Not from the 'depth-theologians' but from St Augustine, we are told that God is 'more inward than the inmost part'. It was St Augustine's commentator, Bishop Ullathorne, who wrote:

> Let it be understood that we cannot turn to God unless we first enter into ourselves. God is everywhere but not everywhere to us; and there is one point in the universe where God communicates with us and that is the centre of our own soul. There he waits for us, there he meets us. To seek him we enter into our own interior.[12]

We need not be daunted to be told that our speaking of God as personal is like breaking the rules of the symbol ∞, and working with it as if it were a finite number. Personality as we know it in ourselves may be argued to be finite. But to speak of an infinite God as personal is simply to have the highest regard we can for those processes and relationships under which his activity is perceived by us. Everyone knows that in his true nature God transcends each of the categories, including personality, that the mind of man can devise. It may be very true, as is maintained by Tillich, that every attempt to picture or describe God, even the use of his name, is to obscure and limit and lose something of him. But when our prime impulse is to address and adore God, such a detachment must seem to the Christian over-austere. If we believe he can reveal himself to us at all, we can only meaningfully envisage him, even communicate with him, in the highest terms we ourselves can know, with every reservation that these terms will be ultimately insufficient. Such terms are for us personal.

The Christian believes it is in this way that he can know and express the most about God. To hold God other than personal, is inevitably – for us – to leave him sub-personal. His existence, far from being the primary existence on which all other being depends, becomes at best a metaphorical construct, built around the abstractions of 'process', 'relationship' and 'value'. But personality seems to be the conception of God that is needed to give real meaning to process and value in the world. It is meaningless to talk of a process (such as creative evolution) or even of a value (such as love) being able of itself to command our allegiance or even to carry any explanation of its own existence.

And if personality is required, in relation to process and purpose, it will be a principle so clearly transcending myself that – rather than 'It' – the better pronoun is found to be 'He'. Ineffable and infinite though he be, we yet truly find that he does enter into a relation with us comparable to that of one person with another. Though we believe with adoration and awe that God is Being itself, eternal and before the worlds, yet he meets with us so accessibly within ourselves, that the proper pronoun can no longer remain 'He'. It must become irresistibly 'Thou'.

RELIGION AND ANTHROPOLOGY

Man can be justly credited with a natural religious function. We are increasingly aware today that the exercise of religion may be deeply necessary to psychic health. Not only has primitive man given it an importance comparable with sex and aggression, hunting and tilling the land. But in civilized man the motivations that have sprung from the religious impulse have been as far-reaching for the welfare of society as for the individual.

The psychologist C. G. Jung has spoken in a broad sense of religion as 'a careful consideration and observation of certain dynamic factors, understood to be "powers," spirits, demons, gods, laws, ideas, ideals or whatever name man has given to such factors as he has found in his world powerful, dangerous or helpful enough to be taken into careful consideration, or grand, beautiful and meaningful enough to be devoutly adored and loved'.[13]

The anthropologist will want to ask, 'How did it all begin?' He will seek to explain the religious impulse from its earliest rudiments, just as the biologist will explain the physical aspects of man according to the theory of evolution. For our religion, like our bodies, is plainly the offspring of remote history. A plausible case can be made – and I think no theologian will want to dispute it – that the religious impulse was perpetuated in us by having a selective advantage from the time of its first appearance.

In Alan Isaacs' recent book *The Survival of God in the Scientific Age* there is a persuasive chapter, deriving our religious ideas from the psychic needs of early man, and from the processes of evolution and selection by which these were satisfied.[14] We must fairly examine this evidence.

Religion is claimed to begin with 'emotional motivations' among early men. The first must have been the fear of death. Primitive man was from the beginning reluctant to believe that his own existence would cease with bodily death. It was early accepted that something disembodied from the individual must survive him, perhaps under the analogies of sleep and dreams. Once attained to, such a concept of spirit or soul would have given enjoyment and compensation. But it did not bring all gain. There can also be fears about what might be the spirit's lot in the world beyond. In his famous Victorian book *Primitive Culture*, E. B. Tylor was the first to use the term 'animism', meaning the endowment of men and things with primitive spirits. This could have led to the recognition of 'spirit leaders' that were the obvious precursors of Gods.

The fear of death seems attested by the discovery of skeletons with tight binding to restrain the activities of the dead, or by the heavy stones placed over the interred body. Rituals of burial represented a farewell and a final disposal. Such considerations led to belief in all-powerful spirits, capable of influencing the conduct of the living. Man began to pray to these spirits to propitiate them against what might happen to him after death.

Early religious ideas must have been reinforced, too, by fear of infertility and the shrinking from loneliness. The anthropologist Margaret Murray writes in *The Genesis of Religion* of the fear and awe that must have inspired primitive men as they watched women in pregnancy and labour. There is much evidence that the worship of goddesses came earlier than that of gods. With men's strong apprehensions lest the fertility of women should decline, prayers were said to the supernatural power held to be responsible for fertilizing women. Perhaps a female deity was supplicated when children were wanted. When Palaeolithic man came to understand his own part in generation, there was a profound revolution in religious psychology, and the figurines used as symbols of fertility gave place to phallic figures.

The fear of loneliness must have been as widespread in the history of the race as it still is among people today. In infancy it is allayed by the contact of the child with the mother or a mother-substitute. The studies of Harlow – on young monkeys – have shown that here, as in man, the mother fulfils a function that is psychologically indispensable. When the belief in parental infallibility loses its hold, man begins to construct omniscient and omnipotent supernatural powers. These have the great advantage over human contacts that they are mental, and hence do not depend on communication of man with man. Christian theology speaks of our yearning sense of incompleteness; we look for fulfilment by union with the transcendent deity that created us. Divested of its theism, the anthropologist would see this simply as an expression of man's universal sense of loneliness.

During man's later history, emotional motivations have been strengthened by rational ones. There are the socially derived motivations by which, in a gregarious society, notions of ownership, rules, restraints and moral codes can be enforced by superhuman agencies. Expediency and brute strength can thus be supplanted by religious belief. The fear of God can be urged upon those rebels who fail to conform.

Religious belief brings with it too the imagined power to explain and influence nature and the material world. Frazer, in *The Golden Bough*, contended that the religion of the supernatural replaced magic when the latter was found not to work.

In short, the religious impulse is seen as part of the psychic inheritance of the race. We should be able to demonstrate its selective advantage and reconstruct its development, just as we can with the evolution of man's bodily organs and their functions. Such conclusions – if they are valid – will leave the theologian undisturbed. For any state of the mind or will, or rather its physical correlates, we can produce a physiological or an evolutionary explanation that sufficiently accounts for all that is going on at the natural level. Theological statements about transcendent causes keep clear of the natural order; they are obstinately incapable of being verified in naturalistic terms. Science neither proves nor challenges them.

Any concept of God that we may upon other grounds have been inclined to form cannot be weakened by showing how man's awareness of God could have evolved, or how advantageous such an awareness was to man's psychic need. God is not thereby to be dismissed as a short name for certain phenomena our minds have become adapted to construct.

We could take an analogy with the physical sense of vision which has also been gradually evolved. This must have had a long history from simple perception of different intensities of illumination from light to dark, through the resolving of shape and movement, to stereoscopic vision and awareness of colours. Visual perception is clearly advantageous to man and will have been initiated and improved by natural selection. It could be said also that colour simply is my private way of perceiving light waves of various wave lengths. But what will not be denied is that our sense organs give us access to properties of the outside world that were real before the existence of ourselves or of any organisms that could perceive them. Such a world in its own right exists; it is conjured up neither by our sensory evolution, nor by the value to us of our being able to detect it.

Evolutionary and emergent explanations can be useful so long as we remember how little they really explain. God is neither validated nor refuted simply because we can surmise how we came to have an awareness of him. God does not become a subjective construct of human protopsychology because our ancestors seem to have had a need of him.

Against the evolutionary and historical explanations so natural to a scientist, William Temple made a firm protest in one of his earliest writings, an essay called *The Province of Science*, in 1904.

> The real cause of a thing's being what it is, is to be sought not in the past but rather in the future. Man is not what he is only because he was once an ape, but he was both apish and is human in order that he may hereafter be divine. The world is not what it is because it was once part of the nebula, but because it is ultimately to become the Kingdom of Heaven. Society may be historically the offspring of sexual passion, and religion of the vilest superstition, but that does not touch the validity of either.[15]

Here – in Temple's argument and in the whole belief of the Christian theist – lies the real unity and permanence that all science is pointing to but cannot of itself reveal: 'in the Eternal Mind in whose consciousness all space and time are comprehended, and in his unalterable purpose which is the sole reality in man or in the world, the sole universal law, the only true uniformity of nature.'[16]

OUTLOOKS ON REALITY

Julian Huxley has relegated God to the last fading smile of the cosmic Cheshire cat; and this dismissal is acceptable enough from a scientist. For God is, by a fair and reasonable definition, that which is unknowable and indeed vacuous to science. Theology can no longer operate today by taking up – on a God-basis – the explanation of phenomena that science is temporarily unable to pursue further. Our talk of God must concern the whole cosmos, but it is conducted in a wholly different vocabulary and from a different vantage point from that of science. Jacques Maritain[17] has spoken of the differences

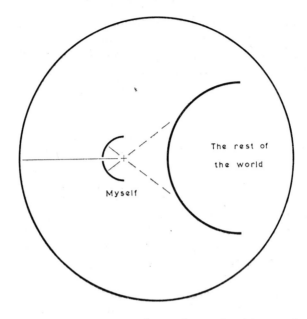

The rest of
the world

Myself

FIGURE 3. A diagram to suggest the two 'convex' and 'concave' outlooks on reality. The cross fixes my own vantage point; and the complete all-including circle is to represent God.

between scientific and poetical language, the one providing exactly defined and unambiguous statements about reality, the other seeking to communicate reality itself. To Charles Davis,[18] the distinction between 'sacred' and 'secular' is found to lie in the different modes by which we apprehend them. We may return again here to Eddington's two sorts of knowledge, symbolic and intimate. We have already designated these as 'convex' and 'concave';[19] for the two aspects of knowledge imply and complement each other, and – in principle – each must run through all reality. But though it is imaginable that a tree or a rock might be known 'concavely', such an intimate vantage point cannot be ours.

If we may for a spell take refuge in a model, as in Fig. 3, I can represent myself as knowing 'convexly' the whole observable universe, everything outside my conscious personality, and even the physical fabric of my body itself. This knowledge can be precisely quantified, and the observations that comprise it can be exactly repeatable; if it is knowledge of another person, our viewpoint is that of behaviourism.

Intimate or 'concave' knowledge is by contrast available to us, from our personal vantage point, in introspection upon our conscious selves. It is only indeed by analogy from such introspection that we can believe in other personalities like our own. There is one other sort of knowledge available to us that must be intimate or concave. This is our knowledge of God. We could even venture to complete our diagram by putting in God, showing him as an enclosing sphere, or – much better – a great luminosity, surrounding and shining through everything it contains. For anything to be looking at God convexly can make no sense; to stand off and observe him would be to make him part of some larger totality. Our finite personalities can arrive at no comprehensive knowledge of God. But it could be possible to obtain a glimpse of him, concavely, by a window that breaks through the opaque sphere of our personality. What is the nature of this window, and how our apprehension by it can be enlarged, must be part of our discussion as this book goes on.

Using the same model, we could begin also to speculate about the nature of God's own knowledge of the world. We must, of course, think of him not simply as a sphere bounding and transcending his world, but as everywhere continuous within it. If he be immanent in the created world, even if not exhausted by it, we shall have to regard him as in some sense concentric with every part of its content. From his vantage point within his world, he then sees and knows concavely every particle and molecule, as it proceeds from, and exists within, his creative and inexhaustible being. He is – in truth – the 'Spirit whose vesture is the magnificence of the material universe'.

God's animating and indwelling the world can be looked upon not just as expressing its present state, but as pointing towards an incarnational view of the whole universe. In his early work 'The Mass on the World', Teilhard de Chardin sees God's immanence as in the highest way congruous with eucharistic teaching. With the radiation of a presence of Christ throughout the universe, the Eucharist takes on for us a cosmic and planetary dimension:

> In its initial and primary meaning the term 'Body of Christ' is limited, in this context, to the consecrated species of Bread and Wine. But . . . the host is comparable to a blazing fire whose flames spread out like rays all round it.[20]

> Do you, Lord Jesus, 'in whom all things subsist', show yourself to those who love you as the higher Soul and the physical centre of your creation? Are you not well aware that for us this is a question of life or death? As for me, if I could not believe that your real Presence animates and makes tractable and enkindles even the very least of the energies which invade me or brush past me, would I not die of cold?[21]

CHAPTER 10

Beyond the Rational

Das Schaudern ist der Menschheit bestes Teil.
Goethe

IF there be indeed a sense in which we can say with Goethe, 'awe' is the best part of man, it will be a part that cannot be comprehended solely by intellectual means. And if our study of values has led us to envisage a purpose underlying the universe, here is something again that will have no place in the field of interest of science. If these matters be in the sense we are suggesting 'beyond the rational', we shall have to find whether our minds can be effective instruments for coming to grips with them at all. We have already refused to take too dismally H. G. Wells's statement that the human mind is no better equipped to discover ultimate truth than a pig's snout; and we must now enquire whether man is really so limited as a God-seeking animal as this would imply.

We can turn first to the quality of awe as a part of man. For this we would today use the now familiar word 'numinous'. The term was first applied by the German philosopher and theologian Rudolf Otto, in his now classic book, *The Idea of the Holy*,[1] written in 1917 to assess the non-rational feelings that blend in with the rational evidence for God's existence.

Under these are the feelings of awe and profound reverence, the sense of the *mysterium tremendum* and our utter dependence and impotence in face of it. Primitive people share these feelings. But what may begin as a stirring of demonic dread can be ennobled and elevated with the growing religious awareness of man. At their highest, these feelings must be integrated with rationality, personality, purpose and morality. But the importance given the numinous should not be allowed to encourage fantastic or extravagant irrationalism. Dr Otto is sharply aware that 'the "irrational" is to-day a favourite theme of all who are too lazy to think or too ready to evade the arduous duty of clarifying their ideas and grounding their convictions on a basis of coherent thought'.[2]

The elements of the numinous reach back – it is claimed – not to experience, but to the *fundus animae* or ground of the soul. Even though we may believe, with Kant, that all our knowledge begins *with* experience, it by no means follows that all *arises out of* experience'. The interpenetration of the rational and non-rational elements of the religious consciousness is like that of warp and woof in a fabric. A closer comparison could be with the permeation of an instinct – for example, the sex drive – by the reason. Instinct is not, like the numinous, transrational, but is the subrational pressing up from the nature that man shares with the lower animal world.[3]

Both the numinous and the instinctive – finds Dr Otto – lie in a close relation to what may be said to lie between them, the reason. Like appreciation of music, the numinous is something 'wholly other' than reason. Where the libretto of a song may express feelings that are rational, the music purely as music makes its appeal to the suprarational. In 'programme music' we may find a sort of illegitimate rationalization attempted, making a unification of the musical and the dramatic. But the music itself is something uniquely mysterious that has no point-to-point correspondence with the rational at all.

Yet if we cannot analyse the numinous we can point to certain elements in it. First, with the *mysterium tremendum*,[4] Otto finds the element of 'awe and hallowed fear', the thrilling yet dreadful stirring of the soul to worship: 'How awful is this place'. There is, too, the element of overpoweringness, of '*majestas*' and of creature-feeling in the face of overwhelming might. This can be illustrated in a passage quoted by William James:

The perfect stillness of the night was thrilled by a more solemn silence. The darkness held a presence that was all the more felt because it was not seen. I could not any more have doubted that *He* was there than that I was. Indeed, I felt myself to be, if possible, the less real of the two.[5]

The numinous holds also an element of incomprehension, the bewilderment or stupor in the face of something not completely understood. (And here Dr Otto points out – aptly I believe – that the often trivially clear-cut and detailed 'findings' of the spiritualist cult are enough to show that the spirit or soul so comprehended is of little interest to the psychology of religion.)

Finally, there is the capacity of 'fascination' that, beyond our rational faculty, lies hidden in the ultimate part of our nature. This can find no satisfaction in the mere allayings of our sensuous or psychic or intellectual cravings. Here – in the basis or ground of the soul – the numinous experience may pass at its highest into blissful exaltation.

> The conception which the saints have of the loveliness of God and the kind of delight which they experience in it are quite peculiar and different from anything which a natural man can possess or of which he can form any proper notion.

At their ultimate depths, the mystics speak of a bliss they agree in affirming is incommunicable. St Catherine of Genoa exclaimed:

> O that I could tell you what the heart feels, how it burns and is consumed inwardly! Only I find no words to express it. I can but say, might one little drop of what I feel fall into Hell, Hell would be transformed into a Paradise.

It is rare that visions are experienced of this intensity and power; and the mystics themselves are emphatic that these are rather of the nature of extraordinary favours, neither necessary to oneness with God, nor even in themselves an assurance of personal holiness.

Yet it is those men and women with the deepest experience of the mystical who are most unshakeable and serene in what they claim to know. Their intimations of God are the richest life can hold for them. A few of the rest of us may in rare moments have been afforded only glimpses of what these insights could mean.

For the response to mysticism is most common in those races of men where the intuitive faculties have not been largely substituted by intellectual analysis. Most of us, with our contemporaries, can find little of the mystical in the active and world-involved lives we count it an Anglo-Saxon virtue to lead. Perhaps this poverty in us could only be a real argument against mysticism if we could feel we had sought or deserved more of it.

It is true that with our modern knowledge of evolutionary psychology, and – most recently – of psychopharmacology, we might plausibly argue that these 'glimpses of real world' are illusory. But if this were really so, our plight would be surpassingly strange and sad. We would be deluded not in an infirmity that wise and rational men have been able to overcome, but in the richest and profoundest apprehensions we can form. For these insights seem to be no psychic cul-de-sac. To the soul that knows them they are a strength and liberation.

THE PSYCHOLOGY OF JUNG

The territory of the mind we called the 'beyond rational' would seem to correspond with C. G. Jung's 'personal and collective unconscious'. Jung's system of psychology has – like Freud's – a descriptive mythology of its own; but far more constructively than the Freudian determinism it enables us to look to the unconscious mind for the creative forces of our being.

Carl Gustav Jung (1875–1961) was at first one of the earliest disciples, and later notably diverged away from Sigmund Freud. More than any other the leaders of analytic psychology, Jung is a psychologist sympathetic to the mystical outlook. To him, the central content of all religions, including myth, folk tradition, poetry and legend, is to be found in the unconscious. He has spoken of these resources as the 'hidden treasure' that mankind has through the ages drawn upon to raise up 'its gods and demons, and all those potent and mighty thoughts without which man ceases to be man'.[6]

We have already had from Freud's psychology a picture of the determinate state in which life is held to be lived from the unconscious. This we have likened to the thraldom of St Paul's 'body of death'. But in Jung's teaching the unconscious mind is not simply a receptacle for the discarded yet persistent rubbish of our conscious experience. It is rather the source of creative powers and energies; and the central figures by which religious ideas are imagined and formulated are the categories that Jung calls the 'archetypes'.

Taking as his territory the 'collective unconscious', Jung has isolated the archetypes as figures of ancestral origin with a deep and personal significance for human beings. The conscious mind cannot grapple with them fully, nor even properly bring them up for inspection. Our thoughts cannot clearly grasp them, because we did not produce or invent them. The unconscious is filled with a profusion of these archetypes, though they may be little revealed in the character we present at the surface.

To look first at the outward face, by which we relate to or conform with the requirements of society, Jung calls this the 'persona', from the mask worn by actors of antiquity to present a given character to the world. Through it we play the part society expects of us, whether it be parson, pop-singer, poet or professor. The persona is a necessity to us in our normal relations with others; if it is not appropriately developed we shall be gauche, ill-established in the world, and apt to offend people.

The other side of the personality, which the persona tends to keep from expression, is the 'personal unconscious' called by Jung the 'shadow'. This can be the being we imagine we are not, the reverse or mirror image of the conscious. Thus a man who is consciously an extrovert will be in the unconscious mind an introvert. The timid man will be unconsciously brave. The differences between the sexes are represented in their complementary aspects in the unconscious mind. In man there exists an unconscious counterpart of woman known as the *anima*. By its help man apprehends the nature of woman: it presents the age-old experience of man with woman which becomes tangible only by actual acquaintance, as with mother, lover or wife. Similarly, there is in woman the unconscious counterpart of man called the *animus*.

The shadow may sometimes be exposed when we act out of character ('something came over me' or 'I was not myself'), or perhaps when we take a strong or irrational dislike to a certain person. The personal unconscious may be said to incorporate all those desires and emotions that are incompatible with our civilized personality. Since the unconscious cannot be touched by ordinary education, the 'instinctive' man may go on showing the same impulsiveness of action as an infant. Not only is the personal unconscious vague and obscure in outline, it is as unavoidable to the complete man as is the dark to the light or the convex to the concave. Man has to live with his shadow and find the moral courage to accept it as part of himself. No full integration, teaches Jung, or no redemption of the whole man, is possible without such tolerance and – in this sense – love of ourselves.

Going beyond the personal unconscious, we reach the 'collective unconscious' with the heritage of the 'archetypes' communal to the whole race. The deepest levels of the collective unconscious may be common not only to all humanity but even shared with our primate and earlier ancestors.

In justification for this doctrine of general archetypal ideas, Jung has pointed to the extraordinary unanimity of theme of the mythologies of different cultures. During analysis certain symbols are said gradually to lose any personal relation to the patient, and fall back to a context only of generalized myths and legends. The old wise man is, for example, the type of the king or hero, medicine man or saviour. Jung likens this to something of an assembly of fathers or dignitaries who lay down incontestable, rational, *ex cathedra* judgements. This archetype may be so overdeveloped in man that he really believes he possesses the 'mana' or magical wisdom that it holds out to him. Such over-possession is called by Jung 'inflation'. The archetype of the great mother may influence our lives in a comparable way, as with the capacities in woman for loving, protecting, understanding and serving. It too can be inflated into possessive motherliness or jealous domination.

As Jung has shown, inflation may confer on us the feeling of Godlikeness: personal courage, infinite wisdom or capacity for forgiveness, however 'beyond ourselves' or unable to be mustered at will these things may normally be.

Man needs humility in the face of these forces he cannot understand. The conscious self or ego may have to relinquish belief in itself and its own omnipotence. We are to find – says Jung – a position 'somewhere between consciousness with its hardly won values and unconsciousness with its vitality and power'. Only thus can a newly organized centre of the personality emerge, transcending and differing in its nature from the ego-centre. This is the entity that Jung terms the self, properly speaking, using the word in the Eastern philosophical manner, for the supreme principle or oneness of being.

While the ego, then, is the centre of the conscious, the self is a harmony of both the conscious and the unconscious. It is like a magnet to the disparate and unorganized aspects of the whole personality. It unites and transmutes opposing elements, and involves the seeming paradox of our highest and lowest being. The idea of the transcending self is formulated by Jung in *The Secret of the Golden Flower*,[7] based upon his long study of the Eastern mind. Yet this is never a cult of oriental occultism. The conscious will – believes Jung – is a precious instrument, painstakingly forged; and with science as its tool the modern mind can open more doors than with bare hands. Science 'only clouds our insight when it lays claim to being the one and only way of comprehending'.[8]

Frieda Fordham (in her study of Jung to which I am indebted here) speaks of Jung's 'self' as consisting

in the awareness on the one hand of our unique natures, and

on the other of our intimate relationship with all life, not only human, but animal and plant, and even that of inorganic matter and the cosmos itself. It brings a feeling of 'oneness', and of reconciliation with life, which can now be accepted as it is, not as it ought to be.[9]

The growth of such a centre, it is claimed, can be clinically observed in patients under therapy. But it need not always be induced by analysis. Sometimes it is enough to free the subject from an unconscious childish dependence, to recognize the cause of a distressing symptom or to make a more satisfactory adaptation to life. But always in therapy Jung expressed himself more concerned with future goals than past history. 'I no longer find the cause of neurosis in the past but in the present. I ask what is the necessary task which the patient will not accomplish.'

THE DISCOVERY OF THE SELF

The self is not only the centre but also the whole circumference which embraces both conscious and unconscious; it is the centre of this totality, just as the ego is the centre of the conscious mind.

C. G. Jung[10]

The mythology – if it can be so called – of Jung has often been criticized as portraying over-elaborately what other psychologists would account for more simply. Yet his account of the 'discovery of the self', in whatever psychological terms we may choose to couch it, has some striking parallels with religious experience. First, unlike determinate Freudianism, it not only takes account of the present predicament of man, but looks constructively forward from it. Christianity has done this, too. In Chapter 2 we have sought to understand the self by the idea of making 'one out of many', or the 'co-ordination of the whole psychic nature for action'. We find now in the Jungian picture what is evidently a description of the will and personality coming into formal existence.

Christian experience can also be understood in the sense of the discovery of the self. This is strikingly appraised in a contemporary essay by Bernardine Bishop, a young Catholic laywoman, in the recent symposium *The God I Want*. She tells how the encounter of Christianity has been transformed for her into a relation of trust and love. 'The God I want is the God who enables us to love and lets us be, lets us be ourselves. The God I want is unknown to me, yet certain; as unknown and as certain as death.'[11]

She looks successively at what she regards as three deficient or 'a-Messianic' forms of Christianity; mechanisms by which she claims the real Incarnation is evaded. These are the cultivations of God the Judge, God the Riddler and, latterly, God the Neighbour. The author recapitulates – as she says – two thousand years later, in her own development, the experience of the early Church in passing from a guilt-ridden régime of law and observance to one of freedom.

Conversion is spoken of in these terms:

> In effect, a new centre is found within the personality to which the individual ego suddenly seems relative, even though it is one's own ego; for it is the centre we all share. It is mysterious, alive with a life beyond one's personal one, and a source of attraction, ordering personality afresh in relation to itself. It is the integrative factor, for in some undefinable way it is not only the centre of personality but the whole.[12]

Such experience awakens us to transcendent mystery at the extreme of human awareness.

> This awakening is beyond our power to bring about, and cannot but be experienced subjectively as a miracle as astounding as the raising of Lazarus. Once it happens, nothing but response is possible, for the inner Christ is born within us, and takes over leadership of the personality from the ego. Hence it becomes a love-relationship, so widely symbolized in religions as father/child love. We commit

ourselves in unconditional trust to the all-accepting source of life and love. That becomes our goal, and the new-found centre of growth within us the principle that we 'follow' to reach it. It is no longer a matter of the ego grinding itself into deformity against stony idols, but the union of the God above and the God within. The ego becomes spectator to that love, and, along with all the other human powers within us, fuel to that fire. Everything we have previously been accustomed in pride or shame to call 'me' is suddenly experienced as relative, created; and therefore acceptable. We can look at ourselves for the first time without fear or favour. We can dare to get to know ourselves, for however terrifying the discoveries we make, the voice of Christ will say, as often before: 'It is I, be not afraid.'[13]

Experience in this mode, existential and intensely personal, with its releasing of new powers and freedom, is something men and women can widely attest; though they might rationalize or comprehend it in varying ways, and would not all agree to preempt it into a specifically Christian setting. For it could be asked, however authentic this experience may be for us, how could it have any bearing upon the claims made about the 'Jesus of history'?

It is to the Church's historical experience of Christ and its present meaning for us that we must shortly turn. But we shall first look, in the chapter that is to follow, at the actual predicament of the world with its problems of pain and sin. We must do so because the Church – in claiming that Christ reveals God to man – has acclaimed him as Saviour within the context of a world that is at odds with God's purpose and sorely needing redemption.

In the personal Christ revealed for us in history, we are to look for the focus on which our living experience converges. To use the words of Bernardine Bishop in the essay already cited, 'My own belief is that historical and psychological reality coincide at the point of the Incarnation, and that Christ is not only the symbol of the Self, but is the Self indeed'.[14]

Such an affirmation, integrating present experience with an historical revelation, is the most important step of our argument at which we have yet arrived. It is our first statement of what Christianity is distinctively and essentially about.

CHAPTER II

Pain and Evil

The night racks my bones,
and the pain that gnaws me takes no rest.
With violence it seizes my garment;
it binds me about like the collar of my tunic.
God has cast me into the mire,
and I have become like dust and ashes.
I cry to thee and thou dost not answer me;
I stand, and thou dost not heed me.
Thou hast turned cruel to me;
with the might of thy hand thou dost persecute me.

Job 30: 17-21

In the last chapter we have been using personal religious experience to build further upon the philosopher's arguments for God. The evidence for God's ultimate self-existence as creator and sustainer of the world might not as an abstract proposition carry conviction. But we have been able to add to it evidence of a 'beyond-rational' kind that would seem to bring the apprehension of a transcendent order within the reach of our own lives.

We have seen the apparent reality of value in the world, and glimpsed the quality of human love, not just what it may feebly be, but what it could fully portend and realize. From this we have posited not only that the ruling principle of the world is personal, but – as the teleological and value arguments would lead us to believe – that it was made with a benevolent purpose for an intelligible good; and that this purpose could involve our individual selves within its loving concern.

Can we yet affirm, though, that, whatever else we may not know about him, God is love? Do we know enough of his dealings with the universe to find love not only the key to ourselves, but to God's rule and governance of the world?

Before we can accept this, I believe we must face squarely the enormous difficulties for such a viewpoint that the world, with evil and pain in it, presents. Even to those whose lives have fallen in secure and comfortable ways, God's benevolence may not be self-evident at all, or – at least – may not be the only face of him we see. I sharply remember the scorn of a Polish war victim, tossed as human jetsam between the Russian and German sides, as he indignantly rejected the supposition that the creator was a loving one. We may recall, too, William Temple's early declaration that the problem of evil and pain remained the only real hindrance to religious belief, as tersely stated by the man who, after describing the appalling sufferings of his wife, ended: 'If Jesus were God, that would not happen.'[1]

The suffering of conscious and sentient beings seems to present an even older problem than moral evil and human sinning. Many would believe that animal pain is in itself enough to cast doubt upon the benevolent design of the world.

Throughout animal evolution, pain – which is the apprehension of the environment in modes sharply unpleasant – must have had a warning role. We can teach animals under experiment to avoid certain actions by small instalments of repellent tastes or electric shocks as 'punishments'. This negative conditioning can be set off against rewards for making the 'right' choices in a given situation. Pain serves in ourselves as the stimulus to instantaneous avoiding reflexes, as against fire or violent impact. It is an effective safeguard against worse injury. Animals that have been experimentally reared without experience of pain may perform poorly or be entirely wanting in these avoiding reflexes.

Over the whole organic world it is a fact that certain properties of the environment, such as heat, light, radiation or pressure, will 'hurt', even denature and kill, living protoplasm. This would not in itself seem to be evidence of a malignant design or a callousness that a benevolent creator might have avoided. It is a state of affairs inevitable where organisms are evolving in tension with a physical substrate. We could – it is true – conceive of alternative ways to safeguard a fragile organism from damage. Some of these indeed work reflexly and silently as part of our 'visceral behaviour', just as a photo-cell might activate an unconscious circuit for the avoidance of light or shade. But for the silent behaviour altogether to supplant our conscious – and hence often painful – contact with the outside world, could only be with the loss of the very properties we call life.

The pain sense is likely to be better developed in animals with complex nervous systems, and with finer and wider sensitivity to stimuli. At the outset of the scientific age, Descartes pictured the whole subhuman world as insentient mechanism. The most primitive animals can indeed have little integrated awareness of their continuing selves; their consciousness of their environment may be in no more than a succession of simple 'present instants'. But at our other extreme of sentience we know but too well how remembered hurt or anticipatory terrors can aggravate present pain. For most animals, we cannot know where on the scale between they would fall. But we readily recognize that animals suffer pain, and that we have a moral duty to minimize it (though this is something the great religions including Christianity have, over the centuries, been lamentably slow to concede).

We can be pretty sure, too, that the anticipation and realization of pain have both increased with the evolution of our cerebral cortex. This cannot mean that we are callously to undervalue animal pain, though it may help us to see the problem in better proportion than Isabella in *Measure for Measure* who tenderly believed that the poor beetle she trod upon felt a death pang as great as when a giant died. For the largest part of our own suffering must lie in our capacity to introspect. Burns' address to the harvest mouse defines the human predicament well:

> Still thou art blest, compared wi' me!
> The present only toucheth thee:

But, och! I backward cast my ee
    On prospects drear!
And forward, though I canna see,
    I guess and fear!

The total burden of human pain is appalling to imagine in all its dimensions. But C. S. Lewis makes the point, in *The Problem of Pain*, that it is not in a supra-individual sense cumulative. The greatest amount of pain conceivable is not the total that can be suffered by millions of mankind but by one individual. When we have reached this, horrible as it may be, we have at least plumbed the whole depth of suffering possible in the universe.[2] Many will think even this comfort sophistical, for the individual quantum is in itself unthinkably terrible.

Psychologists have begun to find, too, how assertively the mind is involved in the measure of sensory pain. A painful sensation is not at all a fixed response to a given harmful stimulus. Perception of pain is modified by our past experience, our expectations and our total cultural background. Pain is evidently not a pure sensory experience at all. Apart from sensation, such as a burn or toothache, localized at a particular place, there is an 'affective' or emotional dimension of pain, the unpleasantness that suffuses our whole experience and is as wide as consciousness itself. It is this anxiety associated with pain that can be relieved by cutting special nerve tracts in the operation called prefrontal lobotomy.

These questions are discussed in a recent article 'The Perception of Pain' by Ronald Melzack, where pain is accounted a complex function of the whole individual, his present thoughts and fears, the meaning he gives his sensations, as well as his hopes for the future.[3] There are many examples of the relevance of the whole experience to pain. In some races the woman shows virtually no distress in child-birth, and works in the fields until the day the baby is born. The husband meanwhile stays in bed, groans with evident pain during the birth, and – with the baby in his bed – gradually recovers from the ordeal through which he has passed.

Dogs reared in isolation from normal stimuli could be so conditioned that they failed to respond to an electric shock or a lighted match. Moreover, the nervous system of the higher brain can modify the message carried from the pain pathways of the spinal cord. Soldiers severely wounded in battle (as studied recently by Beecher of the Harvard Medical School) may not even feel sufficient pain to need morphia. The degree of pain is determined in large part by other factors, perhaps by euphoria at the prospect of release from the ordeal of the battle-field.[4]

'THE SHADOW UPON THE WORLD'

The evil that looks most 'dystelic', most discordant with a loving purpose in the world, does not arise directly out of pain at all. It comes from the fact of human sinning, being the evil possible to the human spirit, malevolent, warped and unloving as free spirits – alone, it would seem – can become. Such evil hardly appears to be bound up with evolution or neurophysiology at all. If only it were, we might hope for it to recede as life became better adapted, or men more rational or medical science more wide-reaching.

The hardest facts to reconcile with God's purpose are perhaps the ills that happen to the young or defenceless or uncomprehending; or the devastation of whole races and communities, the more appalling because it is so inclusive and unmerited. If God were both all-powerful and all-loving, goes the reiterated query, would he let this happen? Hence some have believed that God's sway in the world might not be absolute, or that evil principles could be in combat with or even superior to the author of the universe. Thus the God of the Manichees was thought of not as sovereign and supreme, but as one in a hierarchy: he might be clever enough to create, but too stupid to realize that creation is inherently evil.

Against every short-term indication, I believe that history justifies an optimism about human progress. Over five centuries of our own national story, communication, education and technology have been transformed beyond recognition; and our race has become more widely enlightened and humane. This is an empiric statement for one era of history; it owes nothing to a liberal doctrine of inevitable human progress, and its time-scale is too short for the all-embracing judgement of a Toynbee vista of history. But it seems true for our own day, notwithstanding the new frightfulness of mass genocide, brain-washing and man-inflicted radiation damage that our unregenerate use of science has made possible.

Any natural goodness or noble aspirations of man seem intractably at odds with the evolutionary era we live in. Not only is there the evil, as we have found, of disorder and failure, a system making blind advance by ruthless sacrifice of individuals. There is, too, the suffering by malfunction and disease, and from pathogens and parasites. Viruses and bacteria, protozoa and helminth worms, are pitted in constant war against man and medical advance. So vigorous indeed are these aggressors in the world that many theologians, including William Temple and E. L. Mascall,[5] have conjectured that the cosmic plan may have been blemished or vitiated by a pre-human fall. Finally at the human evolutionary level, there is the capacity for suffering of our own bodies, acutely sentient of the worst that can imaginably be done to them by fellow men. Some would believe that this in itself would be enough to cast doubt over the world's whole beneficent design.

At the middle of the twentieth century we are more conscious, too, of the full potential of moral evil than we were at the opening. Before 1914, it has been said, English Christianity could be essentially optimistic. Theology tended to put its chief stress on the Incarnation, with man's growing enlightenment and emancipation giving the world its noblest meaning. Even in the 1920s, the tenets of modernism would have been that sin is the anachronistic survival of animal traits, that the natures of God and man are one in that perfect humanity can be identified with deity.[6] It cannot convincingly be said that men are worse now than then. So far as technical and economic advance, and public conscience for human welfare can serve, we have built a better world than had before been dreamt of. Yet with two world wars and their aftermath of nuclear threat and crippling armament budgets, the full capacity of human barbarism has seemed to reach the surface in ways and places frighteningly close to hand.

Theology today stresses our fallen state. Theologies of the atonement are no longer only exemplarist; they speak starkly of man's need of redemption. Already in 1939 William Temple could declare: 'The world of today is one of which no Christian map can be made. . . . Our task with this world is not to explain it, but to convert it.'[7] From the Continent, Karl Barth starkly reminded contemporary man that 'in the presence of pure scientific and technical solutions, *he himself* is part of the evil he thinks to overcome'.[8]

The evil around us is evidently cosmic and global. Our whole hive is in an ugly way disordered. In what we describe as the 'free world' our own guilt is assuredly great. From our dismal primacy in the use of atomic warheads on open cities, to the cynical misalignment of priorities in a hungry world that has blemished even the achievement of the moon-landing, to the gathering storms of race hatred and assertive nationalism, we are too closely implicated to find any scapegoat in 'atheistic communism'. For 'godless materialism' we need not look away from home.

Yet there is an equal sense in which the cosmic sin of the world is immediate and personal to us. We know that our own uncaring, our own self-centredness, and our own fundamental want of righteousness, corrupt and vitiate others for whom we are responsible. None of us can be a moral island by himself. Nor are moral events simply bilateral transactions with a single neighbour. Our actions have a radial effect, and their consequences reach out and intermesh to involve countless others we cannot know.

Those who have advocated today the 'ethics of the situation' have approvingly adopted St Augustine's 'Love, and do what you will'. In *Christian Morals Today* Dr Robinson wants twentieth-century man to be allowed to tackle the subject of

ethics on an inductive rather than a deductive basis. No doubt
we shall need in any age to re-think the expression of eternal
moral principles in ways appropriate to contemporary society.
The Bible is to be seen not as morally oracular in every situation
of our own day, but – as someone has said – as a set of worked
examples. Numerous areas of morality today, not least in the
world population crisis, face the Church with the imminent
need for restatement.

But the real difficulty in using St Augustine's general maxim
as a moral talisman is that it begs every operational question.
To make the deductions needed for ourselves, under a situation
of actual moral stress, takes time, disinterestedness and
objectivity that will seldom be ours to command. In a world
where men have not this quality and quantity of love, an
element of tradition and authority must edit each moral
decision.

Man's present actions, Christianity has traditionally affirmed,
are patently astray from God's purpose for him. He is by his
nature prone to go wrong. We need not explore in depth here
the theology of original sin to perceive that such loss of direction
seems inherently a possibility in a creature capable of free
moral choice. Doubtless a different sort of world could be
conceived. God might have constrained human action by
peremptory power. But he could not have so won the freely
given response of the created. To do this he must reveal himself
not in power but in atoning love.

Horrible in its realization as is the evil of human sin, we
doubt that it presents a philosophical problem at all, at least in
any sense that God could have created a different world with
beings in it that were either moral or free. Freedom involved the
possibility of sinning, and man in actuality did sin. To desire a
state of moral automatism, where the laws of conduct and belief
are followed like those of electricity and mass action, is to ask
even God for a logical impossibility.

The meaningful question to ask, and it is still a hard one,
would be: are the attainable heights, not only of creativeness
and intellectual mastery but of the noblest love and self-

sacrifice, worth the blackest the world can show, rendered a hell by human misuse of freedom? For in man alone, prone to go wrong, can moral capacity be said to exist at all. In him only can *privatio* or deprivation of God become *pravatio* or realized sin, of a sort that animal savagery is wholly exempt from and below.

That we are uniquely this sort of creature could be the measure of our unexampled value in the cosmic plan. And if this be true, it must also be the measure of the Creator's sorrow in our fall. Even our own revulsion at the fact of sin can be vivid and real. The scathing anger of a student generation, even when destructive and inept, can have a righteous base. Human anger can be for us a pale reflection of God's burning indignation at sin. But God's wrath, the Christian believes, is ever to be balanced against his atoning self-giving for us. Love mingles with that perfect righteousness that his nature cannot but insist be fulfilled. And if the total redemption of the created be God's purpose, that victory cannot be won while a single soul remains untouched or lost to him. William Temple has written:

> Myriads of worlds following their appointed course through vastness of space exist because He would have it so. But that self-willed souls should be won to love Him, and thus make love and not self the centre of their being – that costs what is represented by Gethsemane and the Cross. The world as a vale of soul-making is full of darkness and tragedy into which God himself must enter.[9]

Here, in the light of the atonement, could not even the fact of sin be – not justified, but in its very anomaly and scandal assimilated into the cosmic plan? This is the paradox of which William Temple could exclaim: 'A sinful world redeemed by the agony of Love's complete self-sacrifice is a better world, by the only standards of excellence we have, than a world that had never sinned.'[10]

It is the same truth that breaks insistently into the paschal liturgy of the Catholic Church: '*O certe necessarium Adae peccatum, quod Christi morte deletum est! O felix culpa, quae talem ac tantum meruit habere Redemptorem! O vere beata nox, quae sola meruit scire tempus et horam, in qua Christus ab inferis resurrexit!'* ('O truly necessary sin of Adam that Christ's death blotted out; and happy fault that merited such a Redeemer! Blessed indeed is this, the sole night counted worthy to know the season and the hour in which Christ rose again from the grave!')

To hold that God subjected the world and every creature in it to evil in order that he might in due time deliver them, might be a perilous way to formulate Christian belief. It is more tenable that evil becomes logically necessary as the negation of the existence of good. One of the best discussions of this question is given by Dorothy Sayers in her study, *The Mind of the Maker*.[11] If evil, she argues, belongs to the category of not-being, two things follow. The reality of evil is then contingent on the reality of good, and the good – by merely occurring – automatically and inevitably creates its corresponding evil.

Charles Williams (in *He Came Down from Heaven*) has given us a fine discussion of the theological problem of evil. From Aquinas it is recalled, 'God would not know good things perfectly, unless he also knew evil things . . . for, since evil is not of itself knowable, forasmuch as "evil is the privation of good", as Augustine says, therefore evil can neither be defined nor known except by good'.[12]

God then knows evil by 'simple intelligence' as not-being. The human situation with respect to evil is different. Having fallen into self-will, men can know it as part of their experience. As God could not do, they have called evil into active existence by associating their wills with it. Dorothy Sayers presents us with a dialogue between Faustus and Mephistopheles; under Faustus's plying with questions the Devil is incidentally too acute a theologian not to be scandalized at the suggestion that God made evil.

Faustus: Who made thee?
Mephistopheles: God, as the light makes the shadow.
Faustus: Is God, then, evil?

Mephistopheles:
    God is only light,
    And in the heart of the light, no shadow standeth,
    Nor can I dwell within the light of Heaven
    Where God is all.
Faustus: What art thou, Mephistopheles?
Mephistopheles:
    I am the price that all things pay for being,
    The shadow on the world, thrown by the world
    Standing in its own light, which light God is.[13]

CHAPTER 12

Jesus Christ

'God said, "Let there be light" and there was light.'
'Jesus cried with a loud voice . . . . My God, my God, why hast Thou forsaken me?'
   These two sayings measure the difference in effort and cost between creation and redemption . . . . the one consorts naturally with the popular notion of omnipotence, the other belongs to a thought of God which conceives Him as Almighty only by his own self-sacrifice.

William Temple[1]

THE world we find around us, vitiated by evil, cruelty and sin can – it would seem – admit of no loving God unless it be one concerned to redeem it. The Christian's God is at once Creator and Saviour, and between these two aspects of his nature there is for us tension and paradox.

A transcendent God, primal act of self-existence, or an immanent God encountered at the depth of our own nature, either of these we could apprehend without shock. God challenges Job: 'Where wast thou when I laid the foundations of the earth? . . . Hast thou entered into the springs of the sea? Or hast thou walked in the search of the depth?' All this we could find abstractly credible of God. But to realize God offering himself with compassion and concern for individual men, we must take to ourselves the cry wrung from Job by his tempters: 'I know that my redeemer liveth . . . whom I shall see for myself, and mine eyes shall behold, and not another.'

Theology uses the terms 'Logos' and 'Son' for the self-utterance of God by which he supremely revealed himself in the world. The Word that had been with God from the beginning, the principle by whom the worlds were made, enters upon the natural order as a human person. He is made flesh and dwells among us. We behold in him the glory of God's own person and the stamp of his very being.

Yet when we have proclaimed, 'The Word was made flesh', we have not yet arrived at the full mystery of Christ. The ultimate truth about Christ is that he came to serve and to suffer. 'When he is reviled, he reviles not again, and when he suffers he threatens not.' For suffer he unfeignedly did. His redeeming act culminated in the Passion and the Cross. God so loves that he gave himself.

To understand Jesus as the effective mediator of God, we must never forget – along with his true Godhead – his perfect and vulnerable humanity. God took manhood upon him without any stint or withholding. He became like us in everything: in the capacity to be hurt, to feel sorrow and even despair, and to know temptation, except alone that he was without sin. Only thus, from our human condition, could he possibly avail for us in our own plight. This is a God that for our sakes endures Gethsemane and Calvary. In the fullness of his sacrifice, he can utter the cry of dereliction in which the Son of God, bearing the sins of a whole humanity, experiences in his own nature the uttermost abandonment possible to human despair.

The world to be redeemed presents its most intractable problem in the freedom of the created. Though we speak of God as indwelling in his creation, it is yet as different from him as creature from creator. That creation is necessary to God in the sense of completing the fullness of his being, is something we cannot dare to assert. Can we believe, though, that mankind is necessary to the satisfying of his love, even to achieve a purpose in which we are as co-workers with him?

For God has endowed each personality with a freedom he will neither bend nor constrain. Though he has 'laid the foundations of the earth and put wisdom to the inward parts and understanding to the heart' he will not by his peremptory power compel a single human will to obedience. This is the value that creation must entail to God, showing us at once the depth of his love and the immensity of his sorrow in our fall.

There can be no stronger assertion than this, William Temple once said,[2] of the superiority of spirit over matter. 'The physical universe is to the Almighty a very little thing. What else is meant by calling Him Almighty? But not every task is even to Him a little thing. The fashioning of a child's soul is a task to call from Incarnate God the Bloody Sweat and the Cry of Desolation. So much greater and more precious is a moral being than all the majesty of the starry heavens . . . "It is too light a thing that Thou shouldst call worlds into being out of nothingness. Thou shalt turn pride into humility and call out love from the selfish heart".'

This chapter is not intended to give an adequate Christology. Its author could not. But of Jesus' person and of his Godhead, there are some things that must be said. The one way in which a revelation of God could be meaningful to man would be through personality; for it is thus alone that love can be expressed. Human and cosmic history at large may show in a general way the power of God and the wisdom of his dispositions. But it is in personality alone that we can receive and intimately know him. This is how we apprehend eternal truth and absolute obligation.

However vitiated our lives may be by sin and self-will, we have the image of God so stamped on our nature as to make it in principle possible that he should visit us. Love cannot be known from the phenomena of nature, nor could it be recognized in a general leaning of the world, on the whole appearing to make for righteousness. Love must be revealed through the meaning and service of a particular human life. As was the constant emphasis of William Temple's preaching on the Incarnation, there is but one possible mode of omnipotence in a world that is to contain free spirits: their creator must show forth his love and win from them their answering love.

THE GODHEAD OF JESUS

No theory [of the Incarnation] is heretical or heterodox unless
it denies that Jesus Christ is both Perfect God and Perfect
Man.

William Temple[3]

Nowhere in his own utterances did Jesus explicitly claim
divinity for himself. His Godhead was discovered by the faithful:
experience of him came first and the mature conclusions from
that experience were drawn only after the end of his earthly
ministry. The Gospels tell of a humanity uniquely shown forth
in a life of sacrifice and service. There was concern and oneness
with the plight of men. An open proclamation of divinity would
have been at cross-purposes with such a mission. 'If I honour
myself, my honour is nothing.' People would have been
incredulous, dumbfounded or intimidated; his purpose was
rather to show them by his acts and life what God must be like.
Poor, born in an outhouse, working, tempted as we are,
scorned and reviled, he was to show them that Jesus Christ does
what only God can do. Charles Gore, in *Belief in Christ*, writes:

> We can conceive nothing further from the method of Jesus
> than that He should have startled and shocked their
> consciences by proclaiming Himself as God. But He had done
> something which in the long run would make any other
> estimate of Him hardly possible.[4]

We must look then to the things he did, and to the things he
expressly claimed, and see what these imply about his nature;
how far they take us from the straightforward ethical Jesus,
around whom later theology is alleged to have fabricated a
God-figure.

Though the gospel is rooted in time, it is on the scale of
eternity. The man it shows us can be no mere holy man. His
own words make claim to a uniqueness in several ways: his

oneness with God, his moral authority over men, his ministry of salvation to them, and his mastery over the powers of evil. He speaks deliberately with the authority of God.[5]

The Sermon on the Mount is sometimes treated as a superb non-supernatural ethic. But arising from the heart of that teaching are the questions R. W. Dale, in his *Christian Doctrine*, is impelled to ask:

Who is this that places persecution for *his* sake side by side with persecution for 'righteousness' sake', and declares that whether men suffer for loyalty to him or for loyalty to right-eousness they are to receive their reward in the divine king-dom? Who is it that in that sermon places his own authority side by side with the authority of God, and gives to the Jewish people and to all mankind new laws which require a deeper and more inward righteousness than was required by the ten commandments? Who is it that in that sermon assumes the awful authority of pronouncing final judgement on men? ... These are not words we ever heard before, or have ever heard since, from teacher or prophet. Who is he? That question cannot be silenced when words like these have once been spoken.[6]

If we are to take the gospel seriously, at the only evaluation even its ethical teaching will evidently bear, Jesus has a place without parallel as the mediator of God to man. In his presence we do not doubt that we are in contact with God in a unique way. In the very perfection of his human nature his life stands forth as miraculous in a degree no other of the miracles of Scripture can attain. In Dr J. S. Whale's memorable sentence: 'His sinless perfection is a miracle, in the sense that history is ransacked in vain for another fact like it.'[7]

His Godhead comes home to us, then, in the same way as it first reached the Church, by following out the implications of his life to where they seem inevitably to lead us. Isolated in the Gospels before its time is St Thomas's utterance in the upper room: 'My Lord and my God.' This is a breaking forth of devotional language that was not for another generation to be fully assimilated into theology. At the moment of martyrdom, St Stephen likewise salutes him: 'Lord Jesus, receive my spirit', asking of Jesus what Jesus had asked of God.

With us, as with the Church, experience comes first. There is the experience of conversion itself; following this, recognition that we are reconciled to God by fellowship with Christ. 'From that comes the apprehension that in Christ is found the explanation of history because He is the revelation of the Father's will and the agent of its fulfilment.'[8]

St Paul appears never to have used explicitly the word God as a title for Jesus. He writes to us in the language of spiritual function and experience. But the insight he reaches is one that could only afterwards be expressed in the sonship and divinity of Jesus and indeed in the formula of the Trinity.

In the opening words of St Paul's epistles, the salutation and grace couple the name of Jesus Christ with God, placing it indeed before the Father's. St Paul affirms, too, that in Christ 'dwelleth all the fulness of the Godhead bodily', that Christ existed before his Incarnation 'in the form of God', that this same Christ is 'the image of the invisible God' and that 'God was in Christ, reconciling the world unto himself'.

It is in the Letter to the Hebrews that the Godhead of Christ becomes fully acclaimed. Here, too, the true humanity is emphasized, that 'in all things it behoved him to be made like unto his brethren, that he might be a merciful and faithful high priest in things pertaining to God, to make reconciliation for the sins of the people. For in that he himself hath suffered being tempted, he is able to succour them that are tempted.'[9]

But this epistle begins with the formal proclamation of Jesus as eternal Son of God. It is this Christ that God has appointed heir of all things, by whom also the worlds were made. And though, through the prophets, God had in early times given a partial revelation of himself, he had now in Jesus spoken to the world by his Son, showing us in Jesus 'the brightness of his glory, and the express image of his person'.[10]

The first letter ascribed to St John is in fact anonymous and its authorship difficult to fix. But it has a kindred style and thought with the Fourth Gospel, and is in fact the first corrective issued by the Church against false teaching about Christ's nature. For by the end of the first century, Gnostic thought had begun to invade the young Church. Christ, the new heresy taught, had only seemed to take a human body. Salvation was dependent not on works after faith but on knowledge of the divine mysteries. Thus was denied the need for forgiveness and for fellowship and brotherly love. In this letter the Godhead and the humanity are made explicit. 'We know that the Son of God is come, and hath given us an understanding, that we may know him that is true, and we are in him that is true, even in his Son Jesus Christ. This is the true God, and eternal life.'[11]

GOD PURPOSIVE AND PASSIBLE?

The only language about Jesus Christ that has ever been adequate to Christian experience is the language of thanks-giving and adoration that fills our liturgies and great devotional writings. If we attempt an exploration into God by human rationality, it is true, in the words of Archbishop Ramsey, that we may 'miss the way . . . by following the false path of a theological science without silence, without penitence, without contemplation, without wonder'.[12]

Yet, however great the prime impulse to worship, our Christian belief raises philosophical difficulties that we cannot refuse to face. To some men the difficulty of conceiving a God of loving purpose may not be the first or greatest obstacle to belief. It could be harder still to conceive a God with purpose at all, in the sense of a desire or design still lacking perfect fulfilment. Can God satisfy the philosopher's demand of him as a metaphysical absolute and at the same time evince such a concern for other beings as to limit his perfect self-existence? For if he be infinite and everlasting substance, in himself complete, he should want for nothing in finality that his creation could supply. When we speak of a God 'without body, parts or passions', how are we to reconcile the patent unfulfilment of the world with anything like the philosophical perfection of his being?

God's nature is eternally to produce, to communicate itself and to love. Yet even so, Bishop Gore would maintain,[13] he could be essentially independent of the world he created 'because God's unique eternal being is no solitary and monotonous existence; it includes in itself the fulness of fellowship, the society of Father and Son and Spirit'. Not many are likely to accept such an answer, which would bring us perilously close not to a trinity but to tritheism. If God had from the beginning existed as a perfectly loving society of three persons, there could have been no possible motive to create the world: the divine love would be already satisfied within the divine being.

Our problem springs from the existence of free created beings. This is for us both the greatest manifestation of God's love and the source of our greatest theological difficulties. Our power to contain the whole truth about God is so limited that we could well exclaim with Richard Hooker: 'Our greatest eloquence concerning him is our silence.' Yet our knowledge of God could be least untrustworthy where our apprehension of him has been closest. Whatever else we may say and hold about him, our concept of God must be founded upon what we know of him as a God of love.

Our apprehension of Jesus in our lives helps us functionally – as it were – towards a knowledge of God that we could never have gained abstractly or by the bare testimony of nature. Of course to many men, to adherents of some great non-Christian religions, even to the atheist jealous for the credentials of the God he is to reject, it may seem impious to attribute properties or characteristics to God at all. But the Christian knows there are some things it is blasphemy *not* to attribute. A God lacking in love and redeeming purpose towards his creatures, and without the capacity to suffer, falls short of the very perfections the Christian has seen his divine Lord reveal.

Some of my readers will know G. K. Chesterton's fine modern allegory *The Man Who Was Thursday*. It is the story of the tribulations and terrors of the six philosophical detectives, Thursday and his companions, during the phantasmagoric pilgrimage when each believes himself to be isolated and in peril of the others. The six at last having been reconciled in the presence of the master detective Sunday, Satan comes also among them and charges the redeemed in this world with never knowing suffering. Thursday, for his companions and himself, throws back the taunt, then turns his gaze upon the immense and silent face of Sunday, who is the peace of God. ' "Have you," he cried in a dreadful voice, "have you ever suffered?"

'As he gazed, the great face grew to an awful size, grew larger than the colossal mask of Memnon, which had made him scream as a child. It grew larger and larger, filling the whole sky; then everything went black. Only in the blackness before it entirely destroyed his brain he seemed to hear a distant voice saying a commonplace text that he had heard somewhere, "Can ye drink of the cup that I drink of? . . .".'[14]

In the Christian's God the capacity to suffer, far from limiting his perfections, fulfils him in the greatest possible perfection. And to a God who wills the fulfilment of the created order, the present world patently lacks completion. It cannot yet be a full expression of the purpose of God. Rather is it an order needing change for that plan finally to be achieved. If God be indeed love, he must will that change and desiderate such perfection for the world and every human creature.

When the Scriptures speak of God's sorrow, his wrath, his indignation at sin, this is not to impute to him changeful or capricious passions or feelings. Nor when we think of him as immutable does this imply indifference or unconcern. It can be part of his unchanging goodness, lively consistency and burning justice and love. All this is exhibited in reaction with the erratic and inconstant quality of our own lives. As the world, and we ourselves in it, fluctuate and change, God's all-loving constancy will appear to men in different aspects and modes.

To those who take seriously the Godhead and the manhood of Christ, age-old questions arise out of his human incarnation without stint or withholding. How can it be that up to his incarnation, the Logos knew all things (presumably ancient history, the composition of DNA, as well as scientific discoveries still to be made by us) and could still become in any valid or availing sense human? And if this Logos, creative and eternal Word of God, were present with the Father 'before Abraham was', what are we to believe happened to his divine attributes during the thirty years of his human life? How did omnipotence and omniscience become suspended as the price of true humanity?

The early Fathers generally held that the divine powers of the Logos were quiescent or sleeping during the Incarnation, or that he 'permitted' human experience to prevail over him. In modern times, the young Charles Gore, with his famous essay in *Lux Mundi* (1889), brought the subject to the surface by questioning the infallibility of our Lord's human knowledge.[15] He had erred, for example, in attributing Psalm 110 to David, as well as in citing the Book of Jonah as an historic record. How much, during his incarnation as man, could the Logos superhumanly know? Was his ignorance, for example, of the date of the parousia (Mark 13:32) real or pretended?

For a 'new' theologian taking a reduced or ethical view of Jesus the man, the problem of a God emptying himself to the limitations of a real humanity largely disappears. It can cease to worry us if we do not believe that Jesus, 'the man like us', partook of God's nature in the way we have affirmed. These questions we can never answer with statements about means and modalities. Nor can we do so from our knowledge of the psychology of the unconscious, for which we would need awareness about Jesus' inner life that we cannot possibly have.

Yet Charles Gore was surely right when he said: 'all real sympathy of the unconditioned for the conditioned demands – as far as we can see – the power of self-limitation.' Love makes itself known in history not by self-assertion, but by self-effacement and utter humility. This is, in its very paradox, the great token of Christ's divinity. St Gregory of Nyssa wrote: 'The sublimity is seen in lowliness, and yet the loftiness descends not.'[16]

Perhaps we can come closest to the truth if we do not think of the Godhead as retreating upon the manhood, but of the manhood as being progressively taken up into God, in the Incarnation, until the very powers of manhood are realized most fully. Through the human life of Jesus, from the childhood in Nazareth to the adult years and the Passion, it is possible to see the divine nature being increasingly set forth. God has limited himself in the freedom that belongs to his omnipotence for the purposes of his own end of infinite love. The divine attributes are not lost but manifested in a life that is both genuinely human and is also a movement of man towards that self-realization that is to perfect his destiny.[17]

Instead of the putting off of divinity, we can begin to think of the fulfilment by which it is put on. This is the Redeemer who, before he was fully indued with his glory and triumph, was to pray: 'Father, I desire that these men, who are thy gift to me, may be with me where I am, so that they may look upon my glory, which thou hast given me because thou didst love me before the world began.'[18]

CHAPTER 13

Revelation and Scripture

Historical and psychological reality coincide at the point of the Incarnation.

Bernardine Bishop[1]

Men when they cry for bread which will nourish them cannot be content with a stone, however sacred.

Yvonne Lubbock[2]

GENERAL considerations about the nature of the world or the possible attributes of a supreme being could never have brought us to a knowledge of Jesus, or a belief in the incarnate Word as the Son of God. A natural theology could teach us no more about our Father in heaven than sociology could tell us of our father in Hampstead.

Revelation must be personal. It must involve not only historic knowledge about a person but a real experience of that person. If there has indeed been a supreme revelation, marked off in kind and depth from any other, it is not surprising but inevitable that this is involved with particular happenings in history. A meaningful showing forth of God's nature and love, in terms of personality, was bound to be in one place and time and not in another; to be shown to people of one race and even local district; in short, to take one specific form rather than the multitude of different forms that it might conceivably have had.

These qualities, that have been called the 'scandal of particularity' must always appear as an impediment to those who insist on regarding God as an austere and infinite absolute. To the reader of Paul Tillich, every human conception of God, every formula and dogma, even the use of his name, must seem to limit him and detract from his totality. The reverent agnostic will thus speak of God as the great unknowable. In fact, it has been remarked, this reticence may not be as reverent as it seems: it assumes not only that man is unable to know God, but that God is unable to reveal himself to us.

Belief in God as incarnate in Jesus Christ can plainly not be natural or innate. It comes to us as a legacy of history. But when we affirm this, we must do so with important cautions. Revelation may indeed depend for its substance on the general facts of creation, and more particularly on special facts of history. But the personal apprehension of God does not come about for man by an intellectual assent to certain items in an historical calendar. Nor can it be assured by a lucid declaration, engraved and lasting for all time.

For to say that revelation is personal does not only mean that it stems from a particular person in history. It means that it is complete only when that person is known and loved. This is a progressive unfolding of truth that must go on for us through our whole lives. Beginning in history, and with the traditions and early teaching we inherit, it is accomplished and completed only by our active part in it. We must think of God as guiding both the natural and the historic process, and supremely also as guiding the minds of men. 'The interaction of the process and the minds of men which are alike guided by Him is the essence of revelation.'[3]

Revelation is for us a personal apprehension akin to mystical experience. It may even be dulled or obscured by embalming it in dogmatic formulations settled once for all. From being guideposts marking out a broad, safe road, the doctrines of the creeds may become even stumbling blocks to the faith. But to agree that dogmas may be reformable is not to undervalue the real historic content of the Gospels. Things did truly happen in history, even though their revelatory power was not for us complete until our minds laid hold of them in faith. When it is said that historical and psychological truth coincide at the point of the Incarnation, this is to believe that revelation is a synthesis of true history and true experience.

Even when the Gospels record tangible events as raw

historical materials, these will be events that the secular world cannot at once assimilate. For when it is claimed that the man Jesus at a particular time in history revealed to us God's nature, this is not to be taken simply to mean that he was a man so good as to present human nature in its highest form. Nor is he for us a man uniquely adopted in due historic course as God. The expressions 'Word' and 'Son' are being used for God's real utterance of himself, because Jesus shows us the real and uncreated nature of God incarnate in a truly human person. When the Creed says 'begotten from the Father before all the worlds, God from God, light from light, true God from true God', it is using the only sort of expressions direct enough to convey the Son's timelessness and eternity. Of his oneness with the Father Jesus repeatedly speaks; when he affirms of himself, 'Before Abraham was, I am', this is not a bold metaphor in temporal form, but the taking to himself of the very character of God. Teilhard de Chardin, in the *Hymn of the Universe*, speaks in these terms:

The prodigious expanses of time which preceded the first Christmas were not empty of Christ: they were imbued with the influx of his power. It was the ferment of his conception that stirred up the cosmic masses and directed the initial developments of the biosphere. It was the travail preceding his birth that accelerated the development of instinct and the birth of thought upon the earth. Let us have done with the stupidity which makes a stumbling-block of the endless eras of expectancy imposed on us by the Messiah; the fearful anonymous labours of primitive man, the beauty fashioned through its age-long history by ancient Egypt, the anxious expectancies of Israel, the patient distilling of the attar of oriental mysticism, the endless refining of wisdom by the Greeks: all these were needed before the Flower could blossom on the road of Jesse and of all humanity. All these preparatory processes were cosmically and biologically necessary that Christ might set foot upon our human stage. And all this labour was set in motion by the active, creative awakening of his soul inasmuch as that human soul had been chosen to breathe life into the universe. When Christ first appeared before men in the arms of Mary he had already stirred up the world.[4]

In our own day as in the past we have had all manner of glosses of 'Christianity not mysterious', seeking for secular man explanations of the Incarnation that do not strain his scientific or contemporary habits of thought. Lloyd Geering is able to write that

the life we have here with all its frustrations and finiteness is capable of maturing to the best we can actually imagine, and *this is the meaning of the Christian doctrine of the Incarnation.*[5]

Elsewhere the same author has made a plea that

the Christian faith must be radically reorientated and concern itself *not with an unseen world but with this world* ... [and declare] something satisfying to modern man who has become painfully aware of his limitations and his *mortality.*[6]

From such a point it is easy to recede to the qualified ethical approval of the man Jesus, as typified in the following words from a lay writer:

The authority of Jesus may consist in a special relationship to God or it may be similar in kind though not in degree to that of other exceptional men. Without being of necessity wholly original, or wholly convincing, let alone divine, he can nevertheless hold our attention and dominate our lives. And if he does so we are surely Christians.[7]

The risk exists always and everywhere that the presentation of the gospel will be incredible to natural man, whether Graeco-Roman sophisticated man, or twentieth-century scientific man. It cannot therefore be the preacher's task to assimilate the gospel into secular belief by explaining away its supernatural content. William Temple once wrote to Ronald Knox:

'I am not asking what Jones will swallow. *I am Jones* asking what there is to eat.'[8] The real risk is not that men will fail to comprehend the gospel, but that they will think they have absorbed its difficulties by bringing it into non-mysterious terms under the natural order. The gospel is thus put under the judgement of a world that should be judged by it.

We freely employ the term 'mythology' today in relation to the narratives of the New Testament. In the sense in which the liberal theologian uses it, mythology does not necessarily connote something fictitious or even historically dubious. It is a framework of events in which general truths may be expressed in a concrete way. A similar mythologic dress – it could be claimed – is given to traditions of state or racial history, whether it is about the founding of Rome or the opening of the American frontiers. Many details that are historically based may have filtered into the mythologic stream. But what is held to be important is their vivid actualizing of universal truth, rather than their factual content in itself. In this way primitive people will use myth to express the rhythm of the seasons and other natural processes, as well as the destiny of tribes and societies and their transactions with the deities.

That the Gospels express general truths about God in a framework of religious myth would be the widespread assumption of liberal theologians in our own day. With Rudolf Bultmann's famous essay (written in 1941, but delayed in English translation until 1955 in A. M. Farrer: *Kerygma and Myth*, Volume I), the demythologizing of Christianity can be said, not to have first begun, but to have entered into the mainstream of English theology.

Today it has become increasingly accepted that the historic life of Jesus presented by the Gospels is clad in such mythologic dress that we can understand its meaning for today only when we get rid of the whole first-century background. The supernatural is to be stripped away as the excrescence that the Church and theologians have laid upon the straightforward gospel message. Jesus of Nazareth was a figure of real, though shadowy, existence who gave himself for others. His moral teaching is the noblest and truest and most profound ethic ever preached by man to man.

The difficulty in approaching the New Testament as straight-forward history – far more than the fundamentalist will want to concede – is that different parts of the record invite such wide differences of interpretation as between fact and religious symbol. Critical judgement has constantly to be brought to bear. This is not simply a literary judgement or an assessment of evidence. It must be a theological evaluation in which the whole Church shares; and it is a responsibility no man can avoid who claims to fall somewhere between the wide extremes of the literal fundamentalist and the wholesale demythologizer.

It is in some ways a handicap to have all the canonical books of the Old and New Testaments bound together under the title of the Holy Bible. For this large library is enormously varied in character, and a relatively large part of it is not offered as historical narration at all. Many of the books are inherited or adopted by the early Church from the Jewish Scriptures: there are books of law and ritual, songs of penitence and praise and thanksgiving, a love-poem and a treasury of aphoristic wisdom. Then there are the annals and state chronicles of ancient Israel and – of supreme importance – the books of the prophetic age. There are historical novels in Jonah and Ruth, visionary apocalyptic in Daniel, and in Job a superb allegoric approach to the most taxing of religious problems, unmerited suffering.

In the Gospels themselves we have an abundance of literary forms and conventions, these, too, of varying historicity. There are first the genealogies of Jesus in Matthew and Luke, neither in our sense historical. The first Gospel traces his descent from Abraham to link him with the salvation history of the Jewish people. Luke derives him from Adam who was the son of God in turn. Many of the stories may be old traditions, such as the tales of the Magi and the shepherds, and reminiscences of the family circle surrounding the birth of Jesus. There are descriptions, too, that could be externalized representations of inner experiences: heavenly voices, the annunciations to Mary and

Zacharias, Joseph's dream. The tongues of flame and sweat like drops of blood would generally be explained today as vivid metaphor.

There are other events far more central to the narrative that it would seem difficult to regard unquestionably as history. These are preserved for us by the credence that belief in a real incarnation may give them as subsidiary happenings. Such events, with their miraculous content, probably did not of themselves produce faith directly. The first generation of Christians evidently did not as a whole know of the virgin conception of Jesus. This may have been a tradition reticently preserved within the holy family and its close circle. It is mentioned only by Matthew and Luke. Paul is wholly silent about it, rather surprisingly since we may assume he would have had the story from Luke. The arguments for regarding it as historic in the traditional way, or for allowing it to be understood symbolically, are well balanced and summarized in so traditional a book as Oliver Quick's *The Doctrines of the Creed*.[9] Though many present-day Christians might be openly agnostic about such a pious tradition, there are some whose agnosticism would be expressed (in the whole light of the Incarnation) in a reverent unwillingness to reject.

From the demythologized gospel of the Bultmann school, and as the end-product of much modern textual criticism, the 'Jesus of history' emerges as an intangible figure without reliable history. Our apprehension of him, and our impulse to worship, is based on the shifting criteria of individual insight. Theology is reduced to ecclesiastical psychology. Jesus becomes for us so subjective as to be ultimately uncommunicable to other men at all.

Yet this would not be a fair statement of the whole Bultmann position. The 'demythologizing' has obviously detached the revelation of God from any special act in history. The Incarnation is now something that happened not to God but to man: a heightened perception on our part rather than a particular incursion of the eternal into the natural. But what is called the 'kerygmatic' element of the gospel is still insisted to be there. When the gospel is preached today, men's lives are transformed from an 'inauthentic' existence of anxiety and despair to an 'authentic' life of freedom and faith. The crucial act and encounter is in the present moment. All the high Protestant value attached to preaching is found here. It has been remarked that for Rudolf Bultmann the Christ event with its power among men took place not in the years A.D. 1–30, but every time Bultmann entered the pulpit at 11 o'clock on Sunday.

It is admittedly difficult for a sceptic to see why this should be so, or why the preaching of Buddha or Islam, or the exposition of Marxist communism or Huxleyan humanism, or the practice of psychotherapy, should not also produce this special 'authenticity'. Perhaps they do. For otherwise the Bultmannist would be driven to justify his unique claims by restricting 'authenticity' to what happens when the Christian gospel is preached. This in fact becomes our position if we *define* the word of God as simply something that has a particular effect upon the hearer. It has been said that to insist upon retaining the 'kerygma' while rejecting the historicity, to combine preaching with the Bultmann attitude to the Gospels themselves, is to substitute magic for myth.[10]

The preaching of a demythologized gospel, in short, puts the same strain on our credulity as the receiving of an historic one. We shall surely go wrong if we detach from its historicity the present power of the Gospels to speak to us. Historic and psychologic truth are blended not only in the Incarnation but in the Christian's encounter in the present moment with Christ through Scripture. We are right to put stress upon 'kerygma', for the Bible does not speak to us alone by simply recounting the Christian claim of history. But it is kerygmatic in its reading and contemplating and preaching, just because we have also been faithful and diligent to conserve it substantially as history.

The power of the gospel is as immediate and existential as the mystical experience of Jesus in our own lives. It is the same experience; for we are reading the gospel not primarily as an historic quest, but to find Jesus in himself, who is the very crown and substance of revelation. His gospel is itself '*evangelium*' with mission power. As the disciple, having met with Jesus, said to the others, 'Come and see', so we can proclaim, who will read the Gospels with an open heart, 'We have found the Messiah'.

OUR USE OF THE BIBLE

To Britain and Northern Europe the Reformers bequeathed a tradition of Bible-reading unique in its fervour. Its flowering was seen not only in John Bunyan, and in the Methodist and evangelical movements, but in the whole acceptance of the Bible as the first or only book of the home.

Today the Christian laity – Anglicans at least – on the whole do little regular Bible study. New liturgical developments have displaced the morning and evening offices with their regular cycle of lessons in which the Anglican Communion once took special pride. Knowledge of the people and themes of the Bible is almost vestigial among ordinary people. At the end of an era of 'biblical Christianity' the Bible has become detached from all apparent relevance to the people's lives. To a younger generation, though new translations in bright covers replace the sober black Authorized Version, the Bible has become an unfamiliar, even an uninteresting book.

What are the reasons for this? No doubt in part it is a reaction from the unbalance of the earlier biblical tradition. Few of us in our lifetime will have been exposed to literalist fundamentalism. Yet old habits of textual exposition have often carried over, sometimes for prepackaged answers to complex moral questions of the present day. The short Bible readings on Sundays or at school are often detached from context or commentary. Even the press is apt to present a 'text for the day' as if there were some magical efficacy in the reading.

Worse than this has been done with the Bible. Many of us can remember the support attracted between the wars by the Bible-based movement known as British Israelitism. Though itself beyond the pale of theological discussion, it has left a legacy of wide distrust of textual exposition, and even of biblical authority itself. Today it is not reassuring to find the most vocal response to secularism in a trenchant 'back to the Bible' call. The Billy Graham evangelism features the portents and catastrophes of the Old Testament as having a detailed relevance for us today. The Bible is presented as God's literally inspired word from cover to cover; where there are discrepancies with science, it is the latter that is said gradually to be 'catching up'.

The social danger of biblical crusades appealing for a 'return to the word of God' is that they imagine some former generation, remote or recent, with a better or semi-ideal Christian understanding to which we need only go back. But to apply as a blueprint for Christian action today the domestic and pastoral ethos of the first century, or of our pioneers of a century ago is to inoculate the contemporary world against all the relevance of Christianity to it. It is forgotten that the Christian creed, as well as the Church's songs of protest and concern, apply uncomfortably to those situations we are so often urged to 'keep religion out of'. Accused of being an agitator, a man of conscience must often answer: The Christian always is, if he is true to his calling.[11]

Psychologically, both Bible and Church can become overdominant in our approach to the faith. There can be more truth than we like to acknowledge in C. G. Jung's plaint in *Psychology and Alchemy*:

The Western attitude, with its emphasis on the object, tends to fix the ideal – Christ – in its outward aspect and thus to rob it of its mysterious relation to the inner man . . . . Yes, everything is to be found outside – in image and in word, in Church and Bible – but never inside . . . . Christian education has done all that is humanly possible, but it has not been enough. Too few people have experienced the divine image as the innermost possession of their own souls. Christ only meets them from without, never from within the soul; that is why dark paganism still reigns there, a paganism which, now in a form so blatant that it can no longer be denied and now in all too threadbare disguise, is swamping the world of so-called Christian culture.[12]

Nothing I have written is to undervalue the Christian's need and love of his Bible. But our Bible study must clearly have restored to it intellectual and devotional strands that in the past we have neglected. Bible teaching requires a creative imagination and a high maturity in the Christian faith.

In his book *Religious Thinking from Childhood to Adolescence*, one of the many of its kind appearing today, Ronald Goldman traces the child's development through an early sub-religious phase rather resembling the crude Mosaic stage where everything is thought of in concrete terms and material facts. Only later, if at all, does the adolescent come to conceptualize adequately about religion. Far too often growth is arrested at the first stage, at a mental age of no more than ten, where a diet of Bible stories may retard a child's thinking simply by reinforcing crude, materialistic and literal religious ideas.

> There is strong evidence to suggest that by ten years of age most children have developed a two-world mentality. One, a theological world where God exists, was especially active in Bible times, but is now in heaven; in which anything can happen and God can and does interfere in the natural world to help 'the goodies' against 'the baddies'. The other is a world of emerging scientific thought, cause and effect thinking, where God does not exist and the mysterious and supernatural is irrelevant.[13]

THE 'RECOVERY' OF THE BIBLE

There is still a real sense in which the Bible has been crucial to the development of twentieth-century theology. The Continental Protestant school of Karl Barth, however otherwise unlike the Bultmannites, has like them stressed the kerygmatic power of the gospel and the salvative function of its preaching.

The first reading of Barth gives a stimulus and shock to any man in whom the complacencies of ethical and natural theology have taken root. Most of the common assumptions of our day come impartially under fire: the drawing of any intimations of God from the created world, the value of piety or good works for man's salvation, or indeed of any power of our own to help ourselves. We are to find God not in nature or in general history or even in the processes of our own lives, but in his decisive revelation of himself in Jesus. To rely upon natural theology is misguidedly to set up criteria that God is presumed or required to fit; whereas he stands judge over all revelations and not we in judgement upon him. Access to God is entirely vertical and one-way, towards ourselves by the sole initiative of God. Who he is and what it is to be divine, we have to learn from the one in whom he has revealed that divinity. If he has revealed himself in Jesus Christ, it is not for us to be wiser than he, and say his revelation is in contradiction with the divine essence.

> We have to be ready to be taught by Him that we have been too small and perverted in our thinking about Him within the framework of a false idea of God . . . . We cannot make [our insights] the standard by which to measure what God can or cannot do.[14]

Anglican theology has never been Barthian. But the liberalism and 'modernism' of the first two decades of the century were followed by a new emphasis upon the Bible in the context of men's own awareness of God. The gospel was seen anew to have a living and contemporary power. Preoccupation with the historical life of Jesus was now matched with a new concern that would understand the gospel primarily through the religious experience of the first Christians and of ourselves today. A radical exponent of this view was the Cambridge theologian E. C. Hoskyns, in the 1920s. In his essay 'The Christ of the Synoptic Gospels',[15] he lays stress on the failure of liberal Protestantism to formulate the *contrasts* of Scripture correctly:

The contrast is *not* between the Jesus of history and the Christ of faith, *but* between the Christ humiliated, and the Christ returning in glory . . . not between a reformed and an unreformed Judaism, *but* between Judaism and the new supernatural order by which it is at once destroyed and fulfilled: not between the disciples of a Jewish prophet and the members of an ecclesiastically ordered sacramental cultus, *but* between the disciples of Jesus who . . . are as yet ignorant . . . of his claims . . . and the same disciples, initiated into the mystery of his Person and of his life and death, leading the mission to the world, the patriarchs of the new Israel of God.

Religious criteria, and the insights of faith, are not only relevant but deeply necessary to our study of the texts. Biblical study, like the whole of our theology, is an activity of believing Christians, to be prosecuted from within the faith, and in the witnessing body of the Church.

Across a whole century, the words of an older Archbishop Temple still ring with an emphasis that seems strong and true:

Our Lord is the crown, nay, the very substance of all Revelation. If He cannot convince the soul, no other can. The believer stakes all faith on His truth, all hope on His power. If the man of science would learn what it is that makes believers so sure of what they hold, he must study with an open heart the Jesus of the Gospels; if the believer seeks to keep his faith steady in the presence of so many and some-times so violent storms of disputation, he will read of, ponder on, pray to, the Lord Jesus Christ.[16]

CHAPTER 14

The Tension of the Church

'I'll do anything for you, Vicar, except come to Church.'
He has heard that, especially from the working classes, for
long enough. The difference is now that he may hear it from
the curate.

Dr J. A. T. Robinson[1]

WE need not set out in detail the possible indictments of the
Church, for the bishops and clergy seem to be doing this well
enough. They must be helping, too, to create the climate of
present disillusion. On the *Observer* front page (14 April 1968)
Dr Robinson can forecast the 'disintegration of the whole
framework of organized religion'. 'The Church may expect a
rapidly increasing brain-drain. For many of the more lively
minded are losing faith in the relevance of the religious casing.'

The current theological debate has rendered the old subjects
of ecumenical conversation out of date. The secular theology
has opened a new cleavage plane (this time a horizontal one)
running through each of the separate denominations. But in the
midst of all this, many remain convinced that criticism should
not be aimed at the existence and credentials of the Church, but
at its incredibly slack performance. O. Fielding Clarke, in his
refreshing book *For Christ's Sake*, wrote:

> Where I disagree totally from Dr Robinson is in the diagnosis
> of our condition and, therefore, in its cure. . . . What Chris-
> tians need to do is not to think up new images but to deliver
> the goods! The bishop complains that the Church is too
> turned in on itself, and his remedy is a century of theological
> juggling with images.[2]

Our children today are understandably preoccupied with the
Church's mission, and with its involvement in the plight of the

world. It is the social radicals that will be more listened to than the writers of theological paper-backs. The Church is being judged on where it stands in issues of peace and war, racial integration, world population control and the care of the starving. In a time when Vietnam and Biafra are ghastly negations of the Christian gospel, the Church is expected to have a courageous concern with secular policy.

Yet it would be taking a short view to say the Church's first priority is to have a contemporary image; or that her prime role is a political one in a world where our statesmen are pursuing yesterday's unrealities. The Church is – and must be – far more than this. For wherever the gospel has been viable in the world the organized Church has existed. Quite simply, to be a Christian at all is at once to be a member of the Church.

Not all Christians have agreed upon what the Church may claim to be. Most would concede it to be the fellowship – closely or loosely knit – of those who have found their life in Christ. But to many Christians, and certainly to those of the largest historical groupings, the existence of the Church and the claim that she is one and holy and catholic and apostolic, are not simple historical conditions that have resulted in the faith being handed down. They are themselves articles of the faith.

The Church is not then simply a confederation of the diversity of Christian congregations or *one* instrument of God's purpose ranged beside many secular ones. And Christianity cannot be merely or primarily a doctrine of salvation to individuals. In a traditional catholic view the Church involves 'the establishment of a visible society as the one divinely constituted home of the great salvation, held together not only by the inward Spirit but also by certain manifest and external institutions'.[3]

This is putting the doctrine of the Church high, believing that all Christians have a role in its society, which is the covenanted means of their unity with Christ and with one another. When the Church is called the 'body of Christ' or is credited with being the extension of his incarnation, this is for the Catholic not simply metaphoric but reflects a firm reality of organization.

In our own day Free Churchmen, as well as Romans and Anglicans, have come to hold a more spacious and central doctrine of the Church. Ecumenical union is not likely to founder now on this issue. Whatever the differences about the nature of the Church, the significant fact is that all are accepting it as necessary for the proper unity of men within the Christian society.

What are the grounds on which the Church makes such all-inclusive claims? First, by its sacraments it lays claim to a unique ministry of grace. In its promise of the Spirit it claims a unique ministry to teach. In its ordering of ministers it has a unique apostolic tradition to preserve. The Church is the necessary vehicle then (for the whole course of history has shown us no other) by which God's saving acts have been made known to every age and to our own. Through the Church alone can our personal experience of God be sharpened and focused upon his revelation in history.

Professor Mascall writes: 'The fact that the Spirit will lead the Church into all truth does not mean that the Church will never be affected by misunderstanding or will never diverge from the path along which God is directing it; it does mean that it will be protected from irreparable catastrophe.' He speaks, too, of the Church as a stream that picks up from time to time a good deal of rubbish in its course but sooner or later deposits it upon some convenient sand-bank.[4]

The doctrine of the Church involves an apostolic ministry and an authority with which all its members are to be in communion. In an age where the principle of hierarchy is everywhere being questioned, many find it strange that the Church still insists on working through a clear-cut personal authority. In fact, this is a functional need that she might have discovered empirically if she had not already had it supplied. In a day of commissions, councils and committees, the Church has not been alone in finding the working shortcomings of a pure democracy. Yet she is perhaps unique in knowing the principle by which democracy can be at once transcended and revitalized. Here again we see that personalism and particularity by which universal truth is safeguarded and witnessed to.

The Church's principal officers are those successors in the line of the Apostles called bishops. These are not simply colourful presiding dignitaries or administrators. They are both shepherds and watchdogs, and their function is to safeguard in their own person the faith witnessed by the Apostles and to hold the Church to this.

It is very true that bishops have not in every age behaved in ways that would appear apostolic. They have hundreds of times been no more enlightened and courageous than a good average of lesser men. George Bell of Chichester stood almost alone among the bishops in condemning the mass-bombing of civilians. Right up to our own day the English bishops have enjoyed an income and way of life strangely at odds with their mission not to be waited on but to serve. How many of the spiritual peers were in the nineteenth century in the progressive ranks on any important issue of the day? How many bishops even today understand the radical social gospel for which younger Christians are – with diminishing patience – looking to the Church?

Yet the vindication of the personal principle has signally appeared in the happenings of our own time. The Second Vatican Council, for which no representative body would have been likely to find the impetus or zeal, was initiated by that apostolic man, John XXIII. With the childlike wisdom of the saints and the craft of the politicians, he set afoot the deliberations that were to transform the face and polity of the Roman Church, cutting through the lethargy and obstruction of the advisory commissions until he could finally exclaim: '*Adesso comincia il mio consilio*' ('Now begins *my* council').

What is the nature of the Church's teaching authority among men? First, it is, in its ideal, and ought to be, so far as possible in its practical expression, universal. It will agree in holding and in handing on a certain consensus of doctrine. In his inaugural lecture at King's College on 'Theology and History', Professor Mascall affirmed that theology is a function of the

Church as the body of Christ, and the theologian is the man to whom the exercise of that function has been specially committed. An important part of his address may be quoted at length:

> The theologian's motto should *not* be 'It all depends on me'. He is not committed to 'beginning all over again'; rather he is 'in a great tradition'. He should neither be a victim of the over-confidence which is convinced that it has given the Christian religion the ultimate and definitive form nor be haunted by the *Angst* which fears that the whole structure of Christian thought may be without solid rational foundations. He is part of something which is greater than himself; he is the heir of the Christian ages . . . .
>
> Thus, as I see it, the task of the Christian theologian is that of theologizing within the great historical Christain tradition; *theologizandum est in fide*. Even when he feels constrained to criticize adversely the contemporary expressions of the tradition, he will be conscious that he is bringing out from the depths of the tradition its latent and hitherto unrecognized contents; he is acting as its organ and its exponent. He will also offer his own contribution for it to digest and assimilate if it can. Like the good householder he will bring out of his treasure things new and old. But he will have no other gospel than that which he has received.[5]

In putting stress on authority and consensus, we are of course far from ignoring the individual freedom which has today widened in theology as never before. Even in 1937 the Archbishops' Commission showed a broad spectrum of individual belief among the Church of England clergy. Today this would be even wider, though doubtless with a different balance and centre of gravity. Sincerely held opinions are no longer today stigmatized or proscribed as heresies, though it is not to be expected that the official teaching – with which the Church catechizes and instructs – will run as wide as all these individual viewpoints and dissents.

Could a biologist illustrate the Church's tension of liberty and consensus by the simple animal Amoeba? The cell's constantly changing boundary with the world represents freedom of enquiry and insight. Small tentacles are put out to explore, to initiate new movements, or to withdraw and regroup. At the centre of the cell lies the nucleus, with its precious body of inherited instructions. Representing consensus, in all places and through all time, it governs the cell and safeguards its action. But the life of the cell must perish when its boundary with the world ceases to be flexible and free.

One of the best expressions of the meaning of authority within the Church comes significantly from the scene of Vatican II, in the journalist Robert Kaiser's lively commentary *Inside the Council*. The Church is to have regard for the impossibility of finality in expressing truths that are themselves eternal. She will not wish to use a crushing magisterial authority where there should be freedom for scholarly enquiry. But her authority is not that of a democracy, coming from the will of its people. Her authority is of Christ. Yet, in Kaiser's words:

> [this does not mean] that the Church must hurl down its commands and anathemas like some sort of Vulcan! Or that it must exert something analogous to the meekness and mildness of Christ who said 'Learn of me'. Is the authority of the Church meant to dominate or serve? If it is to dominate, then there is no need for the bearers of that authority to listen. But if it is to serve, then those bearers of authority have to be attentive to the expressed needs of the world.
>
> A father asks his crying child why she is crying. There is need here for a little dialogue. How much more need should there be when the service is one delegated by Christ himself, the Good Shepherd who once said: 'I know mine and mine know me'? Between Christ (or his Vicars) and his flock there has to be an interchange.[6]

In what sense is the Church as we know it today holy? The blemishes of its past and present will be notorious to any honest student. Yet such disabilities have never been held to invalidate in a total way the Church's witness and powers. They represent the visible character we might sadly expect of a Church militant in an unloving and unenlightened world. John Wycliffe, who was one of the forerunners of the English Reformation, would have held the whole Church to be corrupt and her ministry and sacraments defective until her ministers had become holy. With his theory '*de dominio divino*' he believed that man's responsibility was directly to God, without need of order, hierarchy or authority; and ('*de dominio civili*') that dominion or leadership was founded in grace and that the unworthiness of the holder of an office deprived him of the power of its exercise.

The same thesis is often heard from dissenting individuals at the present day. But it could not have been conceded without disaster by any branch of a Church that has constantly to preach and minister in man's actual sinful state.

The temporal development of the Church during 2000 years is a leading theme of European history. After it had outgrown its early limits, the Church of the Apostles and Fathers took on in the first millennium a federal structure that the Eastern branch still possesses. Following the great East-West schism of the eleventh century, the Latin Church at the height of the Middle Ages assumed a feudal form and asserted a growing temporal power. At the Reformation the corruptions and abuses such a system had engendered were partly cleansed with the breaking away of the Protestant communions and the Roman Counter-Reformation stemming from the Council of Trent.

From this stage began two contrary trends, which have impaired the Church's life and mission up to our own day. Both sides have tended to perpetuate their separation in ways peculiarly lasting and malign. On the one hand the Roman Communion inaugurated what Charles Davis (in *God's Grace in History*) called 'an absolutist system, according to which almost all authority is derived downwards from the top'.[7] This has lasted until the stirring of the deep impulses to renewal and unity, still unrealized, in our own day.

In the Reformed Churches enthusiasm for individual liberty and direct recourse to Scriptures came at the same time as the renaissance of national political consciousness. The Church's oneness and catholic authority were deeply obscured. Sects multiplied, with the arguments the first schismatics had appealed to, seeming ever to justify new and more local splitting. The divisive tendency in Protestantism has had tragic results in weakening the Church's mission and action in the world.

In the Western Church and its divisions, what has been truly called the great fact of our time (and it may well be the greatest movement within the Church since the patristic centuries and the early Councils) has been the visible movement towards ecumenism and ultimate organic union. With all that remains to be done, with the real difficulties in reaching consensus, conversations between Anglicans and many of the great diversity of free churches are now astir.

On the Roman side, the Second Vatican Council, with its treatment of liturgy, discipline and government, has made in ten years a transformation of the Church's visible face such as no previous age had aspired to.

In these achievements and in their promise still to come we may look for a measure of the Church's vitality and survival value. There is increasing consciousness everywhere of the blemishes that led Oliver Quick (in 1927, in *The Christian Sacraments*) to speak of universal schism: 'Perhaps God has concluded all under the sin of schism that He may in the end have mercy upon all through the grace of union.'

The Church's impulse to unity can be seen as of a piece with that unifying that we have found constitutive of our own nature and personality. It can prefigure too that gathering of powers that Teilhard de Chardin has proclaimed in his vision of an advancing, self-unifying noosphere. It is a part of the organic expression of mankind, advancing upon the point where Christ is presently to be all in all. To Teilhard the Church seems implicitly to confirm the idea of a universe dominated by energies of a personal nature: first, in the substance of its creed, next by its existence value, and finally by its extraordinary power of growth.

In Teilhard's view the Church – as the City of God, with the two characteristics of personality and universality united in its theology – presents the most realistic and at the same time the most cosmic of our aspirations and hopes. To him, those who fail to see these in the Church fail completely to comprehend its nature. There is a sense in which the Church is a 'prodigious biological operation – that of the redeeming incarnation'.

Of its 'existence value' there has appeared, in Christian love, a zone of thought in which a genuine universal love has been shown to be psychologically possible and to operate in practice. In its 'power of growth' Teilhard finds the Church 'the *unique* current of thought, on the entire surface of the noosphere, which is sufficiently audacious and progressive to lay hold of the world . . . in an embrace . . . where faith and hope reach their fulfilment in love'. Christianity alone can reconcile in one living act the all and the person, and 'bend our hearts not only to the service of that tremendous movement of the world which bears us along, but beyond, to embrace that movement in love'.[8]

'RELIGIONLESS CHRISTIANITY'

> You never get any of this dry-as-dust theological stuff from him that's done so much to keep people out of the churches. Quite the contrary. Last Easter he gave a sermon on the eleven plus.
>
> *Angus Wilson*[9]

The novelist's imagination is hardly wide of the mark. On Passion Sunday, 1968, I listened at Southwark Cathedral in place of evensong to a Brains Trust discussion on 'Education for the Arts', led by a much-respected politician, Miss Jenny Lee, Minister for the Arts. The congregation faced a long table down the nave, and neither prayer nor benediction followed the main billing. When I found the programme strange, a bystander assured me that people could be attracted this way who would never otherwise come into a church.

It would be easy to make too much of such examples. There could be complaint if the Church were *not* looking for a contemporary image, involving – among other things – beat music, discotheques and mannequin parades. It can be ground to rejoice that the Church is alive to the weekday and worldly, the so-called profane, implications of Christianity. It is good to have a protesting Church (even if it is still a timid one), where the times so scandalously call for Christian protest.

To recognize all this is to grasp an important part, but, I believe, not the whole of the truth about the Church and its life. Here I must refer to Dr Robinson's teaching about 'worldly holiness'.[10] The view he offers about 'engagement' is a popular one today, well enough set out in *Honest to God*, though often reiterated since. Its practical advice is wholly consistent with the idea of God not as transcendental over and against the natural order, but as essentially immanent in ourselves and discoverable by personal relationships 'in depth'.

The secularists sometimes seem so anxious to locate God at the depths of 'our' being that he is in danger of being exhausted in his immanence there. It is hard to see what will become of his transcendent role as creator and sustainer of the world; for it is being stated pretty clearly by the secularists that there is no world transcending this one that it can be our business to cultivate.

The same view carries over into worship and prayer. We are told that it is 'the essence of the religious perversion, when worship becomes a realm into which to withdraw from the world to "be with God" – even if it is only in order to receive strength to go back into it'.[11] The purpose of worship is not to retreat from the secular into the department of the religious, let alone to escape from 'this world'. We can agree that it would be perverse to resort to church on Sunday to find a God who could not be reached on a weekday in other places and modes. Yet it is for this sort of attitude that Dr Robinson appears to be reserving the word 'religious'. It would normally be called pietism or religiosity.

There is a technical sense, it is true, in which we can talk of a 'religious' order, as of a calling belonging – as Robinson would say – to the experts. Of the religious vocation, the prevalent Anglo-Saxon view might be that there could be room for this sort of thing under the diversity of gifts of the Spirit, but that in a world with real problems to be faced, and pressing work to do, it is as well that there are not 'too many like that'. As between Mary and Martha, it is for the busy concern of the latter (whatever tribute we may pay to Mary) that our sympathy is tacitly reserved.

Popular approval has long canonized (in the Celtic heretic Pelagius) a Welshman whose influence across the English border has been disproportionate and malign. Ours is an age that can so fail to understand the religious vocation that it will be sorrowingly said of a new postulant, even by lifelong church people, 'I could understand it, if only it were doing somebody any good!'

About prayer Dr Robinson has this to say: '[It] is the responsibility to meet others with *all* I have, to be ready to encounter the unconditional in the conditional, to expect to meet God in the way, not to turn aside from the way.' Prayer is giving ourselves to people, which is the 'heart of intercession'. 'To pray for another is to expose both oneself and him to the common ground of our being; it is to see one's concern for him in terms of *ultimate* concern, to let *God* into the relationship.'[12]

A similar view is taken of the sacraments. Liturgy is not, for the Christian, a religious rite but 'the proclamation, the acknowledgement, the reception, the adoration, of the holy in, with and under the common . . . . The Holy Communion is the proclamation to the Church and to the world that the presence of Christ with his people is tied to a right receiving of the common, to a right relationship with one's neighbour.'[13] In such an account of the Eucharist nothing is said of thanksgiving or sacrifice, and God would not seem to be specifically active either here or as a real recipient of prayer. We could go about our lives finding the holy in the common without the Church having any particular point or relevance, except for those we are to label the 'religious'.

This would surely bring about a strange and unmodern separation of the people or '*laos*' from the experts. And there is also the separation that Dr Robinson makes, perhaps with rather little historic sensitivity, between what he detects in the 'medieval' and in the contemporary outlooks. He quotes with approval the remark from George Macleod's *Only One Way Left* that traditional prayer forms 'go dead on us' because they are conceived in medieval terms and 'we are not really conditioned to read what they are really saying. For medieval man life was dull, brutish and short. Life here was over against the real life of the Spirit.'[14]

Somehow it is now different for us, 'girt about with possibilities' in a modern age. Dr Robinson's advice for us about prayer is essentially this: first (as we all know very well), a natural discipline of prayer is not easy to acquire or persevere in. Most of us will be constantly dissatisfied with the progress we make. Perhaps we could be wrong then in pursuing prayer at times set aside for it. This may be the way for the experts, but not for us if we are 'not the praying type'. Prayer at times of regular withdrawal is then likened by Dr Robinson to taking cold baths or forced constitutionals, instead of observing the simple rules of good hygiene and enjoyment of life. Hence, it is suggested, since the traditional teaching on prayer 'doesn't work for us', that we should give it up, and join those people whose 'prayer is in the practice of their trade' and in their relations with other people 'in depth'.

A Robinson-type qualifying note is now introduced. Having been cautioned against disengagement as a religious perversion, even to receive strength to return to the world, we are told a little puzzlingly, 'I should be the last to say that periods of disengagement are not absolutely vital'. In one such period of 'withdrawal' he wrote *Honest to God* (an activity incidentally that many of us might rather have counted as 'engagement'). Dr Robinson is convinced that his thinking is only done with pen in hand, writing, and he is really praying for people in involvement with them, as in seeing students, writing and interviewing. 'The pentecostal point, as it were, is in the engagement.'[15]

It is here that the sources of the Christian life seem to be confused with the fruits of it. Certainly allocation of time as between work and prayer will vary immensely with the temperament and kind of vocation. But for the Christian it will ultimately be the life of prayer that is primary: it has been said to be an anticipation of heaven carried over unbroken into that life. It will be enrichment and revelation drawn from prayer that will ensure that we find room for greater calls on our service and involvement. But William Temple's words for such a situation are surprisingly direct: that any man who begins to find it so for him should beware. 'It is not that works are primary and prayer helps them. Prayer is primary and works test it.'[16]

If I may speak from the user viewpoint as a non-expert of forty years' standing, I would find Dr Robinson's advice on prayer misconceived and even harmful. Most of us as adults are probably more retarded in prayer than in any other activity of life. We often cling mechanically to well-worn prayer forms, and it is a commonplace that these 'go cold' when we use them without real effort or depth. None of us need feel guilt at altering or temporarily giving up altogether a too-well-established routine of prayer. But our prayer-life, however fitful and frail it be, seems always to suffer and be diminished if we are for long content to let it drift. We have the strong sense that we are fleeing down the years from the encounter where the richest meaning of life has been in some way glimpsed by us.

One could doubt profoundly whether the apprehension of God does – in any meaningful sense – lie in engagement as such; or whether the world unredeemed by the transcendent has anything holy in it at all. It will be readily enough claimed that one or other form of human relationship is in a real sense 'holy communion', that 'whenever I look down a microscope I find God', or that 'one is nearest God's heart in a garden'. We must be careful we do not by this fall into sentimentality easy to affirm but eliciting from us little in active response.

In all these statements about God in the natural order, or even in human relationships *per se*, I can find only a limited meaning for me. As a busily engrossed man, lecturing, researching, sitting at a typewriter, administering, attending committees – and even synods! – I have to ask myself whether any effective spiritual life is to be culled (by me) from all this busyness with action and execution in themselves. Even where the motivation and enjoyment might be of the highest (as in writing of this present kind), I wonder whether too large a share of combativeness or Pelagian self-justification does not blemish the task.

As well as prayer 'going cold', it might of course happen that giving ourselves to our neighbours in depth could cool off for us in just the same way. In spite of all we are taught about worldly concern and engagement in the common, we might after all find ourselves not very good at loving our neighbour. We may appear – in the result – to be 'not the out-giving type' at all.

What are we to do about this? Are we to be advised to shift from the encounter with our neighbour to a primary concentration with learning to love and tolerate ourselves? This paradoxically might not be bad advice, if – by retreating to make a better advance – it were to bring back the personality to its prime relation with God.

Bernardine Bishop – in the essay I have quoted before – finds the trouble with the 'God the Neighbour' avenue is that we can become dispirited without the illumination of prayer.

> The vital stages whereby Christ becomes, for the individual Christian, an inner reality seem to have got left out . . . . Unless we come to know ourselves, our relations with others will remain charged with projections, compulsive demands, compensations for failures, unadmitted wishes, escapes from loneliness, repressed antipathies, and the nicer we are trying to be, the likelier it is that our aggressions will run underground and emerge elsewhere as cruelty . . . .
>
> God the Neighbour is a healthy sign of restiveness. But he is no answer. Indeed he represents another mechanism whereby the Incarnation is evaded.[17]

TENSIONS

Ut tensio, sic vis
Hooke's Law of Elasticity

A healthy Christian theology must generate tensions out of its very subject matter. These of themselves give it force and strength. In the ideal state they are not to be relaxed but kept taut. With the physical law of elasticity, Robert Hooke three hundred years ago found that *the power is proportional to the tension,* and this truth has in it a broad and useful analogy for theology.

No single age in the Church's history, and certainly no single interpreter, could present a fully balanced statement of Christianity. The pressures and priorities of contemporary thought forms will always preclude this. And the secular world that generates these pressures will seldom be concerned about theology at all, though it will be a stagnant Church that does not take account of such pressures, and a dying Church that lives by its memories of the past.

Political man will all too easily recognize what the Church's social gospel may mean to the causes he holds dear, and in which he may be willing to sacrifice himself. In movements against racism and militarism, world poverty and discrimination, Christian individuals have held an honourable place, though the total of effective Christians in public life has never in our own time been large enough.

A theology that is to proclaim the whole belief of the Church must be conscious of the insights of other times with different priorities and temperaments. The eternal priority is devotion to Christ, in setting forth the truth about his life and person. But in our own day, we are certain to be found taking limited views, or concentrating in areas where, in the climate of the time, stress is thought to be needed. Some of the great books and nearly all the lesser ones are thus in some ways partisan.

From this fact comes the undoubted appeal of the 'new'

writing in theology, of which Robinson's *The New Reformation?*[18] and Lloyd Geering's *God in the New World*[19] are fair examples. This could be why it is good that the 'peace of the Church' should from time to time be shattered, especially where it is a complacent peace, held by inward-looking or nominal Christians. This is certainly not to say that these writers are useful simply because they provoke us to clear-headed answering, or because 'error can be tolerated when truth is free to combat it'. Nor is it because the 'new' writings have reached newspaper headlines and books about theology have become best-sellers.

Writings such as these, even from positions well outside the official teachings of the Church, contribute to the tension under which the Christian faith must exist. The extent to which strangers and many within the Church's fold have been helped by them is something the traditionalists have in humility to take account of. What someone called the 'almost audible sigh of relief' that greeted *Honest to God* points to the real predicament of thousands of people. In the letters quoted in the SCM paperback, *The Honest to God Debate*, one writer could speak of a book that for him 'had drawn the strands together and bedded them in the New Testament', and had removed for him the sense of guilt about 'not being able to believe what I felt I ought to believe'. From another 'perhaps one of the greatest blessings is that you – and the men who have inspired you – have made the Church seem alive again, when for years it has seemed so unbearably dead'. 'What you have started is going to bring the Church back into the market place and involve the spiritual interest of millions who have chosen for a variety of reasons to consider themselves as not "religiously minded".'[20]

In her finest witness the Church has accepted the paradox that is set at the heart of Christianity. There is the truth – at the one pole – of Christ's transcendent majesty, revealing to men the express and glorious image of his Father. And there is the truth that shows him serving and sacrificing, calling for our own commitment and absorption in him, and – through him – with all men, wherever the world has need of our concern.

When we say these truths must be held in a living tension, we must be clear what we fully mean. Tension is not an erstwhile state we shall grow out of as wisdom and enlightenment increase. It is of the essence of the Church's being, supremely necessary if she is to be loyal to her gospel. For the Church's health the tensions of her theology and witness must be as taut as bowstrings.

Tensions will arise from the paradox of Christ's own nature, divine Logos and suffering servant. In our own nature and actions we have already found the tension between the ideas of service and perfect freedom. We have recognized too, in the present chapter, the paradox implicit where renewal and restatement – the popular impulse of ecumenism – have been set in motion by authority, personal and apostolic. The Second Vatican Council has pointed up, too, the tension between the individual's freedom of conscience (ultimately, as the Church teaches, inviolable) and his habit of loyally submitting his insights to the mind of the Church. For there will be tension also, as we formulate Christian beliefs, between the legacy of history and the personal apprehensions of the contemporary age.

The Church's action in the world is bound to raise tensions of itself. So often it will be claimed (frequently by people themselves affluent) that the Church should not have built a cathedral, a theological seminary or a choir school, but should be distributing its money to the poor. It was recently protested – of an undeveloped area – that the Church should not have sent a missionary when what was really needed was a trade union organizer instead.

One way in which the tensions of Christianity are not to be resolved is by the counsel of compromise or the middle path, particularly attractive to those within the Anglican tradition of religious freedom. The *via media* between opposite dogmatisms may be the essence of the British political genius, and even in Church order 'it hath been the wisdom of the Church of England . . . to keep the mean between the two extremes, of too much stiffness in refusing, and of too much easiness in admitting . . .'[21] But the 'middle way' cannot properly be a theological precept at all. Tensions are not to be slackened by avoiding *too much* secular concern, or *too much* withdrawal. The two polarities must interact and give each other life and meaning. The full-ness of devotion to God must be known by the fullness of identi-fication with the world.[22]

Dr Barbara Ward, in recently urging church and secular programmes of aid for undeveloped countries, before the Roman Church and the World Council of Churches, said this:

> To those who say that all this concern with world poverty and development is turning religion into materialism, the Bible has some very uncomfortable answers. God through his prophets says the exact opposite – that religion without concern for my neighbour's physical needs is quite simply not religion.[23]

As always, while the contemporary tide is flowing one way, while today's priorities are strongly social and secular, most of the Church's self-critics are warning us of the opposite dangers of transcendentalism and unworldly pietism! It is widely urged that the clergy will have to justify their separate existence by finding secular weekday vocations; as if the full-time pastoral ministry were not crucially necessary today and alarmingly undermanned. We generally guard ourselves against the excesses into which we are currently least likely to run. This slackening of the Christian tension is nowhere more apparent than in what is today being called 'religionless Christianity'.

Canon David Jenkins has recently spoken trenchantly about the secularizing of the Church's activities in an article 'The Swinging Church Strikes a Wrong Note'. The Church must today be asking what it is her real function to do.

> Why should ordained ministers be encouraged to think they have a role by sticking around with people who in operating social agencies clearly do have one? The Church's existence can only be valid if she has a role which is basically in-dependent of secularization and of the number of people who

at any one time recognized and subscribed to that role. This is the role of living by and pointing to the truths about God and man which are focused in Jesus Christ, and of being a particular channel of resources beyond our own which are available for human living . . . . The Church has nothing to contribute to a secularized world unless she is careful to live both in and beyond that world.[24]

CHAPTER 15

God's Action in History

> Purpose exhibits its own unity in the adaptations to changing conditions of which it is capable. We should therefore antecedently expect, what religious experience is found to affirm, that God not only controls all the world by the laws of its own being, inherent in its elements by His creative act, but that as He made it for the realization of certain values, *so in pursuit of those values He acts directly upon its course as occasion in His all-seeing judgement may require.*
>
> William Temple[1]

ARCHBISHOP TEMPLE's words, with the italics which are mine, bring us to a central affirmation of Christianity, God intervening in particular ways in the course of nature and history.

A great part of God's purpose for the world must be effected by the unswerving regularity of the laws of nature that he has brought into being. At the mental level God could operate – we may suppose – by inspiring the minds and purposes of men, bringing them into closer accord with his own. It may be that many of the effects of prayer are brought about by the reconciling of our minds and wills with God's, rather than trying clamantly to alter his purpose.

But beyond this there is still the idea of God acting within the course of nature, in ways relevant to a specific human situation. This is the sort of action traditionally called 'miracle', and it has been considered to be of a different order from God's general causation of all events. It is this special category of action that is being widely rejected today, not only by the avowed secularists but by many, including clergy, who would claim to stand well within the fold of Christian orthodoxy. Such supernatural interventions – it is alleged – make breaches in the smooth course of a world running under nature's orderly laws.

Yet such a smooth course can at best be ascribed only to one

P201-2

aspect of the ordinary world we know. Our own bodily
activities might themselves seem to fall into two categories.
There is first the 'silent' behaviour of our viscera and our hearts
and lungs, and our physiological regulators, 'servo-systems' over
which we normally have no purposive control. This could well
enough be said to follow from natural laws, although in a
palpably complicated biological situation. Secondly, there is
our willed and purposive behaviour; and this – whatever the
problems it raises for psychology and philosophy – introduces
a novel element not finally to be accounted for in physical
terms.

To this extent there seems already a dualism (if we can
provisionally accept such a figure of thought) in the way
phenomena happen. Although this is an orderly world with
regular physical laws, our free actions neither depend upon nor
disrupt such a system. Freedom does not forcibly set nature
aside, but feeds in new material, upon which nature's laws will
operate.

The philosophical problem of myself acting freely is as
profound as the problem of God acting by miracle. Both would
require the sort of world that does not run on deterministic
tramlines. Moreover, until we think of God as able to act
directly upon the world's course for the realization of certain
values, there would seem to be no possibility of his discriminant
compassion or concern for particular individuals ever being
effective. By no providence are we to be kept by him as the
apple of an eye, or to be hidden under the shadow of his wings.
No longer is this a God that, when I call upon him, will hear me.
We should have not a Christian world, but a sub-Christian
world; the austere and brave world of those good men Spinoza
and Einstein, yet still a sub-Christian one.

The efficacy of prayer must presuppose final freedom of
action for God in his universe, whether upon the minds or
bodies of men or upon inanimate nature. This remains true
whatever the new insights we are gaining about prayer. For at
the present day, as ingenious man's command of nature is more
widely achieved, we are ceasing to use intercessory prayer as a

list of wants to be gratified by special interventions. We would no longer call for public prayer upon an outbreak of typhoid or plague, when we need better sanitation or vermin control. We do not so rely upon God's provident care as to neglect the benefits equally given by him, whether of blood transfusions, antibiotics or safe contraceptives. These are parts of the natural order that intelligent people are to make use of. If they seem to curtail the scope for God's special intervention, they will be welcomed as instances of his beneficial ordering of the world, rather than taken as a refutation of any of the Christian teaching on prayer.

It is clear there will be pitfalls in keeping open a place for the 'special intervention' of God if we are to think of such activity as confined to conspicuous reversals of the natural course which we can isolate as 'prodigies' or 'miracles'. God's total governance of the universe must – in the economy of grace – be such of a piece that it is meaningless to talk of 'first order' or 'second order' activity at all. If we need to postulate his special intervention in the world, this need not be expected to happen fitfully or profusely. Yet to look for results from intercessory prayer (whether or not these be frequent or unequivocally recognizable) is to envisage no more violation of the laws of nature than asking me to turn on the light.

OBJECTIONS TO MIRACLE

Modern man's scepticism over miracle does not arise merely from a dislike of the untidiness of a world where God will intervene capriciously; though the idea of a creator constraining himself within the majestic regularities of his own laws makes a strong appeal to many who would never acknowledge themselves deists. A more telling objection to miracle is perhaps in the particularity it implies. This is like the objection to man's uniqueness and value in the face of astronomic space and time. To many it appears inconceivable that God – infinite act of being and author of creation – should concern himself with chosen individuals, now or two millennia ago, in our own speck of the universe. Such an objection pleads a rational and realistic world against the claims of special dispensation and the trans-natural. Its strength is that it looks alarmingly like common sense.

Miracles have moreover seemed an affront to many with mature religious beliefs. Not only have thousands of unedifying claims of the miraculous gained a superstitious credence through the centuries; but their very idea in principle is seen to make God too trivially concerned and parochial. To Hinduism and other ancient Eastern faiths, it is intolerable that God should be so humbled. The objectors are really saying again, with modern emphasis, 'This man blasphemeth'.

Special objection is taken to those nature miracles, such as transmuting water into wine or multiplying loaves and fishes, that are to us physically unimaginable. For miracles of other kinds can often seem to be made credible under a naturalistic view. Healing miracles, including rigorously investigated modern examples,[2] can be labelled psychosomatic, or hypnotherapic. Raising from the dead could be recovery from cataleptic trance. Virgin birth could be parthenogenetic (for biological parthenogenesis could be quite credible in the human species and scientists have in recent times seriously entertained examples of it), though the offspring would genetically be daughters and never sons. These explanations are all meant to remove the difficulty of the event being miraculous at all. But even explanations involving hallucinations or visionary exaltation in the beholder must still leave the difficulty of trans-natural causation. They help not our ultimate understanding but simply our imagination in laying hold of the event. We must avoid the fallacy of discounting a miracle merely because its circumstances are physically imaginable, or because it is only 'a very little one' (as the maidservant in the Captain Marryat novel who excused on such grounds a baby whose existence needed apology).

The great host of these objections – 'folly to the Greeks', 'scandal to the Jews' – come from a timidity in grasping what God's incarnation could really imply. God's discriminant concern in particular situations – a God who acts – is at the very core of Christian belief. Incredibly, sometimes, to us, his action involves not the cosmos in broad abstract, but our own unedifying selves. This is of a piece indeed with the Christ-child's lowly birth among us, of which C. G. Jung has memorably said: 'There can be no birthplace more lowly than the foul rag-and-bone shop of our hearts.'[3]

It is highly to be expected that such a transaction will affront purely rational belief, and that scientifically oriented men will, regretfully or impatiently, reject it out of hand. How much easier, it will be exclaimed, it would be to propagate among humanists and all men of good-will the ethical gospel of the Sermon on the Mount, if only the supernatural were not so obstinately part of the package!

Despite all this we have still the astonishing claim of a God taking our own nature upon him in human life and form. It is not simply that the virgin birth need hold the central importance long given to it, if not in theology or in apostolic writings, at least in popular piety. Many Christians indeed have held that a natural birth would seem more appropriate than a miraculous one for the incarnation of the Son of God. Whatever their historic credibility, it cannot be that these events of the nativity (which the earliest believers could not have known about and upon which Mark and John and Paul are silent) are the real credentials of Christ's divinity.

But those who would demur at the outset over the biological anomaly of a virgin conception will, as they study the Gospels, be confronted with 'greater things than this'. In an age where the common emphasis is on an 'ethical teacher' or 'Jesus, the man like us', we are brought back to Christ's challenge to his own followers: 'Who say ye that I am?' To answer, we have to stretch all our apprehensions, our mystical sense and those faculties that lie deeper than reason, into some conception of what God's incarnation could portend for the natural order:

The real central miracle ... that staggers the imagination is the

Incarnation. If we once believe that God himself entered into human life and passed through a human experience, then a belief in the Virgin-birth follows naturally and brings no new difficulty. The historical Incarnation involves a break with the past and a new and unprecedented divine activity, beside which the wonder of the Virgin-birth sinks into insignificance.[4]

At the supreme affirmation of the Creed, that the Son of God was incarnate and made man, the head and knee were traditionally bowed. Faced with the Incarnation and its whole import, it must be that all the faculties of the mind and intellect, as they behold it, are bowed too.

Intellectual men, seldom commanding a surplus of rich possessions, are apt to read complacently the warning about the camel at the needle's eye. Yet the pride of a sophisticated mind could in the end offer a disability still greater – as being the corruption of a nobler faculty – than the mere acquisitiveness of the rich. In our own natures, the last enemy to be destroyed may in the end be the greatest. It may be the infirmity not of oligarchs nor of merchant-princes but of the intelligentsia. We are in sad case if it be claimed that our intellectual stringency must hold us back from the apprehension of God.

Writing of the knowledge of God, Father Gerald Vann says:

We leave far behind us the mental ability which comes of book-learning or the analysis of experience by a keen intellect: we are in the realm of the wisdom which comes direct from God, and which you are likely to find in the unlettered and simple more often perhaps than in the brilliant and the learned, since it is the fruit of the soul's docility to God.[5]

COULD IT HAPPEN?

When it is alleged that there has been a miracle, the scientist must be allowed the first question. We shall not be concerned at this stage with the authenticity of a particular instance of the miraculous. We are simply asking whether the laws of nature prevent us at the outset from entertaining any such category of claims at all.

The method of science is first observational. If we could be allowed ocular witness of a miracle (whether as a bystander in New Testament times, or with a modern work of healing), the empirical fact (it will be said) would have to be accepted, even if we could not at present explain it. Above all, we should not try to argue a fact away out of a sceptical predisposition.

We shall be over-optimistic if we expect scientists always to behave as observers like this. In speaking, for example, of telepathy, a nineteenth-century scientist protested that neither the testimony of all the Fellows of the Royal Society nor the evidence of his own senses would lead him to believe in the transmission of thought from one person to another independently of the recognized channels of sense. T. H. Huxley, faced with the reluctant witness of a committee of the Dialectical Society to a series of paranormal phenomena, refused to join the committee and continue the investigations. 'Supposing the phenomena to be true', he wrote, 'they do not interest me'.[6] There are thus *a priori* assumptions by which scientists may claim in advance that certain events cannot occur.

For, as well as to observe and record, the scientist has the task of discovering relationships and causes linking natural phenomena. He will thus have much to say about the *probability* or lack of probability of certain classes of events. The probability of a miracle happening is so unquestionably minute that we should in fact expect a scientist to try stubbornly to explain it on other grounds, or even – in the short run – to reject the evidence.

It is commonly suggested that what appears miraculous today will eventually be understood within a wider framework of natural law. Not only did primitive people attribute earthquakes and tempests directly to their deities, even Newton provisionally reserved the earth's spin on its axis to the special action of God. Could there – it will be asked – even be natural laws so rarely exemplified that their results – like the visit of a comet – could seem to us prodigious and unique? Such arguments could be welcomed where they make a *class* of event less mysterious to science. But as explanations they would say nothing of an event's causation, only adding something to its plausibility.

For scientific laws are statements and predictions about probability. A purposeful act – whether it be postulated of man or of God – is in this sense not a member of a class of events, but in its own right unpredictable and unique. It is a misunderstanding of scientific law to think of our own purposes coming under its ordinance. To take one example of such an act of purpose, Archbishop Thomas Cranmer, when he was burned at the stake, first thrust into the flames his right hand with which he had written his much-repented recantation. This was a highly unusual piece of human volition. If any natural law was in question, we could call it the physiological law of reflex pain avoidance. Yet confronted with this information about Cranmer, we do not feel obliged to say that any law of nature has been breached, or that we must extend the principles of physiology to take account of any new facts.

Even if we set out on the impossible task of scanning Cranmer's motivation, psychological history and personal conditioning, we should still be avoiding the real question. For the Archbishop's action originated with human decision and will. It is true that certain psychological or emotional predispositions of its author could have made it more likely; but it is not, in its happening, to be accounted for by any appeal to physiology or by any facts about the natural system.

Someone may still answer that for Cranmer's action we have an efficient cause within the natural system, namely the firing of a neurone and the contraction of appropriate muscles. What makes God's miraculous action within the natural order inconceivable is that we cannot imagine efficient causation getting a toehold within the system at all. But this is a metaphysical difficulty we are not meeting for the first time with God. If it is to puzzle us philosophically (as well it may) it will be as an impediment to the whole purposeful order. For the explanatory gap runs not between God on one side and the created world on the other, but cleanly through our own selves, between our conscious purposes and their fruition in nerve impulse and action.

Again, it will be objected, our purposive action (although it might fairly be said not to be *ordained* by natural law) is nevertheless located in a physical frame where the laws of science must operate. Nothing can happen that is 'impossible' by these laws, from our own volition or even with the uniqueness of a miracle.

We shall have to ask, then, what is the real binding force of those principles we call the laws of nature? Soon after the quantum revolution in physics, as early as 1928, in his Gifford Lectures published as *The Nature of the Physical World*, Sir Arthur Eddington gave a survey of the status and kinds of natural law at work in the universe.[7] He distinguished three possible categories.

The first, which includes all the laws of conservation, as of mass, momentum, energy, electric charge and the rest, Eddington calls the 'identical laws'. These cannot be violated, because they are not – in a proper sense – controlling laws. They are indeed tautological in that they apply to different but overlapping aspects of nature, or to different measurements of a single physical property. A statement in terms of one conservation law will carry necessary implications under another. These 'identical' laws will remain unbroken while two and two make four, for they are obeyed in the same sense as a 'law' relating the measurements made by a foot and a metre ruler.

The second category of Eddington's contains the important 'statistical laws' which are responsible for most of the uniformity we see in everyday nature. We have already found this uniformity, governing the behaviour of immense numbers of molecules, to be a matter of very high probabilities. This is the level at which the ordinary world can be said to be determinate. At the plane of single events, as exemplified in the behaviour of the elementary particles of quantum mechanics, the physicist can find no determinism. In the same way the actuary can make accurate mass predictions but can never foretell the fate of an individual life-policy holder.

We have already surmised that the freedom of quantum mechanics might operate at significant points within the human brain. But there is nothing we can say with certainty in physical terms of the impact of mind or will upon the body. We cannot even be sure that a volition and the firing of a neurone stand in a temporal causal relation at all. The mind, we have insisted, is untranslatable into any currency of particles and energy. It cannot be discussed at all by analytic statements made about brains or neurones or molecules. Nor can we hold it to be bound by the statistical laws that apply to these entities in the world of nature. It is true that our minds are constantly assailed and engaged by what the world, through our senses, puts into them. But the phenomena of ordinary perception themselves pose an obstacle to understanding tantamount to a miracle. We have, too, the unexplained operation of psychosomatics, and its special area of hypnotherapy, for which there is an abundance of evidence an unbiased observer must admit. But these do not really pose new or strange problems: there is just the same mystery in the way human volitions are from moment to moment registered as events in the physical world.

Questions of God acting in nature would seem to present the same difficulties, no more and no fewer, as questions of mind acting in body. Eddington has claimed, quite realistically:

> Either the physicist must leave his causal scheme at the mercy of supernatural interference from me, or he must explain away my supernatural qualities. In self-defence the materialist favoured the latter course; he decided that I was not supernatural – only complicated.[8]

Eddington's third category is that of the 'transcendental laws', the only ones – as he maintained – that could be genuinely decisive for or against particular events. Where statistical laws are characterized by continuity, transcendental laws would have the property of dealing in discrete whole numbers. They would avoid fractions in the way quantum theory does. If transcendental laws exist, they will be harder to find because we will no longer be getting back from nature merely what we have put into it. Such laws would be foreign to any scheme we could ourselves subconsciously have constructed ('God made the integers', it has been said, 'Man made all else'). Indeed, if the capacity to predict be really one of the requirements of a valid scientific construct, the transcendental laws might not form a proper part of the scientist's conceptual apparatus at all.

If the real causation of events is by conative minds, ultimately sovereign over the natural world, these would be disclosed by purposeful acts, whether of man or of God. A purposeful self is adaptive and self-adjusting. It is a property of minds to act appropriately to an external situation. One pitfall in thinking of God like this is, of course, that it could picture him as being so out of control of his world that he must need periodically to step in, to catch up with or accommodate to events. But part of the element to which God will react (if the idea be tolerable even as a figure of thought) will be the changing situation brought about by human freedom. None of God's action in the world need seem capricious or uncertain from moment to moment. The change and instability in the world would result from human self-will and inconstancy. This is the situation that, for each of us, God's immutable love must be reacting to, so that even he can appear to us to 'act' and 'change'.

I know that I am most completely 'myself' when I use the freedom that pertains to final causation. Moreover, if I am to allow any place in the cosmos for such original action of my own, I must needs think of God as having at least the same order of sovereignty within the world. Admittedly it is philosophically unusual to infer what must be infinite and essential in God by analogy with what is so partial and rudimentary in myself. Yet both would seem to be mysteries of the same order, if not of the same depth. And both pass so unnoticed by science that they demand or admit of no explanation within the world-frame that scientists use.

It seems probable then that, while the scientist deals with large-scale phenomena, statistically predictable, the '*noumena*' that are the real sources of events must always elude his grasp. For these we have to look to conscious and purposive minds. If something to be called 'miraculous' were at times a component of God's action, such events need not appear wild or erratic, but reasonable and even predictable. They could disclose a world that is organic to God in the sense that our natural bodies seem to be to ourselves. They could still be as harmonious with the laws of nature as my own purposeful acts, which occur within a behaviour pattern largely reflex and determinate. Like such acts, they would be a most highly significant species of event, even though (cosmically speaking) excessively rare and seemingly untypical.

DID IT HAPPEN?

The second question is the historian's, and it is concerned with both evidence and inherent probability. Both are needed to establish credibility where an event has not been directly witnessed. In an approximate way they will be looked for in inverse ratio to each other. Where an event is highly likely to happen, it may be accepted on evidence rather slight. The less its intrinsic likelihood, the higher the standard of evidence that will be looked for. Scientific investigation would, of course, follow a wholly different procedure: if the evidence is open to doubt, an event can generally be repeated by controlled experiments as many times as is necessary. But the historian is under the handicap of dealing with the unique. The evidence is hearsay; the event was perhaps experienced by a few witnesses in the distant past and their accounts may be factually sketchy, or may even disagree in important details. The tests to be applied will be the apparent reliability of the witnesses, and the coherence of the story, both within itself and externally.

The inherent probability of the gospel miracles is admittedly so small, that even with what would normally be good evidence many a man would remain doubtful. No detached person is likely to be won to the Christian faith by the claim that its founder worked miracles; and we must not be affronted if well-disposed non-Christians generally hold the gospel evidence too slight to carry conviction in view of the enormous improbability it involves.

It is often asked, if some miracles are to be admitted, where the believer will stop short of credulous acceptance of claims made for every local relic and shrine. It will not be enough to reply: 'I shall believe where the evidence seems sufficient, and reject where it is not'; for it is not solely evidence that we are weighing. The Church has not indeed been over-ready to admit instances of the miraculous. As E. L. Mascall points out, traditional theology has been so anxious to see a consistent world of natural law, rather than one with frequent miracles, as the basis of God's activity, that it has in fact based its classical arguments for God's nature and existence on the former rather than the latter. [9]

We may centre our historic discussion of miracle upon one instance, the alleged bodily resurrection of our Lord Jesus Christ; for we shall be dealing here both with an age-long affirmation of the Church as well as one that is widely contested by anti-supernaturalist teaching today.

As a familiar secular gloss on the Resurrection, an example may be cited from Lloyd Geering: 'From shortly after his death men found themselves strangely moved and renewed by the power and spirit of the same Jesus and when the Gospel of Jesus Christ is proclaimed, it is still found to speak with power, His power. The Lord is risen indeed!'[10]

The Apostles – for some reason – interpreted these subjective impressions as a bodily resurrection; because – it is said – of the supernaturalism that permeated Jewish thought, or because Jesus during his life had spoken to them of his rising.

Without doubt, such teaching has wide acceptance in some of the Churches today. It is said to be a viewpoint from which Christianity can be made credible to many who are labouring under intellectual difficulties presented by the Creeds, even to humanists and men of good-will who may be constructively Christians without acknowledging it.

There are obvious difficulties in this position. First, it would evidently not unite all Christians. There are still multitudes of men and women, many of them dedicated in their lives, some of them sophisticated in modern science, whose joyful hope springs from their belief in Christ's resurrection. It would be a greater loss than is sometimes assumed if these were dismissed as simple conservatives who have not caught up with the fresh insights of current theology.

Second, a rejection of this part of the gospel must loosen Christianity from its essential base in history. It is, of course, difficult to expect firm pronouncements without appearing to beg open and legitimate historical questions. Few Christians today would give the same literal acceptance to everything miraculous in the long and uneven anthology of the Bible. Clearly scepticism about the miracle of Moses' staff will have smaller consequences for Christianity than rejection of the historical resurrection. But if subjective judgement is to be recommended, many believers will feel their whole position exposed and vulnerable. If some things are to be stubbornly held *de fide*, and others to be left permissive, is not the boundary line personal and likely to shift with time? One man will query Enoch's passage to heaven, another will have doubts about the bodily resurrection. These are difficulties to be squarely faced, for they apply in some degree to the interpretations made by us all.

Where individual judgement is used, it must be guided by historical and critical insight. It is theoretically possible for a document to turn up that would invalidate a New Testament statement, however unlikely it may be at this distance in time that new historic light will be shed. Changes in doctrinal emphasis have generally been based on theological or even scientific grounds, rather than on new historical findings. There is no safe high-water mark above which the Christian can retreat with his corpus of belief. He holds his beliefs in the faith that their basis in history (which is crucial to them) will not in fact be overturned by fresh historical evidence.

There are some who would contend that the real risk of faith cannot be the historical one. No present reality such as our faith in Jesus Christ can be dependent upon a past event. The risk must rather be eschatological, that God will in the end turn out not to justify our trust in him. But if we were altogether to sever our beliefs from their background of past events, we would be no longer professing a religion of the Jesus of history.

Dr John Knox, in *The Church and the Reality of Christ*, has ingeniously tried to overcome this difficulty by holding that we are dependent for our knowledge of the resurrection of Jesus upon the Church's memory of it. It is the present existence of the Church which is the great verifying fact; and it is the Church's living tradition – unbroken from the Apostles to ourselves – that must give the event a greater authenticity than the secondary evidence of any historical writing.[11]

We must accept indeed that our beliefs cannot rest solely upon the satisfactory solution of historical questions. There is a component of faith as well as history, to which we must shortly turn in the next section. It would be wrong to assume that if only the historical evidence were strong enough, all rational men would be Christians.

While we speak of individual judgement in assessing Scripture and history, we must not forget the Church's role. Theology is ultimately – we have maintained – a function of the Church as the body of Christ. The theologian is a believing member of that body to whom this special activity has been entrusted. The Church is moreover the believing company of Christians across all the ages; so that no theology can be entirely contemporary, but must take account of the interpretative genius of Christian men and women of other times. The discovery that men of other ages had different world-views or philosophic backgrounds from ourselves should not oblige us to dismiss these from consideration. We ought not to expect that theological truth about God's relation to man and the world, or man's interpretation of sacred history, should undergo the same revolutions that render the science texts of ten years ago value-less today, or enable intelligent sixth-formers to know better than Darwin or Rutherford.

To invoke the tradition of the Church is not simply – as G. K. Chesterton approvingly said – to give votes to the dead as well as the living. It is rather to recognize that no single age can generate out of its own pressures and priorities a balanced theology. If the Church has in her keeping a body of revealed truth, we may expect her to seem conservative in expressing it, however startling and radical such teaching may be in its contemporary application.

Sometimes theological judgements of former times have come to seem defective or unbalanced, and have had to be corrected. This is going on all the time, and the Church today is increasingly loath to use the stigma of 'heretic'. Nor has any essential doctrine of the Church been so lost; for it is only in a limited sense that the heresies of one generation can be said to have become the orthodoxy of the next. In emphasis and exposition, it is true, there will be constant movement and new light. The visible face of Roman theology has been transformed in this last decade, and much more will happen in our own time.

In Anglican theology there was – in some ways – a compar-able time at the publication of *Lux Mundi* in 1889, with the essay that brought the young Charles Gore under censure for trucking with Darwin, or doubting the inerrancy of the Old Testament or Jesus' omniscience while on earth. Yet Gore lived to become during the first part of the twentieth century the entrenched champion of Catholic orthodoxy.

At the time of his ordination in 1908, William Temple's beliefs about the historical resurrection had been held to be insecure. Yet as a prelate, philosopher and theologian, his influence on the Church of his day was to be massive. He was the man who was to teach: 'To believe in miracle is to take divine personality in deadly earnest.'

To turn to the scriptural evidence itself, we all suffer the disability of being hardly impartial in face of the record. The traditional Christian may fear to acknowledge that the evidence may not sustain the faith he has been taught to build upon it. The secularist may equally be unjudicially anxious to reduce the meaning to much less than the words say. In presenting the argument in these pages, I cannot believe that I am altogether disinterested in the conclusions reached. Still, the record calls to be examined, and objectivity need not be quite lost by the predispositions we have to acknowledge.

It has recently been reputably argued that the Gospels and the Acts of the Apostles contain evidence of the sort a secular historian would be delighted with. On the assumption, in fact, that the events narrated really happened, the historic record and the sequelae in the apostolic Church could not really be expected to be stronger than they are. In his Sarum Lectures (1960–61), *Roman Society and Roman Law in the New Testament*, the historian A. N. Sherwin-White has in a notable passage chided the 'form critics' of the New Testament for their unwarranted scepticism. He comments favourably on the amplitude and credibility of our materials for a life of Jesus, as compared with those for his greatest contemporary, Tiberius Caesar. Of the Acts of the Apostles, Sherwin-White holds the confirmation of historicity to be overwhelming. For the character and outlook of St Paul, it has been said that we have a fuller and far more revealing record than for any other figure in the ancient world, save possibly Cicero. It is a fact, and not one to be complained of, that a sacred book will generally receive more searching scrutiny than a secular one. But it could appear that doubts of the resurrection narrative have often arisen not from an anxious study of the record, but from attitudes conceived on general philosophical grounds, and reflected in a sceptical predisposition brought to their editing.

The central difficulty of a 'reduced' or demythologized Christianity is that it is obviously not what the Gospels are about. Whatever we may personally think of the credibility of the New Testament, it will be common ground that its writers believed in the historicity of what they had written. W. M. Ramsay's vindication of Luke as a meticulous historian is for example well known.[12] The third Gospel is flawlessly accurate in every detail of dates, secular or priestly titles and offices, and contemporary happenings for which there is independent check. There is no detectable break in his narrative style between history and the alleged 'veridical myth' which – if it be not historic – must have been clearly known to Luke as an imposture and literary fabrication.

There is broad agreement in the historic record, (1) that the tomb was empty, (2) that the figure the Apostles and others beheld after the alleged rising was Jesus of Nazareth, (3) that the body so beheld had properties and capacities that were different from those of the natural body, (4) that the appearances, though some of them common to many (the greatest reported number is five hundred), were never to an indiscriminate public but always among the followers of Jesus.

We may refer for a recent discussion of the resurrection narrative to that of Dr A. R. C. Leaney (Selwyn Lectures 1966: *The Christ of the Synoptic Gospels*) where he deals with reports of three transnatural events, the Virgin Birth, the Transfiguration and the Resurrection. He is firm in the view that the Gospels contain a great amount of material that is altogether credible, which it is hard to think anyone would invent, like the statements describing Jesus as a man of Nazareth, his taking a house as a mission centre at Capernaum, and so on. Its point was to show that Jesus, a man about whom other and wonderful things might be narrated, was a man well known in a local time and place. Most of his contemporaries rejected him, not because he was an impostor making claims he could not perform, but because he had done great deeds and yet they knew him as an ordinary man. This was a 'stumbling block' to them. In Dr Leaney's assessment, the plain historical material in St Mark's Gospel fastens Jesus to history as firmly as he was nailed to the cross.

After a consideration of the virginal conception and the transfiguring of Jesus before three of his followers, Dr Leaney concludes that these narratives 'convey truth as the evangelist and others of his day saw that truth'. They have been therefore held by some to be non-historical, yet veridical.

Jesus may not have been transfigured before the three apostles, but he *was* a divine being . . . let it be emphatically stated that this is *our* way of looking at the material and not that of the evangelists. Their way of looking at it is to record it in order to teach us something about their divine subject, but also because for them it actually did happen. Had they not thought so, they would not have recorded it.[13]

The narratives of the Resurrection are central and crucial in a way that the virgin birth and the Transfiguration, whatever view we take of their historicity, cannot quite be. We cannot moreover, maintains Dr Leaney, interpret them as we could the others on the basis of the Old Testament or contemporary Judaic imagery. 'The situation out of which they arise is remarkable. It is the situation which must have existed. We can say "must have" because history in its general and secular sense needs an explanation of the rise of the Christian Church on the ruins of the ministry of Jesus.'[14]

In the name of common sense, he goes on, we can repudiate any suggestion of trickery or stealing of the body by the disciples. Such a deception is morally inadequate to the heroism of the early Church or to its inception at all. The only evidence which the historians possess is the New Testament and if they do not believe it they must explain how it arose, for it is clear, unambiguous and unanimous.

There is and can be no objection to thinkers making efforts to work out an existentialist philosophy which will include confrontation with the crucified and relate their acceptance of his complete obedience to God to their own choice of an 'authentic existence'; and to regard such acceptance as the resurrection for them . . . What must be firmly stated is that such ways of looking at the matter cannot be called expositions of the New Testament, that is, of the only historical evidence we now have.[15]

The resurrection belief can hardly be attributed to the

disciples' expectations as a result of Jesus' teaching. None of his friends at first recognized their Lord. Reference to resurrection within his lifetime had been tied to the Pharisaic belief in a general resurrection. Matthew evidently thought this was already happening, with his premature account of saints coming out of their tombs. Paul lived his whole life in the imminent expectation of such a resurrection.

Though Paul – and after him the Nicene affirmation – speaks of Jesus having risen 'according to the scriptures' and John remarks that 'until then they had not understood the scriptures which showed that he must rise from the dead', it is hard to ascertain which Scriptures these might be. And although Jesus had prophesied his own rising, the disciples had evidently not understood his message, for his death left them frightened and despairing.

Is there, asks Dr Leaney, at the conclusion of his argument, a viable alternative to a programme of demythologizing and reinterpreting the Scriptures in terms of existentialist philosophy? It must be that we should try to enter deeply into the meaning of the Gospels for those who wrote them, and of the language they were impelled to use.

> At least, it may be pleaded that before we demythologize, we must understand the myth. When we do, it may turn out that we shall be obliged to say, annoyed to find how old-fashioned we sound, that the 'myth' 'became flesh and dwelt among us'; assuredly we shall not behold his glory unless we have the obedience of faith.[16]

SHOULD IT HAVE HAPPENED?

The final question is a theological one. It concedes that the intrinsic possibility of resurrection is so small that few will believe it who do not have experience of the Jesus it authenticates to men (and this in spite of the admitted historical difficulties involved in its dismissal). But what Christians find about him through faith may incline them at certain points to accept evidence about him which would be inconclusive about any other man. Farrer writes (in *Kerygma and Myth*) about the use of faith to strengthen evidence: 'it is possible through faith and evidence together, and through neither alone, to believe that Christ really and corporeally rose from the dead.'[17]

Questions freely asked today by those who would demythologize the Resurrection are: What does it do for our faith? What are the Gospel writers 'trying to say'? It will be stressed that we would teach a child today that Jesus loves him now, rather than that he rose from a grave 2000 years ago; and that in our active and involved life we may not often use resurrection teaching unless we be comforting the bereaved or aged. And it will be persuasively argued that the real message of the Gospels is of Jesus' final sacrifice and total self-giving for others: to follow this with a resurrection story is to impose a contrived happy ending.

All these reactions seem to assume that the Resurrection can be a piece of religious symbolism, perhaps saying something 'to us', but able to be taken up or left aside according as we may personally find it helpful. But if there be any suggestion that these events were historically true, they will be a part of God's saving acts, and thus must matter enormously. Whether or not some might think it appropriate for God to have managed his self-showing differently, the contrast between Christ humiliated and Christ risen and alive for ever, will be the great hinge-line on which history turns.

Nor will the chief significance of the Resurrection be in solving the historical puzzle of the rise of the Church out of the Apostles' despair. It is full of immediate power for us today. For it is only through the church that arose from it that we can today know anything about Jesus as a man of history. Such a confrontation is as necessary for us as for Thomas in the upper room, when - ahead of his time – he exclaimed, 'My Lord and my God', or for Saul when, on the Damascus Road, he asked fearfully, 'Lord, what wilt thou have me do?'

It is from the Apostles' conviction of a saving act in history that we can then refer our present experience of Jesus to the incarnate Christ of the Gospels. It is the Church's dynamic – in the faith of the risen Jesus – that has kept alive for us all that we can know of him today. As heirs of this belief, we are asking a high luxury of intellectual scepticism if we are to abandon it in our own time.

But some will ask, cannot the moral teaching of Jesus 'authenticate' the gospel, and provide the dynamic for its acceptance and spread? We must ask in answer: Does it do so today? Or did it for Jesus' own contemporaries? If it were a matter of admiring his good life or the Sermon on the Mount, good men have acclaimed these in every age whether they have called themselves Christians, humanists, or even atheists.

What such an ethical religion cannot tell us is whether these subjective apprehensions of authenticity or ultimate value in depth have any relation to the realities of power in the universe. Each of us would have admired the life of Jesus, and even tried to emulate it – if we had ever heard of it. But without his victory over death, we could have no particle of assurance that the love he showed was capable of ultimate triumph, or showed us anything at all about the governing principle of the world.

With all our hearts we would want to believe that love was the strongest stuff in the universe; but in the face of the world we see, it would need an unreasoning optimism to do so. Charles Gore could understandably exclaim that without the Resurrection, we could better believe that the ultimate power of the world was incarnate not in Jesus Christ but in Nero. However this may shock some of us in the security of studies, common-rooms and laboratories, there are many who bear the cross of the world's unlovingness who could draw no hope from a world unredeemed by Christ's sacrifice and triumph.

The very beauty and nobility of Jesus' character could even give added cause for gloom. That he, whose constant account of his mission related to the power with which he would reconcile the world with himself and his Father, should in the final hour be shown up as forsaken and deluded, would in itself be the deepest prognostication of cosmic despair.

We see constantly in the life of Jesus that God's love had to be revealed not as a *tour de force* of cosmic power, but in a human life, self-giving and self-emptying. The corollary of that life is shown in the Resurrection, authenticating in power what was first – and could only have been – perceived through love.

The triumph over death not only affirms Jesus' power. It reiterates his love. To his chosen followers, the forerunners of the lasting apostolate, he gave his last commission for the founding of a Church. His purpose among them cannot have been simply to vindicate himself in power, but to continue his same mission of love: commanding them to show it forth to all men wherever they might be, and assuring us that – in all the doubtings and perplexities of our secular time – he would always be with us, even until the consummation of the world.

Last Things

I look for the resurrection of the dead and the life of the
world to come.

Nicene Creed

LONG before the 'new theology' had arrived, the widespread
belief among secular men was that our 'personal survival' (so
far as it was thought important) lay in what we have created in
the world during our own span, or perhaps in our physical
continuity in our children.

> Man is mortal. What we value in life we have in the world
> here and now. In contrast with this very vital, vivid kind of
> life that you and I know here, all thought of immortal souls,
> life after death, heavenly existence, are but pale shadows in
> comparison.[1]

This is from the theologian Lloyd Geering; but some of the
scientists are found saying similar things. The highest reverence
the humanist Sir Julian Huxley would acknowledge (and it is a
prospect of real nobility) is for the process of 'emergent
evolution', with the continuing mental and ethical improvement of man. There will be a progressive increase in our
humanity and rationality and our command over the resources
of nature.

In Geering's words again:

> The life we have here with all its frustrations and finiteness,
> is capable of maturing to the best we can actually imagine,
> and this is the meaning of the Christian doctrine of the
> Incarnation.[2]

Bertrand Russell expresses his humanism in a more personal key:

> I believe that when I die I shall rot and nothing of my ego will survive. I am not young, and I love life. But I should scorn to shiver with terror at the thought of annihilation. Happiness is none the less true happiness because it must come to an end, nor do thought and love lose their value because they are not everlasting.[3]

A world-view centring upon man's efforts and aspirations in this life can contain much that is powerful and valuable. And if our notion of immortality is to be the still too common folk-belief that we are to wait for the hereafter to balance the deserts and accounts of this life, such a teaching would be better forgotten by the Church. For no man looking from himself to God's righteousness could hope for a future life by right of personal desert. G. K. Chesterton once recalled an old man who affirmed that he would thank God for his creation though he knew he were a lost soul. It has always been a strand in Christian devotion to wish to serve God for himself alone with no regard for hopes of heaven or pains of hell. St Francis Xavier expressed this in his fine hymn:

> My God, I love thee; not because
> I hope for heaven thereby,
> Nor yet because who love thee not
> Are lost eternally.

Remember, too, the noble love of God of the prophets of ancient Israel, for whom the after-life was at best shadowy and bleak, devoid of any heavenly reward. T. H. Robinson[4] writes of Jeremiah:

> the whole drama, good and evil, joy and suffering, the presence or absence of God, must be played out on the stage of this life. For the dead there was only Sheol, and the meanest life on earth was preferable to that. The full heroism

of a man as Jeremiah is not understood until this is appreciated. For him there was no martyr crown of glory. For him there was no triumph in another life. For him there was no prospect of the solution of doubt and the vanishing of shadows in the fuller light of God's immediate presence .... A life of suffering, of torture, of loneliness, of despair, lived in the service of a God who had ruined him and for the sake of a people who persecuted him – this was to meet with no reward save that sunless and godless Sheol which was the common lot of righteous and wicked alike.

But engagement with the world can only be a partial fulfilment, the fruit and not the source of the Christian life. To hold that we are mortal is to fail to understand our full selves. First, it is psychologically shallow to assume that concern for survival after death must be a self-centred assertion of the ego. With life in Christ, the personality has been integrated anew, with the ego made relative to the new centre. In the words we have already quoted from Bernardine Bishop:

> It is no longer a matter of the ego grinding itself into deformity against stony idols, but the union of the God above and the God within. The ego becomes spectator to that love, and, along with all the other human powers within us, fuel to that fire.[5]

It is in this newly won trust that we can love ourselves as carriers of Christ. It is here that the personality becomes conscious of a self-value impossible to extinguish or despise. We are become adopted of God in a sense that it will be blasphemy to under-represent. In nothing less than the life breaking beyond physical death can the enduringness of God's love for his children be expressed. It is from this that the hope of eternity arises which we could not with the wildest presumption claim in our own deserts.

Fully to believe this cannot be a beginning point; it must be the seasoned maturity of the Christian's faith. Whatever the

Church sets out in its confessions and formularies, no man will place eternity at the centre of his own creed, until he can plumb these depths from which the Christian hope arises. Like all belief this is fashioned out of tension with doubt. Just as we grow in our integrated personalities, and in realizing our full freedom, so we make progress in understanding our indestructible relation with Christ. We see more deeply the inexhaustible moral content of the world. The sense of sin is uncharacteristic of natural or secular man. It is the saints who best know their unworthiness in their own ego, and their indelible worth in the redemption of the Spirit.

So little moral progress do we make in our lifetime that we cannot believe this stops with physical death. He who has aroused this craving for righteousness in us, and quickened it by himself being born in us, will surely not leave his work unfinished. This day and hour are already significant because it is here that our eternal life has begun. We are weaving by our actions here 'the spiritual body which will be the garment and instrument of our spirits in the world to come'.[6]

We have faced the apparent unlovingness of a world in which there is evil and pain, and tried to answer the case it presents against belief in a loving God. For myself, the real 'dysteleology' or aimlessness of the world would arise if it had nothing personal in it outlasting extinction. Since God is eternal, an eternal purpose would seem necessary to realize his loving activity. With whatever incredulous sense of personal un-desert, I must believe that this purpose extends to those he has loved and made in his own image.

Nothing less can redeem the cosmic plan from a callous non-morality. Although our individual life-span be rich with love and creative achievement, if its duration be as of a match briefly lighted and passing its flame to the next, the total sequence – however prolonged in time – can have no lasting significance or hope. William Temple wrote, in his Gifford Lectures, *Nature, Man and God*:

. . . if this life only is permitted [men], it will one day make no

difference whether we have striven or not for noble causes . . .
An earth as cold as the moon will revolve about a dying sun.
Duty and love will have lost their meaning. The President of
the Immortals, if there be either immortals or president, will
have finished his sport with man. And how shall the argument which posited the righteousness of that same Potentate
allow us to rest in any such connexion? . . . If at the end there
is to be nothing but cold dead cosmos – which might as well
be chaos – then, though their presence shines like a jewel in
the prevailing gloom, yet it were more creditable to the
Determiner of Destiny that virtue and love had never
bloomed. That they should appear to be discarded makes the
ultimate principle of reality more ruthlessly non-moral than
if it had never given birth to them at all.[7]

RESURRECTION

But some man will say, How are the dead raised up? and
with what body do they come?

1 Corinthians 15:35

With the conclusion we have reached about the status of mind
in the world, the assertion that personality is extinguished with
the death of the brain would seem far from self-evident. With
naturalistic understanding of personality, making it simply a
late-in-the-day emanation from the organic world, we might
indeed have doubted that it could outlast bodily death. But here
we have concluded that mind is essentially untranslatable into
terms of space and time. It is an entity in its own terms, neither
composed of parts, measurable nor palpable. However closely it
may be in register with the phenomena of physiology, the death
of the personality would seem to require a greater homogeneity
between these things than we have been able to find. To the
cautious sceptic, extinction, not survival, may raise the greatest
problems for the rationality of the world.

Yet if extinction seems morally incredible, the survival of
death raises every manner of challenge from contemporary

philosophy. Eternity is impossible for us to conceptualize, difficult even to talk or think about with any clarity of idea. Neither a science of metaphysics, nor even a companion study of 'metachronics' would help us to speak confidently about a translation into an order so unimaginable.

The Christian doctrine of death and survival confronts us then with a mystery. Personality and body, it is insisted, are fundamentally a unity. As Professor Mascall has pointed out, it may surprise even the regular church-goer to find how different is the Christian doctrine of body and soul from the popular view of 'an angel driving a machine' or the Platonic idea of a psyche that is destined to emerge from its bodily prison.[8] In *Christian Theology and Natural Science*, he quotes effectively from a fragmentary sixteenth-century work, *De Resurrectione:*

> God calls even the flesh to the resurrection and promises it eternal life. To announce the good news of salvation to man was in effect to announce it to the flesh. For what is a man if not a reasonable being composed of soul and body? Shall we say that the soul in itself is the man? No, it is the soul of the man. And the body alone – is that the man? By no means; we should rather say that it is the body of the man. Since, then, neither soul alone nor body alone are man, but the thing called man arises out of their union, when God called man to the resurrection and the life, he called no mere part of man, but the whole man, body and soul together in one.[9]

What can these traditional teachings mean for modern Christians? We surely need not interpret them in any material terms of molecular regeneration and survival. Christian philosophy has developed very fully the doctrine of man as body and soul. Nor are these to be thought simply complementary or interlocking; they subsist in such a unity that we cannot think of one as separable from the other. This is an opposite view to the Hellenic one, that the body corrupts while the soul takes wing and returns itself to pure spirit. It contrasts, too, with the teaching of Descartes, at the so-called dawn of the scientific age, holding body and soul to be two separate and parallel entities.

To modern minds the implications of a bodily resurrection invite sophisticated ridicule. Yet such a doctrine is needed to present our survival with the completeness that personality entails. A disembodied continuance without the lineaments of our personal selves, would seem vacuous and unimaginable: so far is Christianity from refusing to take the body seriously. The clause in the Creeds affirming the resurrection of the body is a heritage from the Jewish emphasis on the wholeness of personality. Though we do not think in terms of fleshly continuity, we need not abandon the truth this doctrine captures and focuses for us. Archbishop Ramsey, in *The Resurrection of Christ*, stresses that this teaching, for fifty years virtually the stone cast aside, is today become for us the keystone of the arch.[10]

'God calls even the flesh to the Resurrection and promises it eternal life.' We are raised, then, in our total personal nature. In some manner, when the tedious extension of time and space shall have ceased, each of my qualities and modes of apprehension will be represented in my raised body. Just as in the resurrected body of Christ, each of his attributes was tangible and complete, so I shall be no less a person and personal than I am now.

Christianity takes its firm stand not only upon a certain record of history, but upon the wholeness of personality. It can neither despise nor undervalue the body; nor can it think of survival in pale terms of extruded soul-stuff. Jesus was incarnate and was raised from the tomb, without subterfuge or withholding, in a human body. His risen appearances are irreducibly connected with the disappearance of a fleshly body from a tomb.

But our understanding of the Resurrection will certainly go wrong if we start with the assumption that only the material and the molecular can in the last resort be the substrate of anything real. From this point the mind is reduced to the emanation or physiological function of the natural body; and secular theology follows logically enough by rejecting the transcendent, or what it calls the 'supernatural'. The resurrection of the whole person is then pronounced inconceivable because we have insistently tied the idea of personality to particles, molecules and the laws of nature.

Christians have through the ages believed death to be real and terrible, accounting it the last enemy that shall be destroyed. In a penetrating study of the theology of death, the Swiss theologian Oscar Cullmann has contrasted the Greek and Christian views.[11] We are shown Socrates discoursing serenely upon immortality up to the moment of the spirit's liberation from the body. Very differently, Jesus, in his last hours, was sorely afraid of death, not physically but of the apparent finality of death itself. In the darkness that had to veil his divine sight to make his human sacrifice real and availing, he cries out in his sense of dereliction. He is meeting death not as a friend, but in all its horror, being at that moment in the hands of God's worst enemy.

By his dying, Jesus conquers death by entering upon its own territory. To understand the Christian faith in resurrection, we must – Cullmann writes – disregard completely the Greek thought that the corporeal is bad and must be destroyed Death is not then beautiful as the escape of the soul from the body's trammels. On the contrary,

> the death of Jesus is as loathsome as the great painter Grünewald depicted it in the Middle Ages. But precisely for this reason the same painter understood how to paint, along with it, in an incomparable way, the great victory, the Resurrection of Christ . . . Whoever paints a pretty death can paint no resurrection. Whoever has not grasped the horror of death cannot join Paul in the hymn of victory: 'Death is swallowed up – in victory! O death, where is thy victory? O death, where is thy sting?'[12]

In writing to the Christians at Corinth, Paul is speaking of what is to us unsearchable. 'Behold, I shew you a mystery; We shall not all sleep, but we shall all be changed.'[13] To St Paul, soul and body are not opposites in the Hellenic sense. Though the Church is widely credited, in modern folk belief, with teaching the Greek idea of the severance of the psyche from the flesh, this has never been the Christian view of what happens at death.

Soul and body subsist together as inner and outer man. The inner cannot properly exist without the outer, the soul needing the body for its full life and expression. At the resurrection of the body affirmed in the Creeds, both will be raised in their full integrity. Soul is not to be released from body, but both from 'flesh'. Though St Paul uses the Greek word '*sarx*' for flesh, its meaning is very different from the Hellenic one of organic body. St Paul means by 'flesh', not the biological body, but its world-limited and egocentric plan of desires and aspirations. Flesh, like spirit ('*pneuma*'), is a transcendent power that can have both the inner and the outer man in its thrall. Flesh is the power of sin and death, and – as such – God's greatest antagonist. It is moreover in full possession of this 'body of death'. This is why death is equated with sin, being sin's wages, and why the body possessed by sin is subject to ills, sickness and death.

Against the power of the flesh is the power of spirit. Though flesh has established its dominion over the body, it has never fully possessed the inner man, where the quickening power of the spirit already resides. This is what becomes active when the desires of the ego are overtaken, and the self is integrated around a new centre, as we become 'carriers of Christ'. The whole hope of man is for the spirit to take control and so begin to reign. 'No wonder', exclaims St Paul, that 'we do not lose heart! Though our outward humanity is in decay, yet day by day we are inwardly renewed. Our troubles are slight and short-lived; and their outcome an eternal glory which outweighs them far. Meanwhile our eyes are fixed, not on the things that are seen, but on the things that are unseen: for what is seen passes away; what is unseen is eternal.'[14]

We groan indeed, we who are enclosed within this earthly frame; we are oppressed because we do not want to have the old body stripped off. Rather our desire is to have the new body put on over it, so that our mortal part may be absorbed into life immortal. God himself has shaped us for this very end; and as a pledge of it he has given us the Spirit.[15]

Thus can the body itself be set free and it is in this that we are shown a mystery. The substance of the body resurrected will no longer be that of flesh but of Spirit. 'As we have worn the likeness of the man made of dust, so we shall wear the likeness of the heavenly man. What I mean, my brothers, is this: flesh and blood can never possess the kingdom of God, and the perishable cannot possess immortality. Listen! I will unfold a mystery: we shall not all die, but we shall all be changed . . .'[16]

It is because sin has come by the free-will of fallen man that a saving act is necessary to God's plan. The Holy Spirit is the power alone able to conquer death and win all creatures back in such a redemptive process. We see his power in the healing of bodily ills and sicknesses; for under the dominion of the Spirit, the body is to be perfect. With each of the healing miracles, Jesus was found saying that sins had been remitted or forgiven.

The new world of Spirit was inaugurated in the resurrection of Jesus Christ. In his rising from the dead, he became 'the first-fruits of them that slept'. Resurrection is tied then to a total process of divine deliverance. So far it is seen fulfilled only in Christ; but we are taught in the New Testament that the state of eternal life has already begun for us, where the body is under the command of the Spirit. The victory has been won, and Jesus himself has died and expiated sin.

Oscar Cullmann draws his argument to a close in these fine words:

Christian faith proclaims that Jesus has done this and that. He arose *with* body and soul after He was fully and really dead. Here God has consummated the miracle of the new creation expected at the End. Once again He has created life as in the beginning. At this one point, in Jesus Christ, this has already happened! Resurrection, not only in the sense of the Holy Spirit's taking possession of the *inner* man, but also resurrection of the *body*. This is a new creation of matter, an incorruptible matter. Nowhere else in the world is there this new spiritual matter. Nowhere else is there a spiritual body – only here in Christ.[17]

LAST THINGS

But if we thus died with Christ, we believe that we shall also come to life with him.

Romans 6:8

It is upon these 'last things' that the bravest spirits have fixed their hope, in a kingdom whose consummation we cannot evenly dimly see or imagine. About the states of time, or the order of things that lie between, we can know nothing. 'Those that sleep in the Lord' wait – we trust – as we wait, however different may be the dimension of time, or the state of interim existence till the tally of their brethren shall be complete.

We know that the victory is already won in Christ which remains to be consummated in God's new creation. Christ is the first-fruit of the redemption that shall be wrought also in us.

Bring us, O Lord, at our last awakening into the house and gate of Heaven, to enter into that gate and dwell in that house, where there shall be no darkness nor dazzling, but one equal light; no voice nor silence but one equal music; no fears nor hopes but one equal possession; no ends nor beginnings, but one equal eternity; in the habitation of Thy glory and dominion, world without end, Amen.

John Donne's prayer for the life of heaven is more than three centuries old. As rational man I can make nothing of what it asks. As moral creature I cannot find that I merit it. Yet with some part of me I seem to long for it. The kingdom we look for is not to be extrapolated out of this natural order. Here in this world – full of power to hurt us, and empty in its own right of meaning – there can be no explanations that satisfy, until, laying hold of Christ, we can be changed and redeemed in him, and, looking upon death, ask: Where is its victory?

I perceive too that those who have travelled furthest in the faith, and sought for its truths most deeply, need no excusing or modern-day toleration as weaker brethren out of touch with the world-view of a scientific age. Hard though it may be for Western minds and contemporary man to apprehend, the procedure of our English St Anselm may yet be in the right order: CREDO UT INTELLIGAM: I believe in order that I may understand.

Notes

INTRODUCTION

1. Op. cit. (Fontana, London, 1966), p. 22.
2. Alan Richardson well discusses this trend in *University and Humanity*, SCM Broadsheet 4 (SCM Press, London, 1964).
3. 'Belief is Being: Thoughts on the Survival of Christian Belief', loc. cit., ed. M. de la Bedoyere (Constable, London, 1966), p. 9.
4. *Theology and History* (Faith Press, London, 1962), p. 16.

CHAPTER I

1. *The Concept of Mind* (Hutchinson, London, 1949), p. 76.
2. Ibid.
3. Ibid., pp. 76 ff.
4. Ibid., pp. 79 ff.
5. I. T. Ramsey, *Miracles: An Exercise in Logical Mapwork*, (Clarendon Press, Oxford, 1952), p. 9.
6. Yvonne Lubbock, loc. cit., p. 10.

CHAPTER 2

1. *The Concept of Mind*, p. 81.
2. *Christus Veritas* (Macmillan, London, 1924), p. 68.
3. Ch. 4, 'The Nature of Man'.
4. *Christus Veritas*, p. 53.
5. *The Neurophysiological Basis of Mind* (Clarendon Press, Oxford, 1953), p. 271.
6. *The World and God* (Nisbet, London, 1936), pp. 160–1.
7. Romans 7: 24.
8. *Mens Creatrix* (Macmillan, London, 1917), p. 144.
9. *Christus Veritas*, p. 59.
10. Ibid., pp. 60–1.
11. Ibid., pp. 66 ff.
12. Ibid., p. 69.

13. Good elementary reading on animal behaviour will be found in N. Tinbergen, *The Study of Instinct* (Oxford University Press, London, 1951); Aubrey Manning, *An Introduction to Animal Behaviour* (Arnold, London, 1967).

14. For details of octopus behaviour studies, see J. Z. Young, *Doubt and Certainty in Science* (Reith Lectures, BBC, London, 1951); M. J. Wells, *Brain and Behaviour in Cephalopods* (Heinemann, London, 1962); J. Z. Young, *A Model of the Brain* (Clarendon, Oxford, 1964).

15. *On Aggression* (Methuen, London, 1966), p. 213.

16. Ibid. pp. 213–14.

17. *Christus Veritas*, p. 69.

CHAPTER 3

1. Bertrand Russell, *Autobiography* (Allen and Unwin, London, 1967), Vol. I, p. 40.

2. *The Concept of Mind*, p. 76.

3. See also the discussion by K. R. Popper, 'Indeterminism in Quantum Physics and in Classical Physics', *British Journal for the Philosophy of Science*, 1950.

4. Basic Books, London, 1964.

5. Ibid., pp. 187-8.

6. *The Concept of Mind*, p. 80.

7. E. Schrödinger, *What Is Life?* (Cambridge University Press, London, 1944), p. 87.

8. Penguin, Harmondsworth, 1961, Chs. 1 and 2.

9. *The Successful Error* (Sheed & Ward, London, 1941), p. 64, quoted by Mascall, *Christian Theology and Natural Science* (Longmans, Green, London, 1956), pp. 217 ff.

10. Teilhard de Chardin, *The Phenomenon of Man* (Collins, London, 1959).

11. *Metamorphoses*, VII, 21.

12. Romans 7: 19, 24.

CHAPTER 4

1. This the theme of Professor Tyndall's well-known British Association address, at Belfast, 1874.

2. *Appearance and Reality* (Swan Sonnenschein, London, 1897), p. 358.

3. An excellent introduction may be found in Peter Nathan, *The Nervous System* (Penguin, Harmondsworth, 1969).

4. Cambridge University Press, London, 1961.

5. 'The Physiology of Imagination', *Scientific American*, September 1958.

6. *The Machinery of the Brain* (McGraw-Hill, Maidenhead, 1963), quoted in Peter Nathan, *The Nervous System*, p. 115.

7. *Man on his Nature* (Cambridge University Press, London, 1940), p. 312.

8. T. H. Bullock and G. A. Horridge, *Structure and Function in the Nervous Systems of Invertebrates* (Freeman, London, 1965), p. 329.

9. This section relies much on Eccles, *The Neurophysiological Basis of Mind* (cited above); see also the excellent discussion in Mascall, *Christian Theology and Natural Science*, pp. 225 ff.

10. *Boyer Lectures* (Australian Broadcasting Commission, 1964).

11. Sir Charles Burt, *Observer*, London, 16 April 1967, critically discusses the claim made for computers.

12. O. E. Lowenstein, *The Senses* (Penguin, Harmondsworth, 1966), p. 209.

13. *The Physical Basis of Mind*, ed. Peter Laslett (Blackwell, Oxford, 1950).

14. *The Physical Background of Perception* (Clarendon Press, Oxford, 1947).

15. *The Physical Basis of Mind*, p. 6.

16. Ibid., pp. 54-5.

17. Ibid., pp. 70-4.

18. Ibid., p. 79.

19. *The Concept of Mind*, pp. 63 ff.

20. Ibid., p. 169.

21. *Christian Theology and Natural Science*, p. 223.

22. *The Concept of Mind*, p. 195.

23. Ibid., p. 186.

24. *Christian Theology and Natural Science*, p. 222.

25. SCM Press, London, 1965.

26. *The Concept of Mind*, p. 81.

27. See discussion by Viscount Samuel in *The Physical Basis of Mind*, p. 69.

28. *Man's Place in Nature* (Collins, London, 1966), p. 18.

29. A. S. Eddington, *The Nature of the Physical World* (Cambridge University Press, London, 1928), p. 321.

30. Ibid.
31. Ibid., p. 324.
32. Ibid., pp. 325–6.

CHAPTER 5

1. *Human Disease* (Penguin, Harmondsworth, 1957), p. 253.
2. Ibid.
3. Kimber, London, 1969.
4. Ibid., p. 118.
5. Ibid., p. 230.
6. A. A. Mason, *British Medical Journal*, ii, 422 (1952).
7. F. R. Bettley, *British Medical Journal*, ii, 996 (1952).
8. *Mind and Body*, pp. 38 ff.
9. Ibid., p. 481.
10. Ibid., p. 482.

CHAPTER 6

1. *The Mysterious Universe* (Cambridge University Press, London, 1930), p. 148.
2. *Principles of Human Knowledge* (1710), § 6.
3. Op. cit., Chs. IV ('Relativity and the Ether'), V ('Into the Deep Waters').
4. Ibid., p. 120.
5. Ibid., p. 135.
6. Ibid., pp. 135–6.
7. *Christian Theology and Natural Science*, p. 49.
8. Ibid., pp. 82 ff.
9. Ibid., p. 82.
10. *Process and Reality* (Cambridge University Press, London, 1929).
11. *Space, Time and Deity* (Macmillan, London, 1920).
12. *The Idea of Nature* (Oxford University Press, London, 1944).
13. *Origin of Species*, Ch. XV, conclusion.

CHAPTER 7

1. There are many introductory books about evolution. For a beginner we would recommend, for its lively style and sureness of touch, Ruth Moore, *Man, Time and Fossils* (Cape, London, 1962). The best advanced treatment is still Julian Huxley's

highly documented *Evolution: The Modern Synthesis* (Allen and Unwin, London, 1963, 1st ed. 1942).

2. *The Laws of Physics*, p. 160.
3. *God's Grace in History*, p. 22.
4. Sir R. A. Fisher's *Genetical Theory of Natural Selection* (Clarendon Press, Oxford, 1930), is difficult for the general reader; its main conclusions are dealt with by his contribution to the symposium *Evolution as a Process*, ed. Julian Huxley, A. C. Hardy and E. B. Ford.
5. J. D. Bernal, *The Origin of Life* (Weidenfeld and Nicolson, London, 1967).
6. *Evolution: The Modern Synthesis*, p. 572.
7. The idea of 'exosomatic evolution' is well developed by Sir Peter Medawar in his *Lamarckianism and Other Essays* (Allen and Unwin, London, 1954).
8. Teilhard de Chardin, *The Phenomenon of Man*, p. 289.
9. Reprinted in P. B. Medawar, *The Art of the Soluble* (Methuen, London, 1967).
10. *The Phenomenon of Man*, pp. 292–3.
11. Ibid., p. 295.
12. Ibid., p. 296.
13. Ibid., p. 292.
14. Ibid., p. 298.

CHAPTER 8

1. *Our Experience of God* (Allen and Unwin, London, 1959), p. 65.
2. *God's Grace in History*, p. 14.
3. Ibid., p. 37.
4. *Religion without Revelation* (Parrish, London, 1957), pp. 58, 62.
5. SCM Press, London, 1963, pp. 37–8.
6. Ibid., p. 56.
7. Paul Tillich, *Systematic Theology* (Nisbet, Welwyn, 1953–7), Vol. 2, p. 8.
8. *Honest to God*, p. 29.
9. *The Honest to God Debate* (SCM Press, London, 1963), p. 199.
10. Yale University Press, New Haven, 1941.
11. Op. cit., Preface, p. xvi.
12. Ibid., p. 64.
13. Ibid., p. 88.
14. William Temple, *Christus Veritas*, pp. 7–8.

15. W. R. Matthews, *The Purpose of God* (Nisbet, London, 1935), pp. 71 ff.
16. Hume, quoted by Matthews, op. cit., p. 84.
17. For Russell's treatment of Spinoza, see *History of Western Philosophy* (Allen and Unwin, London, 1946), pp. 592 ff.

CHAPTER 9

1. Op. cit. (Penguin, Harmondsworth, 1966), p. 128.
2. Op. cit. (Methuen, London, 1956), p. 87.
3. *Scientific American*, September 1958.
4. Galatians 5: 16–17.
5. Ibid., 19–23.
6. *The Universality of Christ* (SCM Press, London, 1921), p. 61.
7. 1 Corinthians 13: 7–10, 13.
8. *The Phenomenon of Man*, p. 295.
9. J. A. T. Robinson, *Honest to God*, p. 49.
10. See John Wren-Lewis's essay in *Faith, Fact and Fantasy*, ed. C. F. D. Moule (Fontana, London, 1964), p. 101.
11. *God and Philosophy* (cited above), pp. 38 ff.
12. W. B. Ullathorne, *Groundwork of the Christian Virtues*, p. 74.
13. *Psychology and Religion* (Yale University Press, New Haven, 1938), p. 5.
14. Op. cit., pp. 127 ff.
15. William Temple, *The Province of Science* (1904), p. 21.
16. Ibid.
17. *The Degrees of Knowledge* (Bles, London, 1959).
18. *God's Grace in History*, p. 14.
19. See above, p. 66.
20. Teilhard de Chardin, *Mon Univers*, quoted in the introduction to *Hymn of the Universe* (Collins, London, 1965), p. 15.
21. Teilhard de Chardin, *Hymn of the Universe*, p. 25.

CHAPTER 10

1. English translation, Oxford University Press, London, 1929.
2. Op. cit., Foreword.
3. Ibid., pp. 116–20.
4. Ibid., Ch. 4.
5. William James, *Varieties of Religious Experience* (Longmans, Green, London, 1902), pp. 66–7.

6. C. G. Jung, *Two Essays on Analytical Psychology* (Routledge & Kegan Paul, London, 1966), p. 67.
7. With R. Wilhelm (English translation, Routledge & Kegan Paul, London, 1962).
8. Commentary on *The Secret of the Golden Flower*, pars. 2–3.
9. Frieda Fordham, *An Introduction to Jung's Psychology* (Penguin, Harmondsworth, 1953), p. 63.
10. *Psychology and Alchemy* (Routledge and Kegan Paul, London, 1953), p. 41.
11. Op. cit., ed. J. Mitchell (Constable, London, 1967), p. 160.
12. Ibid., p. 155.
13. Ibid., p. 157.
14. Ibid., p. 155.

CHAPTER 11

1. William Temple, *The Kingdom of God* (Macmillan, London, 1912), p. 57.
2. C. S. Lewis, *The Problem of Pain* (Bles, London, 1940), p. 104.
3. *Scientific American*, February 1961.
4. Ibid., p. 4.
5. *Christian Theology and Natural Science*, pp. 32 ff.
6. See for full discussion, A. M. Ramsey, *From Gore to Temple* (Longmans, Green, London, 1960), Ch. 2 ('The Incarnation, Man and Nature').
7. Quoted by Ramsey, ibid., Ch. 10 ('William Temple'), p. 151.
8. Address, World Council of Churches, Amsterdam, 1948.
9. William Temple, 'Creation and Redemption', University Sermon, 1925, *Cambridge Review*.
10. William Temple, *Mens Creatrix*, p. 286.
11. Methuen, London, 1941, pp. 76 ff.
12. Op. cit. (Heinemann, London, 1938), p. 17.
13. Dorothy Sayers, *The Devil to Pay*, Canterbury Festival Play (Gollancz, London, 1939), p. 106.

CHAPTER 12

1. 'Creation and Redemption', loc. cit.
2. Ibid.
3. *Christus Veritas*, p. 121.

4. Op. cit. (John Murray, London, 1922), p. 68.
5. J. S. Whale, *Christian Doctrine* (Cambridge University Press, London, 1941), Ch. V.
6. *Christian Doctrine* (Hodder & Stoughton, London, 1894), pp. 166-7.
7. Op. cit., p. 104.
8. William Temple, *Christus Veritas*, p. 109, and the discussion following, has been much relied upon here.
9. Hebrews 2: 17–18.
10. Hebrews 1: 1–3.
11. 1 John 5: 20.
12. *Sacred and Secular* (Longmans, Green, London, 1965), p. 26.
13. *The Incarnation of the Son of God*, Bampton Lectures (John Murray, London, 1891), V, p. 137.
14. *The Man Who Was Thursday* (Arrowsmith, London, 1908; Penguin, Harmondsworth, 1967), pp. 328–9; 183.
15. 'The Holy Spirit and Inspiration' in *Lux Mundi* (John Murray, London, 1889).
16. *Oratio Catechetica Magna*, XXIV, quoted in Ramsey, *From Gore to Temple*, p. 35.
17. Valuable help has been gained here from E. L. Mascall, *Christ, the Christian and the Church* (Longmans, Green, London 1956).
18. John 17: 24.

CHAPTER 13

1. *The God I Want*, p. 155.
2. *The Future of Catholic Christianity*, pp. 15–16.
3. William Temple, *Nature, Man and God*, pp. 312-17.
4. *Hymn of the Universe*, pp. 76–7.
5. Address to Canterbury (N.Z.) University students (1967). (Italics mine.)
6. *The Outlook*, September 1965. (Italics mine.)
7. John Grigg, *Manchester Guardian*, 19 December 1966.
8. See F. A. Iremonger, *William Temple* (Oxford University Press, London, 1948), p. 162.
9. Nisbet, London, 1938, p. 156.
10. For a discussion upon the historic standing of the Gospels, see Ch. 5 of E. L. Mascall's *The Secularisation of Christianity* (Darton, Longman and Todd, London, 1965).

11. Trevor Huddleston, *Naught for Your Comfort* (Collins, London, 1956), should be read here, esp. Chs. 4 and 13.
12. Op. cit., pp. 7–12.
13. Ronald Goldman, *New Zealand Theological Review*, 1 (4), 241 (1966).
14. Karl Barth, *Church Dogmatics* (T. & T. Clark, Edinburgh, 1956), IV (1), p. 186.
15. In *Essays Catholic and Critical*, ed. E. G. Selwyn (S.P.C.K., London, 1926), p. 177.
16. Frederick Temple, quoted in *Christus Veritas*, p. 105.

CHAPTER 14

1. *Observer*, London, 14 April 1968.
2. Op. cit. (Religious Education Press, Wallington, 1963), pp. 62 f.
3. Charles Gore, *Catholicism and Roman Catholicism* (Mowbray, London, 1923), p. 1.
4. E. L. Mascall, *The Secularisation of Christianity*, p. 234.
5. E. L. Mascall, *Theology and History*, pp. 16–17.
6. Robert Kaiser, *Inside the Council* (Burns & Oates, London, 1963), p. 197.
7. Op. cit., p. 64.
8. Teilhard de Chardin, *The Phenomenon of Man*, pp. 297–8.
9. *Late Call* (Secker and Warburg, London, 1964), p. 190.
10. J. A. T. Robinson, *Honest to God*, Ch. 5.
11. Ibid., p. 86.
12. Ibid., pp. 99–100.
13. Ibid., p. 88.
14. George Macleod, *Only One Way Left* (The Iona Community, Glasgow, 1956), p. 151.
15. *Honest to God*, pp. 99 ff.
16. And see William Temple, *Readings in St John's Gospel* (Macmillan, London, 1945), pp. 302-6.
17. Bernardine Bishop, in *The God I Want*, pp. 158–9.
18. J. A. T. Robinson, *The New Reformation?* (SCM Press, London, 1965).
19. Lloyd Geering, *God in the New World* (Hodder and Stoughton, London, 1968).
20. J. A. T. Robinson and D. L. Edwards, *The Honest to God Debate*, pp. 48 ff.

21. Preface, *Book of Common Prayer.*
22. Sister Edna Mary, in *The Religious Life* (Penguin, Harmondsworth, 1968), has given an admirable contemporary account of the religious vocation in its relation to works.
23. *Zealandia* newspaper, 27 February 1969.
24. *The Times*, 10 February 1967.

CHAPTER 15

1. *Christus Veritas*, p. 100.
2. See a discussion 'Miracles on Trial' by Charlotte and Denis Plimmer, *Observer*, 11 February 1968.
3. Quoted by Bernardine Bishop, op. cit., p. 142.
4. E. J. Bicknell, *A Theological Introduction to the Thirty-Nine Articles of the Church of England* (Longmans, Green, London, 1955), revised H. J. Carpenter, p. 81.
5. *The Divine Pity* (Fontana, London, 1956), p. 79.
6. Recounted by Sir Arnold Lunn, in Lunn and Lean, *Christian Counter-Attack* (Blandford Press, London, 1969).
7. Op. cit., pp. 237 ff.
8. Ibid., p. 309.
9. E. L. Mascall, *The Secularisation of Christianity*, pp. 197 ff.
10. Lloyd Geering, *The Outlook*, September 1965.
11. These and related questions are excellently discussed in Ch. 5, 'Fact and the Gospels', of E. L. Mascall's *The Secularisation of Christianity.*
12. W. M. Ramsay, *The Church in the Roman Empire* (Hodder & Stoughton, London, 1893).
13. *The Christ of the Synoptic Gospels*, Supplement to *The New Zealand Theological Review* (Auckland, 1966), p. 29.
14. Ibid., p. 34.
15. Ibid.
16. Ibid., p. 37.
17. *Kerygma and Myth* (S.P.C.K., London, 1953–62), I, p. 220.

CHAPTER 16

1. Lloyd Geering, University of Canterbury address, 1967.
2. Ibid.
3. *Why I am Not a Christian* (Allen & Unwin, London, 1957), p. 43.

4. *Prophecy and the Prophets in Ancient Israel* (Duckworth, London, 1952), pp. 137–8.
5. *The God I Want*, p. 157.
6. W. R. Matthews, *The Hope of Immortality* (Epworth Press, London, 1966), p. 46.
7. Op. cit. (Macmillan, London, 1934), pp. 452–3.
8. E. L. Mascall, *Christian Theology and Natural Science*, pp. 208 ff.
9. Ibid., pp. 209 f.
10. Op. cit. (Bles, London, 1945), p. 114.
11. Oscar Cullman, *Immortality of the Soul or Resurrection of the Dead?* (Epworth Press, London, 1958).
12. Ibid., p. 27.
13. 1 Corinthians 15: 51.
14. 2 Corinthians 4: 16–18.
15. 2 Corinthians 5: 4-5.
16. 1 Corinthians 15: 49–51.
17. Op. cit., pp. 38–9.

Acknowledgements

The author and publishers wish to acknowledge their indebtedness for permission to reproduce copyright material as follows: Scripture quotations from the Revised Standard Version of the Bible, copyright © 1946 and 1952 by the Division of Christian Education, National Council of Churches, and from the New English Bible, second edition © 1970, by permission of Oxford and Cambridge University Presses; from *Structure and Function in the Nervous Systems of Invertebrates*, by Theodore Holmes Bullock and G. Adrian Horridge, published by W. H. Freeman and Company, London and San Francisco. Copyright © 1965; from *Human Disease*, by A. E. Clark-Kennedy, published by Penguin Books, Harmondsworth; from *Immortality of the Soul or Resurrection of the Dead?* by Oscar Cullman, published by Epworth Press, London, and The Macmillan Company, New York; from *The Neurophysiological Basis of Mind*, by Sir John Eccles, published by the Clarendon Press, Oxford; from *The Nature of the Physical World*, by A. S. Eddington, published by Cambridge University Press, London; from *God and Philosophy*, by Etienne Gilson, published by Yale University Press, New Haven; from 'The Swinging Church Strikes a Wrong Note', by David Jenkins, reproduced from *The Times* by permission; from *Psychology and Alchemy*, by C. G. Jung, edited by G. Adler, M. Fordham and H. Read, translated by R. F. C. Hull, and published by Routledge & Kegan Paul, London, and the Bollingen Foundation, Princeton University Press, Princeton, copyright © 1953 and 1968 by Princeton University Press; from *Inside the Council: The Story of Vatican II* (U.S. edition: *Pope, Council and World: The Story of Vatican II*), by Robert Kaiser, published by Burns & Oates, London, and The Macmillan Company, New York. Copyright © Robert Blair Kaiser, 1963; from *The Christ of the Synoptic Gospels*, by A. R. C. Leaney, published in *The New Zealand Theological Review*, Auckland; from *The Senses*, by O. E. Lowenstein, published by Penguin Books, Harmondsworth; from *Christian Theology and Natural Science*, by E. L. Mascall, published by Longmans, Green, London, and Archon Books, Hamden, Connecticut; from *Theology and History*, by E. L. Mascall, published by the Faith Press, London; from *The God I Want*, edited by J. Mitchell, published by Constable, London, and the Bobbs-Merrill Company Inc., Indianapolis; from *Honest to God*, by John A. T. Robinson, published by SCM Press, London, and in the U.S.A., 1963, by The Westminster Press, Philadelphia. © SCM Press Ltd, London, 1963. Used by permission; from *Prophecy and Prophets in Ancient Israel*, by T. H. Robinson, published by Duckworth, London; from *The Concept of Mind*, by Gilbert Ryle, published by Hutchinson, London, and Barnes & Noble Inc, New York; from *The Devil to Pay*, by Dorothy Sayers, published by Gollancz, London; from *Essays Catholic and Critical*, edited by E. G. Selwyn, published by the S.P.C.K., London; from *Man on his Nature*, by Sir Charles Sherrington, published by Cambridge University Press, London; from *Christus Veritas*, by William Temple, published by Macmillan, London and Basingstoke, The Macmillan Company of Canada, and St Martin's Press Inc, Macmillan & Co Ltd, New York; from *Nature, Man and God*, by William Temple, published by Macmillan, London and Basingstoke, The Macmillan Company of Canada, and St Martin's Press Inc, New York.

Index